VISIONS
OF
AMERICA
AND
EUROPE

Significant Issues Series
Timely books presenting current CSIS research and analysis of interest to the academic, business, government, and policy communities.
Managing editor: Roberta L. Howard

For four decades, the **Center for Strategic and International Studies (CSIS)** has been dedicated to providing world leaders with strategic insights on—and policy solutions to—current and emerging global issues.

CSIS is led by John J. Hamre, formerly deputy secretary of defense, who has been president and CEO since April 2000. It is guided by a board of trustees chaired by former senator Sam Nunn and consisting of prominent individuals from both the public and private sectors.

The CSIS staff of 190 researchers and support staff focus primarily on three subject areas. First, CSIS addresses the full spectrum of new challenges to national and international security. Second, it maintains resident experts on all of the world's major geographical regions. Third, it is committed to helping to develop new methods of governance for the global age; to this end, CSIS has programs on technology and public policy, international trade and finance, and energy.

Headquartered in Washington, D.C., CSIS is private, bipartisan, and tax-exempt. CSIS does not take specific policy positions; accordingly, all views expressed herein should be understood to be solely those of the authors.

The CSIS Press
Center for Strategic and International Studies
1800 K Street, N.W., Washington, D.C. 20006
Telephone: (202) 887-0200 Fax: (202) 775-3199
E-mail: books@csis.org Web: www.csis.org

VISIONS OF AMERICA AND EUROPE

SEPTEMBER 11, IRAQ, AND TRANSATLANTIC RELATIONS

EDITED BY

CHRISTINA V. BALIS
AND
SIMON SERFATY

THE CSIS PRESS

Center for Strategic
and International Studies
Washington, D.C.

Significant Issues Series, Volume 26, Number 3
© 2004 by Center for Strategic and International Studies
Washington, D.C. 20006
Printed on recycled paper in the United States of America
Cover design by Robert L. Wiser, Silver Spring, Md.
Cover photograph: Colorful globes © Sanford/Agliolo/CORBIS

08 07 06 05 04   5 4 3 2 1

ISSN 0736-7136
ISBN 0-89206-441-2

Library of Congress Cataloging-in-Publication Data
Visions of America and Europe: September 11, Iraq, and transatlantic relations /
Christina V. Balis and Simon Serfaty, editors.
    p. cm. — (Significant issues series ; v. 26, no. 3)
Includes bibliographical references and index.
   ISBN 0-89206-441-2
1. United States—Foreign relations—Europe. 2. Europe—Foreign
relations—United States. 3. International relations. 4. Security,
International. 5. United States—Military policy. 6. War on terrorism,
2001. 7. World politics, 1995–2005. I. Balis, Christina V. II. Serfaty, Simon.
III. Title. IV. Series.
D1065.U5E986 2004
327.4073'09'0511—dc22
                              2003025524

CONTENTS

v

PART IV. CONCLUSIONS

PREFACE

Contemporary history is, by definition, exploratory, and to some degree even speculative. Subsequent events may challenge early assessments or they may uphold lessons drawn but not heeded at the time. This volume is such an effort. It both explores and speculates on events likely to make an impact for years to come, although the final verdicts on these events must inevitably be left to future diplomatic historians.

By now, it is widely agreed that the terrorist attacks of September 11, 2001, marked a turning point in the relations between the United States and Europe. A transatlantic debate that started in earnest in early 2002, first over an alleged "axis of evil" and next over the prospects of an imminent war in Iraq, continues into 2004, but with implications yet unknown for the future of transatlantic cooperation, European integration, and U.S. leadership. This volume, a compilation of essays by leading U.S. and European analysts, seeks to identify the forces that have shaped respective policies and public perceptions on both sides of the Atlantic in recent times. It attempts to trace the origins of the transatlantic rift post-September 11 and to illuminate the current and future challenges for bilateral relations and for the relationship between Europe and the United States. Five national European perspectives—from France, Germany, Great Britain, Italy, and Russia—complement the views of three perceptive U.S. critics.

Early drafts of the chapters were presented at an authors' conference held at the Center for Strategic and International Studies (CSIS) in March 2003. Most writing was completed by late summer 2003, thus excluding from consideration any subsequent developments at the national and international levels. We thank our colleagues on both sides of the Atlantic who accepted our invitation to participate in this project. We also thank those who contributed with their participation and constructive comments to the authors' conference, including Michael Calingaert, David P. Calleo, Desmond Dinan, James M. Goldgeier, Jussi M. Hanhimaki, Gebhard L. Schweigler, Justin Vaisse, and Jenonne Walker.

As with most of the CSIS Europe Program's activities, this project would not have been possible without the generous assistance of the German Marshall Fund of the United States. Our sincere thanks go to Craig Kennedy, Karen Donfried, and their colleagues at the Fund for their continued support.

Christina V. Balis
Simon Serfaty

PART ONE

INTRODUCTION

ONE

ANTI-EUROPEANISM IN AMERICA AND ANTI-AMERICANISM IN EUROPE

Simon Serfaty

America was not born into the world to become a European power. If anything, the opposite is true.[1] For more than 150 years, several generations of policymakers in the United States struggled to keep the "contests, broils and wars of Europe" over there in the Old World. To accomplish this fundamental goal, Thomas Jefferson imagined a "meridian of partition through the ocean which separates the two hemispheres, on the hither side of which no European gun shall ever be heard, nor an American on the other."[2]

Admittedly, there were moments of courtship between the distant relatives, but these were limited and discreet—with France as America's favorite partner in Europe, mainly because of Britain, France's vilified neighbor across the Channel. For the "traveled inhabitant[s] of any nation," noted Jefferson, France was the "country on earth [they] would rather live" in, besides their own.[3] With time, however, even these few bilateral relationships between the United States and other states across the Atlantic faded as the fragmentation of Europe's political and economic space became less and less comprehensible and more and more dangerous. Territorial consolidation, wherever it occurred, was a matter of growing interest, first in Italy in 1866 and next in Germany in 1871. If Europe's past had been America's anti-model, the United States might now emerge as Europe's model for the future. "The adoption in Europe of the American system of union," said President Ulysses S. Grant with specific reference to Germany's unification, "under the control and the direction of a free people educated to self-restraint, cannot fail to extend popular institutions and to enlarge the peaceful influence of American ideas."[4] But no occasional bilateral flirtation ever blossomed into a permanent relationship. America was an accomplished free rider. Sheltered by the British Royal Navy in the Atlantic, which kept the Old World at a distance, and by British diplomacy in Europe, which ensured a balance of power on the continent, the United States would, in time, ascend to the dominant status to which it seemed destined.

World War I did not end the U.S. predilection for separation from European continental affairs—on the contrary. To be sure, there was the unprincipled brutality shown by the countries of Europe during the war, but there was also the inability on the part of the Europeans to start anew in the aftermath of a conflict that had ended Europe as they themselves had come to know or imagine it.[5] At Versailles in 1919, the punitive peace treaty imposed by the victorious powers on the main defeated state, and its annexed Covenant for a League of Nations, proved reckless and self-defeating. The European continent left behind by an embittered America was like a huge whale stranded on the beach. As the Old World slowly and painfully died, it stank and polluted everything around and beyond it.[6] Only memories still linked America and Europe, those "mystic chords" that never quite cease to bind immigrants to their native land, even as they commit themselves in full to the values of their new habitat. Otherwise, Americans still showed little interest in a world across the Atlantic that had caused so much pain and seemed to share little of the community of values built in the New World.[7]

In 1945, however, European countries that were aware, at last, of the depth of their decline "invited" the United States to stay and help them become a bit more like it. The idea of a new Europe—united, democratic, peaceful—was the very idea that had given birth to the New World —a nation that began as "the haven of the disinherited, the underside of Europe" before "two generations of common schooling, intermarriage, ward politics, and labor unions create[d] social peace" among people who had come to the United States to be rid of a thousand years of wars, pogroms, and massacres.[8]

Agreeing to Europe's invitation was decided reluctantly and enforced cautiously.[9] Indeed, for the United States to stay in Europe was not a hegemonic project. Vague sounds of a European Third Force were heard from both Britain and France, but Europe's disarray was total because, unlike in 1919, the understanding of its decline was real. Although it was hardly necessary for America to stand in the way of objectives that could not be met, Europeans could (and did) rely on U.S.

policies as an alibi for explaining what they could not do—and did not expect to pursue anyway. Their willing accommodation of the American ideas for sheltered unity was a statement of collective failure, as well as of national weakness: past collective failures that demanded that Europe be reinvented in the wake of the two suicidal conflicts waged over the previous 30 years; and postwar national weaknesses that demanded an outside help that only the United States could provide. Thus emerged a transatlantic blueprint for a new Europe. The war had been won, but it would now have to be ended once and for all—a prospect that would be achieved (and even imposed) on U.S. terms.

For Europe, the rewards of followership included rehabilitation, reconstruction, and security for winners and losers alike. For the United States, the rewards of leadership included not only the nifty returns expected from its significant investments for prosperity and peace in Europe, but also the intangible satisfaction of consolidating Europe's political space à l'américaine. Early in the nineteenth century, America's birth and maturity into the dominant power it had become called for less Europe in America. By contrast, late in the twentieth century, Europe's rebirth (including more democracy, more affluence, and more security) would have to rely on more America in Europe (meaning more money, more troops, and more leadership).

NEITHER MARS NOR VENUS

Half a century and many lives later, this vision has actually worked. As an ever-closer Europe and its ever-larger union move closer to their finality, the nation-states of Europe are being recycled within the new institutional framework now limiting the sovereignty that used to define them.[10] This territorial *synthesis* has not been limited to the states of Europe. It is also visible across the Atlantic, where a web of entangling interests has consolidated space as irreversibly as across the European continent.

Does Europe matter to the United States? That the question would be raised at all sounds absurd. It is with Europe that the United States maintains its most *complete* relationship, one that is found nearly nowhere else. Born out of the two world wars, this relationship grew during the Cold War into a Euro-American community of increasingly converging (and even common) economic interests and compatible (though distinguishable) political values. But with the Cold War over, the goal has changed as both sides of the Atlantic now need to fashion a community of action wherever these interests are recognized to be at risk and whenever these values might be at stake.

At first glance, such a Europe should be cause for much satisfaction in the United States. Americans who travel to the Old World to mingle with the strange breed of people they still expect to meet there—poets, philosophers, and artists all enjoying a life of intellectual leisure in a delightfully scenic setting of old castles and romantic cafés—still seem surprised by the changes they encounter. Europe's foreignness seems gone, or at least it is losing much of its past romance. Now emerging is a new European identity—people who have become more "like us" after the landscape was cleansed of its historical debris of violence and war. At the same time, many in America seem to believe that whether individually or as a union, the states of Europe are evolving on a planet of their own—the "post-historical paradise" found on Venus where "international laws and rules" prevail over the "possession and use of military might" found on Mars.[11] The role reversal that is thus discovered, rather belatedly, is stunning. It is America's turn to manage the geopolitical travails of the harsh Hobbesian world, while Europe enjoys the rewards of its belated conversion to the saintly features of an elusive Kantian world. "We" started as New England and "they" are ending as *Nous sommes tous Américains*"—to use France's ultimate declaration of faith after the infamous events of September 11, 2001.[12]

The new Europe that no longer equates the nation's fiber with its people's former enthusiastic will for wholesale death is evoked in the United States with a tone that is turning increasingly dismissive, disdainful, and condescending. Seemingly, General Patton has no use for Mother Teresa and for a "culture of appeasement" that sows the seeds of future wars likely to be waged by, and at the expense of, other countries. "Grow up and join in—or pipe down and let us do it," British-born "journalist" Andrew Sullivan warned "Europe's appeasers" in "a message long, long overdue" centered on, but not limited to, an impending war against Iraq. A culture of "numbing pacifism" has left most Europeans without "moral fiber," deplored Richard Perle and many others. It has been cause for Europe's repeated miscalculations—"in politics, economics, social and family life, and moral reasoning"—further rooted in a systematic denial of U.S. policies, during and past the Cold War.[13]

U.S. dismissal of Europe takes many forms besides the recall of its worst moments during its long and admittedly prejudiced history. A sense of American righteousness defines a catalogue of mistaken European challenges to U.S. leadership, challenges that were kept inconsequential by the U.S. determination to act against the will or preferences of their fearful allies. "Why, with a record so active and glorious, is American foreign policy held in such low esteem?" asks Walter Russell Mead.[14] Triumphant tones are extended to a broad past of U.S. victories and European tragedies. Thus, the "glorious" record returns to the earlier part of the century to resurrect U.S. efforts to save Europe from itself, in war (in 1917 and 1941) as well as in peace (in and after 1919 and 1945)—without a thought (or a word) for the U.S. indifference during the prewar and interwar years that introduced or separated World War I, World War II, and the Cold War. Glossing over the enlightened postwar policies adopted after World War II, such court history also emphasizes the role played by the United States during the waning days of the Cold War, when President Bush *père* once again saved Europe from itself in the face of a dangerous Anglo-French opposition to Germany's unification in 1989; when President Clinton extracted Europe from its own insufficiencies in the Balkans in 1995; or more recently when the United States struggled to define a post–Cold War world order that the Europeans again resisted in such vital areas as the deployment of missile defense systems and the management of rogue states.

But that is not all. There is also the important matter of power (especially U.S. military power) and the will to use it (especially European will). Americans would readily forgive Europe's weakness if it were not for the obstacles raised by some European states to the use of military force by the United States—countries like France and Germany that are "old and in the way." As Americans dwell on Europe's habit of "appeasement," the mood turns ugly and confrontational. Many Europeans would agree that World War I might have been avoided had they shunned "a fervor" for war "bordering on a religious experience."[15] But even more Europeans would take exception to the idea that World War II could have been avoided, had they shown equal willingness to fight the evil regime in Germany in the 1930s instead of allegedly "prais[ing] Hitler as a man of peace" and reportedly surrendering "with scarcely a fight."[16] Without a fight? During the six weeks of fighting that preceded France's surrender in June 1940, the French suffered casualties of 92,000 killed and about 200,000 wounded before leaving it up to a few of them, regrouped in London, to salvage a small measure of national pride and renewal. However poorly and ineffectively, they fought while others slept.

There is enough historical blame and shame to pass around. In June 1940, the French defeat was not due to a lack of equipment or even a will to fight, but to a massive failure of inept strategic planning and discredited political leadership. Nor can the Nazi sweep of Europe be attributed merely to France's appeasement, defeat, and surrender. It was also the product of a broader failure of the West to build a cohesive alliance because of the flawed assumption that the French military shield would be enough to contain Germany's revisionist outbursts. But still, when that assumption proved wrong, the British, too, fought with a spirit and a resilience that invite admiration: in the period 1939–1941 alone, casualties from Britain and its empire exceeded 180,000, including nearly 50,000 dead—not to mention the suffering endured while Hitler began a systematic destruction of Britain's cities.[17] That this part of the war would have been fought while waiting for the United States to settle a bitter internal debate over its stake and participation in the war is no cause for historical pride in America. Troubling, too, is the fact that, meanwhile, the Roosevelt administration maintained full diplomatic relations with the Nazi regime that was praised by then-ambassador to Great Britain Joe Kennedy, the father of a future and revered president. After that, the war went on for another 29 months, and millions of additional casualties, before U.S. forces landed in Normandy to write some of the most glorious pages of the nation's history (and underwrite Europe's subsequent debt to American power). As the interwar history is remembered, rooted habits of indifference and appeasement are uprooted all over the transatlantic field. Indeed, how sad it is to remember that when the evil could no longer be ignored, following Japan's surprise attack against Pearl Harbor, it was Hitler who declared war on the United States rather than the other way around.

While U.S. views of Europe can be seen to reflect exasperation over Europe's resentment of the United States, many other explanations compound that resentment and place European anti-Americanism and U.S. anti-Europeanism on parallel tracks. For some, anti-Americanism is just a matter of ideology—rooted mainly in an ideological Left that directs its venom most directly to Republican conservatives and their "belief in individualism, liberty and self-reliance."[18] Thus, a new partition is emerging as Europe allegedly promotes a societal agenda of values-based issues such as the environment, the death penalty, gun control, and other questions that happen to define the Left-Right divide in the United States. For many, it is a matter of values, as Europeans do not share Americans' religiosity while Americans question Europe's faith in the providential role of the state.[19] For others, it is a matter of attitude, as it is argued that the ghosts of Europe's past *grandeur* are still sighted amidst the ruins of its current decadence. Even as these memories fade, they are replaced by an arrogant pride in Europe's willingness to relinquish most of its sovereignty to the various institutions that define Europe as the new Old World. For a few others still, anti-Americanism is a pervasive plot, usually carried out by France on behalf of a narrow view of Europe that wants to assert itself at the expense of a U.S.-led NATO.[20]

This exercise in mutual schizophrenia ("go home, but don't leave us") and paranoia ("why don't you love us?") barely hides the deep ambivalence shown by each side of the Atlantic toward the other. That ambivalence is multidimensional. At the broadest level, it involves America's comfort zone with Europe—united but up to a point, and strong but also without excess. That, in the end, explains Washington's need for privileged partners that would enable it to isolate challenges to U.S. leadership—de Gaulle's image of a Trojan horse brought into Europe via Britain to give the nascent European Community the American voice it was expected to adopt. That, too, is not a plot designed to ensure America's hegemony. Instead it reflects America's concern over the consequences of Europe's failure—the sense, sharpened by past experiences, that whereas the "United" States of America can pursue a single foreign and security policy, Europe's unity remains dependent, for the better and for the worse, on a fragmented union of incoherent states that are still looking for ways to develop a common—let alone, single—foreign and security policy. The rein must therefore be kept short, or else the countries of Europe may be tempted again to start something that they cannot end—whether a war, a revolution, or even a currency—but that the United States cannot ignore because of the interests at stake.

I LIKE YOU—AND NEITHER DO I

While Americans like Europe but do not seem to like Europeans much, Europeans like Americans but do not seem to like America much. That at least may look like an improvement over earlier days, when the "ugly American" reigned—not only "unloved" but also "voracious, preachy, mercenary, and bombastically chauvinistic."[21] The tone then was disturbing. "Americans," wrote Vincent Auriol, the first president of the

French Fourth Republic, are "naïve, ignorant, and understand nothing." Thirty years later, another French socialist leader about to be elected president, François Mitterrand, found such traits "*sympathiques*." His concerns, however, had moved from Americans and their intellectual skills to their country and its political motivation. "I like Americans," he now claimed, "but not their policies. . . ." "I note," added Mitterrand, perhaps carried away by the partisan rhetoric made necessary by his alliance with the French Communist Party, "that the United States has not ceased waging an economic war against us." Later, Mitterrand still dismissed Ronald Reagan as "a man without ideas and without culture" but, small blessing, with "great good sense and profoundly good intentions."[22]

Similar pronouncements were made elsewhere in Europe and throughout the Cold War even though, predictably, they sounded at their worst whenever they were spoken with a French accent. These did not simply reflect a French view, however. "Does Britain like us?" anxiously asked one of *Newsweek*'s postwar special reports in late 1947. Such concern was astonishing: America had just committed itself to the reconstruction of Britain and its European neighbors. Yet with one out of three Englishmen said to be anti-American, anti-Americanism had reportedly "spread from the wealthy and intellectual classes down into the lower middle and working-class strata." Denis W. Brogan, an early British guru of anti-Americanism, was already warning of an emerging "omnipotence of American power." As Brogan put it, "America *has* plenty, but not plenty for all the world, and there must be weary moments in which the leaders of America wonder whether it would be better to move up to the top of the queue nations whose political vocabulary have rather better manners."[23]

Why go on? Whether addressed to the country and its culture, or its institutions and its people, Europe's ambivalence about the United States has been a persistent feature of transatlantic relations. Being an American in most parts of Europe is not unlike being French in most parts of America: not a death sentence, to be sure, but certainly a life sentence. Upon arriving in the United States in the 1950s, Stanley Hoffmann found it "easier to be French abroad than in France," because it is there, in the United States, that he could best uncover his "Frenchness"—on the basis of which Hoffmann made it a point to teach France to Americans, a task for which even his enormous skills would not quite suffice. The same was true of U.S. citizens who traveled to Europe after the war and always found the experience challenging. "It was the American in myself I stumbled upon while trying to discover Europe," thought Norman Podhoretz in the 1950s. "For protest as we all might . . . we were in a million small details marked off . . . as an identifiable national type."[24] Indeed, identifiable it was. Europe's disdainful outlook on America's intellectual life always came together with a skeptical look at America's right to lead.

However exasperating this sort of obsessive anti-American reflex in Europe may be, it is on the whole rather inconsequential and even boring.[25] Yet its most recent resurgence throughout Europe has been special in several respects. First, it includes such traditionally pro-American countries as Germany, thereby making it more difficult to isolate France from its indispensable European partner, as was done by previous administrations at the time of other French challenges to U.S. leadership. In addition, Europe's hostility to U.S. policies has not grown from the top down. Rather it has emerged from the bottom up, as public opposition to the use of military force in Iraq grew even among countries whose government was openly and adamantly supportive of the United States. Finally, Europe's opposition gained further significance when the Franco-German coalition of the unwilling was extended to Russia, thereby creating an "axis" that was fundamentally unprecedented in European history and potentially consequential for both transatlantic relations within NATO and intra-European relations within the EU.

How conclusive this triple play might be (transatlantic rift, intra-European split, and a new Franco-German *Ostpolitik*) is unclear. Suffice it to emphasize that its intensity also betrayed European anxieties about the person of the U.S. president. Admittedly, such a focus was hardly new. Each presidential election has provided Europeans with a good opportunity to bemoan a U.S. leadership that is reduced to a caricature that seems to encapsulate everything Europe fears most about America—its political leaders as well as the power these leaders inherit, with a preparation usually deemed to be insufficient or fatally flawed. From Kennedy, who was said to be too young, to Reagan, who was thought as too old, and from Nixon, who was feared for being too imperial, to Clinton, who seemed too isolationist, no president has ever satisfied Europe's standards of leadership upon his arrival at the White House. A president's popularity came later, usually following his successor's election.

Nonetheless, in early 2001, Europe's response to President George W. Bush remained especially sharp after it had often crossed the boundaries of tolerable language during the earlier presidential campaign. At best, Bush was said to be a younger version of Ronald Reagan—a comparison that was not meant to be flattering. His "axis of evil" speech of January 29, 2002, boosted by a desire to attend to security matters left unfinished by his father during the first war in the Persian Gulf, drew immediate parallels with Reagan's earlier battle with the "evil empire."[26]

Yet, rather than echoing Reagan, the younger Bush was emulating Harry S. Truman. In March 1947, Truman's message to Congress had also evoked the new security conditions opened by the end of World War II and the rise of the Soviet Union. At the time, a single coalition was deemed sufficient to defeat the threat raised by the new and elusive enemy that was feared as a central threat to the democratic way of life. To contain and ultimately roll it back, a single North Atlantic coalition was formed, beginning with the 1947 Marshall Plan as a down payment for the 1949 Washington treaty and the 1957 Rome treaties. This was meant as a single but multidimensional coalition within which economic reconstruction, political rehabilitation, and military security were goals that could be separated but were not separable.

To combat the new, post-9/11 security conditions, Bush planned to rely on the overwhelming abundance of American military power to launch the many missions that would have to be assumed before victory could be achieved. Like Truman, Bush responded to a morality of convictions that presented the world in strictly messianic terms—"with us or against us" to exorcise a new "evil" and bring the perpetrators to justice "dead or alive."[27] Like Truman's, too, Bush's strategy was global ("wherever they are") and time-consuming, as the president called on his compatriots to remain "steadfast and patient and persistent." Finally, and also like Truman, Bush with his knowledge of history limited to that which he has lived drew from these fragmented memories the strength of his convictions. Truman had been a product of World War I (which he courageously fought) and of Munich (which he bitterly deplored). By contrast, the young Bush claimed to be "a product of the Vietnam era" (even though that era produced a war during which he did not serve and from which he did not dissent). As he later confided, in order to explain his post-9/11 mind-set, "I remember presidents trying to wage wars that were very unpopular, and the nation split. . . . I had the job of making sure the American people understood . . . the severity of the attack."[28] In short, Bush concluded in early February 2002, "this nation won't rest until we have destroyed terrorism. . . . I can't tell you how passionate I feel on the subject. . . . There is no calendar, there is no deadline."[29]

There, however, ends the comparison. Having scared the hell out of the American people (as Truman had been urged to do) to "make sure they understood" the severity of the postwar challenge they faced, Truman quickly learned to look the other way as he ignored his own doctrine—from the coup in Czechoslovakia to the Communist revolution in China—and attempted to keep wars limited wherever he had to wage them, including Korea. If America was vulnerable to a new Soviet threat, which it was, that vulnerability was moral and political rather than physical and territorial. For Bush, however, the stakes are higher: to lead the nation on a crusade that is designed to restore America's territorial invulnerability and even "to save civilization itself." Given the enormity of the "vitriolic hatred of America" that inspires that threat, the enemy must be "rounded up" or "smoked out" until he is found "dead or alive."[30] The commitment may well be sufficient to rally the American people around their president, à la Truman,[31] but it has also been credible enough to scare everybody else, including people in Europe, away from America.[32]

On January 29, 2002, the president's annual State of the Union message aroused Europe's latent fears and led transatlantic relations to take a sharp turn for the worse. What caused offense in that speech was its form as well as its substance—what Bush said (and how he said it), as well as what he might do (and to what ends). Coming barely three months after Europe's forceful display of solidarity through both NATO and the European Union, the president's failure to mention either NATO or the EU was astonishing. So was the positioning of Iran, Iraq, and North Korea along an "axis" that left most of continental Europe fearful of what might come next. To make matters worse, the president's reference to a quartet of groups that formed the hard core of a "terrorist underworld . . . including groups like Hamas, Hezbollah, Islamic Jihad, Jaish-i-Mohammad" read mostly like Israel's hit list—a recurring point of tensions between the United States and the states of Europe. Altogether, the speech deepened Europe's apprehension that, as had been shown in Afghanistan, America's allies were being moved to a secondary role even for the treatment of issues that were of direct concern to them, and which they were committed to defeat in coordination

with their senior partner across the Atlantic. In contrast to the spontaneous calls for solidarity heard in September 2001, the January 29
speech therefore started a slow descent toward what 14 months later
would be viewed as "America's war."[33] Now, unlike 1947, and perhaps
more like 1919, America and Europe live in two different time zones—
one that began with the collapse of the Berlin Wall on November 1989
and ended Europe's century of total wars, and the other that was born
with the outrageous attacks against New York City and Washington
and started America's wars against global terrorism.

DOES IT MATTER?

Does Europe's anti-Americanism matter? Certainly it is not related to
the United States' concern over a spreading "hatred" of Americans
around the world. In Europe, anti-Americanism may be an admittedly
exasperating attitude, an occasional ideological project, an effective
political tactic, but it is not a broad strategy—a plot explicitly aimed at
killing Americans. To be sure, such plots can be developed in terrorist
cells implanted throughout the Continent, but they involve agents or
misfits without any link to their momentary territorial base, which
they hate no less (and often even more) than the United States. Nor
does a hard ideological Left still rely on superficial anti-American
projects to keep its base motivated and mobilized. In a Europe inhabit-
ed by centrist republics, a few political inches to the left or to the right
do not make much difference for transatlantic relations. When there is
a difference, it is usually found among those, Left and Right, who still
believe in escaping an institutional cage whose key has been lost in the
web of EU rules and regulations known as the *acquis communautaire*. In
short, Europe's obsession with anti-Americanism remains benign—
which was also the case during the Cold War when it hardly ever stood
in the way of U.S. leadership.

Similarly, complaints in Europe about U.S. foreign policies have not
stood in the way of an ever more united Europe that has remained ever
closer to the United States. Consider this basic reality: from one bout of
discord to the next, Europe has moved steadily to a condition that
leaves it more united, more stable, more democratic, more affluent,
and more safe than at any time in its history. The test of American politics, first articulated by Ronald Reagan during the 1980 presidential
campaign, applies to transatlantic politics: Was Europe better off in
1983 or 1953, or in 1923 and 1913, than it is in 2003?[34] The answer is not

in doubt, and there should be little debate either as to where much (but hardly all) of the credit should go. Indeed, Walter Russell Mead is right to ask, with an undertone of astonishment and exasperation, "Why, with a record so active and glorious, is American foreign policy held in such low esteem?"[35]

Mead's question is not new. It has been raised before, and it could remain unnoticed except for a sense that the renewed spread of anti-Americanism in Europe and the rise of anti-Europeanism in America respond to new and somewhat unprecedented cleavages between the two shores of the Atlantic (and even within Europe). For one, Americans and Europeans no longer view the security environment of the twenty-first century similarly. This "vision gap" began with the end of the Cold War, when the collapse of the Soviet Union and the end of communism denied the Western alliance the glue that had kept it together in the past. In the end, Henry Kissinger had it right in 1973, the first year of his so-called Year of Europe: where Europe's world vision is regional, the American vision is global. In a sense, the only isolationists left are Europeans who are so very focused on the "finality" of their institutions that they are unwilling to commit resources and time to conditions outside Europe. It is as if Europe is still running away from its past through its repeated admonitions to America: whatever you do, don't rush into policies that might be causes for confrontation and don't allow for confrontations that might escalate into a war.

Before September 11, 2001, that plea defined Europe's concerns over a host of new U.S. initiatives that were designed to end the Cold War but that many Europeans feared for their potential to arouse conflict with defeated states like Russia, ascending powers like China, and rogue states like North Korea. Since September 11, priorities have changed, of course. But even as Americans and Europeans agree on the immediate threats they face (which they now do, except when it comes to China), they do not perceive these threats with the same intensity and, therefore, the same urgency. Accordingly, Europe is more cautious as it denies the urgency of the threat (though not in the case of the Middle East), while on the whole Americans are more prone to take risks as they emphasize the imminence of the threat (especially with regard to states like Iraq that have already demonstrated a willingness to use such weapons of terror as chemical weapons).

The defining issue for this widening transatlantic gap was not the end of the Cold War, as might have been expected, but instead the events of

September 11, 2001, because these events pointed to a strategic divorce caused by the different historical experiences lived on both sides of the Atlantic. Thus, however shocked and spontaneously moved the Europeans might have been on the days that followed the attacks, the "day after" seemed to call for a return to the pre-9/11 conditions of interstate relations. In a world that remains tragic, the fate of great powers is to endure the pain that inevitably results from their status. Thus, even assuming that America has drifted toward the planet of Mars in the course of the three global wars it waged in the twentieth century, the Europeans remain all too aware of Mars's proximity to Venus, where they now seem happy to settle after many centuries of exhausting warfare. For Americans, however, September 11 threatened to open a "new normalcy" that does not suit America and its history. That new normalcy has to do with the relocation of war from the "over there" of yesteryear to the "over here" that tens of millions of Americans had to watch on television over and over.[36] When Europeans assume that history is moving on as usual, Americans insist that its reels must now be rewound so as to restore the conditions of invulnerability and even invincibility that have characterized their nation up to now.

The gap that underlies, and derives from, this strategic gap is not between power and weakness, but between force and order. The belief held in Europe is that the threats singled out after the Cold War, as well as those identified since September 11, can best be addressed by the use of nonmilitary power and a reliance on institutions. A reluctance to use force, compensated by a willingness to make generous use of economic power (including money and trade) and sign many more treaties, is offered as evidence for a more mature institutional order. Indeed, some view the enforcement of this model as Europe's new role—"to check the U.S. hubris" as part of a new *mission civilisatrice* whereby Europe would tame America and right its course.[37] But whereas such an approach was one that Americans once used to embrace when it came to taming Europe, it is no longer one Americans are willing to follow or even acknowledge, at least not now and certainly not exclusively: September 11 brought war onto their territory, and war accordingly must be returned to its evil sources. Admittedly, on the day after the war has been won militarily, it will have to be ended by nonmilitary means, thus calling for a different toolbox and different workers to be recruited. But peacekeeping depends on peacemaking, and even though military power is not sufficient for the former it remains nonetheless indispensable for the latter—hence the repeated U.S. criticism of Europe's culture of appeasement and its neglect of defense spending. Hence, too, Europe's increasingly harsh criticism of the United States' predilection for the use of military force and its dismissal of elementary questions of justice.

I lead you, hear you, and like you—and neither do I. So goes America's dialogue with Europe, and Europe's dialogue with America. More than ever before, this is a dialogue of the deaf—two monologues that are misheard and misrepresented. Should this condition continue, the transatlantic rift that erupted in 2002 with past tones of *déjà dit* could soon drift into the *jamais vu* of an existential divide between the United States and Europe. The danger of such a drift has less to do with recurring patterns of anti-Americanism in Europe than with a rising new anti-Europeanism in the United States. The former can be managed, and indeed the challenge for Americans will be merely to learn to live with "the resentments, irritations, and real grievances that inevitably accompany the rise to power of one nation, one culture, and one social model in a complex, divided, and passionate world."[38] The latter may be more defeating, however, should the idea that the risks raised by a united and strong European counterweight justify U.S. policies that would aim at dividing the EU rather than urging it on toward finality. After World War II, it was a conservative Christian writer, François Mauriac, who claimed that his "love" for Germany justified his passion for more than only one Germany. Now, it is the turn of American neoconservatives to proclaim their love for the EU with demands that there be more than one union only.

To avoid such an unwanted outcome, Europe will have to be seen for what it does even as the United States is heard for what it says—the former to demonstrate the constructive followership it accepts and the latter to explain the benign leadership it asserts. In short, exasperated Americans should understand at last that U.S. interests in Europe are far too significant to be left to apprehensive Europeans alone. In turn, apprehensive Europeans should also understand that a continued U.S. interest in Europe is far too important to be left to exasperated Americans alone. For this elementary truth to be not only understood but also enforced, the United States should reach out to its like-minded allies in Europe more than it has since September 11, 2001; at the same time the states of Europe should be more willing to reach out to their senior partner across the Atlantic than they were during the difficult debate that accompanied the war in Iraq 18 months later.

Notes

[1] A shorter version of this paper appeared as "Lo specchio dell'altro. L'antieuropeismo americano," *Aspenia* 19 (December 2002): 158–169, and, in its English version, as "A Dialogue of the Deaf," *Aspenia* 19–20 (2003): 69–80.

[2] Arnold Wolfers and Lawrence Martin, eds., *The Anglo-American Tradition in Foreign Affairs* (New Haven: Yale University Press, 1956), p. 162.

[3] Charles G. Cogan, *Oldest Allies, Guarded Friends: The United States and France Since 1940* (Westport, Conn.: Praeger, 1994), p. 200.

[4] Quoted in Detlef Junker, *American Perceptions of the German Empire, 1871–1945*, Occasional Papers, no. 12 (Washington, D.C.: German Historical Institute, 1995), p. 12.

[5] See the still-moving account by Stephan Zweig, who made of his faith in Europe "a religion." *The World of Yesterday* (Lincoln: University of Nebraska Press, 1964), p. xx.

[6] The image is adapted from Theodore H. White, *In Search of History: A Personal Adventure* (New York: Harper & Row, 1978), p. 275.

[7] "Many of us," remembered President Truman, "were apprehensive lest the isolationist spirit become an important political factor." Harry S. Truman, *Memoirs*, vol. 1, *Year of Decisions* (Garden City, N.Y.: Doubleday, 1955), p. 97.

[8] Jacques Barzun, *God's Country and Mine* (Boston: Little Brown, 1954), p. 10.

[9] Geir Lundestat, *Empire By Integration: The United States and European Integration, 1945–1997* (New York: Oxford University Press, 1998).

[10] See my "American Reflections on Europe's Finality," in *The European Finality Debate and Its National Dimensions*, ed. Simon Serfaty (Washington, D.C.: The CSIS Press, 2003), pp. 1–20.

[11] Robert Kagan, "Power and Weakness," *Policy Review* 113 (June–July 2002): 3.

[12] Thus read *Le Monde*'s main title two days after the infamous attacks. Jean-Marie Colombani, "Nous sommes tous Américains" (We are all Americans), *Le Monde*, September 13, 2001).

[13] "America won't listen to Europe's appeasers," complained Andrew Sullivan at a symposium whose tone bordered on hysteria. ("Friends? Foes? Disconnected Strangers? Europe and America over the next generation," with Jeffrey Gedmin, Andrew Sullivan, Jonathan Rauch, Mark Steyn, Michael Kelly, Jonah Goldberg, and John O'Sullivan, *American Enterprise* 13, no. 8 [December 2002]: 30–35.) Richard Perle is quoted by Edward Pilkington and Ewen MacAskill, "Europe Lacks Moral Fibre," *Guardian* (London), November 13, 2002.

[14] Walter Russell Mead, *Special Providence: American Foreign Policy and How It Changed the World* (New York: Alfred A. Knopf, 2002), p. 30.

[15] This phrase is attributed to the historian Peter Gray by David Gelernter, "The

Roots of European Appeasement," *Weekly Standard* (September 23, 2002): 19. Also, Karl Zinsmeister, "Old and In the Way," *American Enterprise* 13, no. 8 (December 2002): 9.

[16] The allegation comes from Michael Ledeen, quoted in Stuart Reid, "The Anti-Europeans," *American Conservative*, January 27, 2003. On the French surrender, see Niall Ferguson, "Europe Response to Iraq Reflects an Old Rift," *New York Times*, February 23, 2003. In early 2003, such rhetoric became depressingly common and increasingly disturbing, as, for example, the statement, "We should just have let the Kaiser keep the place [Belgium] in 1914." (Andrew Roberts, "France Has Always Been Selfish, But What's Germany's Problem?" *Daily Telegraph*, February 11, 2003.) And Tony Blankley, former speaker of the house Newt Gingrich's long-time press secretary before he turned himself into a columnist and a pundit, wrote, "should, in time, any of the current EU nations feel tainted by doing commerce with the French blackmailer and coward, our [free trade union] should be open to them." ("France Blackmails Poland," *Washington Times*, February 19, 2003.)

[17] David Reynolds, "1940: Fulcrum of the Twentieth Century?" *International Affairs* 66, no. 2 (1990): 327–329. Philippe Burrin, *France under the Germans* (New York: New Press, 1996), p. 5. See also the remarkably accurate postwar assessment, written by Alfred Vagts, "Battle and Other Combatant Casualties in the Second World War," *Journal of Politics* 7, no. 3 (August 1945): 285.

[18] Will Hutton, *The World We're In* (Boston: Little Brown, 2002), p. 357.

[19] Tony Judt, "Anti-Americans Abroad," *New York Review of Books* 50, no. 7 (May 1, 2003): 24–29.

[20] See the author's *La France vue d'Amérique: Réflexions sur la francophobie à Washington* (Paris: IFRI, 2002).

[21] Simon Schama, "The Unloved American," *New Yorker* (March 10, 2003): 34.

[22] Vincent Auriol, *Mon Septennat, 1947–1954* (Paris: Gallimard, 1970). Quoted in Alfred Grosser, *Les Occidentaux* (Paris: Fayard, 1978), p. 139. François Mitterrand, *Ici et maintenant* (Paris: Fayard, 1980), pp. 242, 231. Mitterrand's appraisal of Reagan was shared by Helmut Kohl, as reported by Mitterrand's close associate Jacques Attali. Quoted in Harvey Sicherman, "The Rest of Reagan," *Orbis* 44, no. 3 (Summer 2000): 443.

[23] Special report, unsigned, "Does Britain Like Us? Anti-Americanism Is Growing . . . Fed by Fear, Envy, Frustration, and Years of Want," *Newsweek*, December 22, 1947, pp. 26–27. Denis W. Brogan, "The Wicked Uncle," *Spectator*, October 31, 1947, p. 550 (emphasis in original). For a post–Cold War equivalent of Brogan's analysis, see Oliver Todd's indictment of America's transformation "from a protective force into a predatory force" in *Après l'empire: Essai sur la decomposition du système américain* (Paris: Gallimard, 2002).

[24] Norman Podhoretz, *Making It* (New York: Random House, 1967), p. 85. Stanley Hoffmann, "To Be or Not to Be French," in Linda B. Miller and Michael J. Smith, eds., *Ideas and Ideals: Essays on Politics in Honor of Stanley Hoffmann* (Boulder, Colo.: Westview Press, 1993), p. 32.

[25] Jean-François Revel, *L'obsession anti-américaine* (Paris: Plon, 2002). Note the subtitle Revel gave to his book—*son fonctionnement, ses causes, ses inconséquences* (its functioning, its causes, its inconsequences).

[26] For example, see Alain Franchon, "Les années bis," *Le Monde*, February 16, 2002. See also Thomas Friedman's explicit distinction between anti-Americanism and anti-Bushism in "Let Them Come to Berlin," *New York Times*, November 3, 2002.

[27] The theme in this section is more extensively treated in my "Power and Order," in *Beyond Power and Paradise*, ed. Tod Lindberg (Stanford, Calif.: Stanford University Press, forthcoming).

[28] Bob Woodward, *Bush At War* (New York: Simon & Schuster, 2002), p. 96.

[29] Remarks to the New York Police Department Command and Control Center Performance, New York, February 6, 2002.

[30] Quoted in the *Washington Post*, January 27, 2002, p. A13.

[31] For a critical view of recent political scare tactics à la Truman, see E. J. Dionne, "Inevitably, the Politics of Terror," *Washington Post*, May 25, 2003, p. B1.

[32] Pierre Hassner, "Friendly Questions to America the Powerful," *In the National Interest* 1, no. 13 (Fall 2002); www.inthenationalinterest.com/Articles/Vol1Issue13/Vol1Issue13Hassner.html (accessed June 5, 2003). See also Lawrence F. Kaplan, "Return Address," *New Republic*, June 10, 2002, p. 19.

[33] "La guerre américaine a commencé" (The American war has begun), *Le Monde*, March 21, 2003.

[34] Reagan's widely remembered question to the American people, posed in his closing remarks during the October 28, 1980, presidential election debate, was " . . . are you better off than you were four years ago?"

[35] Mead, *Special Providence*, p. 30.

[36] Vice President Dick Cheney first used the term "new normalcy" in an interview published in the *Washington Post* on October 21, 2001.

[37] Charles A. Kupchan, "It's Up to EU to Check U.S. Hubris," *Los Angeles Times*, November 10, 2002.

[38] Walter Russell Mead, "Review Essay: Why Do They Hate Us? Two Books Take Aim at French Anti-Americanism," *Foreign Affairs* 82, no. 2 (March/April 2003): 142.

PART TWO

AMERICAN VISIONS OF EUROPE

TWO

AMERICAN VISIONS OF EUROPE AFTER 1989

John L. Harper

"There is a pressing need for vision in our world," observed Jacques Delors a year after the fall of the Berlin Wall, "and particularly vision on a world scale."[1] To meet that need, Delors urged that the European Community (EC) pursue new ambitions and realize the partnership of equals dreamed of by Jean Monnet. Delors was also responding to the American vision of a "new world order" sketched out after the outbreak of the first Persian Gulf crisis and on the eve of the reunification of Germany. The U.S. initiative, in turn, reflected criticism of President George H. W. Bush's admitted shortcomings in the realm of "the vision thing." I set out at the time to explain the visions of Europe that had influenced an earlier generation of policymakers.[2] By vision I mean a kind of ideal and ultimate design, representing the intermingling of uniquely personal and broader cultural influences, never fully realized or realizable, but conditioning the thought and action of statesmen.[3] After briefly setting out those early postwar visions, this chapter will try to determine what became of them after the Cold War and the light they shed on the American approach to Europe after September 11, 2001.

RETIRE, RESTORE, OR EMBRACE?

What to do with Europe was the central problem of American foreign policy in the past century. In essence, the problem was how to save Europe from its destructive impulses and prevent its conflicts from engulfing the rest of the world. Different people proposed different solutions, but there were three main tendencies or approaches among the American elites, each represented by Franklin Roosevelt, George Kennan, and Dean Acheson.

Franklin Roosevelt's outlook combined an old American confidence in his country's moral superiority and destiny, an animosity toward the European state system, and a finely honed instinct to divide and rule. Roosevelt was no doctrinaire Wilsonian or multilateralist. His vision of Europe was of a continent reduced to a state of weakness and irrelevancy, in effect retired from its long and checkered career at the center of world politics. In May 1942, Roosevelt told the Soviet foreign minister that four essentially non-European powers—the United States, Britain, the Soviet Union, and China—should monopolize military power and be "the policemen of the world." On Germany, FDR observed, "There are two schools of thought—those who would be altruistic in regard to the Germans . . . and those who would adopt a much 'tougher' attitude. . . . Most decidedly I belong to the latter school."[4]

A high official's appraisal of Soviet war aims was a fair summary of what Roosevelt himself had in mind:

> Germany is to be broken up and kept broken up. The states of eastern, southeastern, and central Europe will not be permitted to group themselves into any federations or associations. France is to be stripped of her colonies and strategic bases beyond her borders and will not be permitted to maintain any appreciable military establishment. . . . The result will be that the Soviet Union will be the only important political and military force on the continent of Europe. The rest of Europe will be reduced to political and military impotence.[5]

Roosevelt opposed schemes for European unity and a European regional organization for at least three reasons: they might appear threatening to Moscow, or become vehicles for committing U.S. ground forces to Europe (he believed air power would suffice to punish future aggression), or perhaps lead to a Europe beyond outside control. Part and parcel of Europe's demotion was the loss of its overseas possessions and the emergence of the United States as the leading power in what became the "Third World." FDR foresaw a set of U.S. bases spanning the globe and a new U.S. role in the Middle East, including patron-client relationships with Saudi Arabia (whose king he met after Yalta) and Iran.

The wishful thinking and contradictions in Roosevelt's vision reflected the wishful thinking and contradictions in popular attitudes: Americans wanted to make the Old World pay for its sins and impose a definitive solution to the problem of internecine conflict. But they recoiled from the prospect of U.S. entanglement and preferred to focus on what many, including FDR himself, considered to be America's more natural and vital concerns *outside* of Europe, leaving others to enforce the peace. For many months Roosevelt refused to accept a U.S. occupation zone in southern Germany because he feared it would become a trap. At Yalta, he famously told Churchill and Stalin that American troops would have to leave the Continent within two years after the war.

Well before 1945, State Department officials like Adolf A. Berle, William C. Bullitt, and George F. Kennan began to denounce plans to abandon Europe and promote the idea of European unity.[6] While they did not foresee a long-term U.S. presence, they feared Soviet expansionism and recognized that the United States must remain in Europe for a transitional period. European unity acquired strong support in Washington for at least three reasons. First, a single market would mean greater economies of scale, higher production, and a larger market for U.S. exports. An integrated Europe was also an essential component of the kind of open world economy that had broken down after 1914. Second, a single market would bring American-style prosperity and an end to political extremism. Third, economic integration, leading (so it was assumed) to political integration, would mean the end of the wars that had necessitated costly U.S. interventions. A federation would provide a framework in which to revive the German economy, a prerequisite for the revival of the rest of Europe. A united Europe would have two additional benefits: it would give Europe the strength and cohesion to be able to counterbalance Russia without having to rely permanently on outside support as well as share America's burdens in other parts of the world.

The strongest U.S. supporters of European unity were those who did not believe that the United States could afford—nor that it was consistent with American principles—to maintain a protectorate over Europe. According to U.S. officials in 1950, when the objective of meeting and deterring a Soviet attack had been achieved, it was "hoped that the United States would be able to leave to the European nation members the primary responsibility, with the collaboration of the United States, of maintaining and commanding" an integrated Western force. According to Eisenhower, "it is not possible—and most certainly not desirable—that [Western] Europe should be an occupied territory defended by legions from abroad." As he put it in November 1955, U.S. policy should encourage the emergence of a "third great-power bloc."[7]

Secretary of State Dean Acheson, whose creed included patient consultation of the Europeans, was one of the first to conclude Europeans did not *want* to be left to their own devices and that doing so risked losing control of a vital part of the world. Despite U.S. pressure and impressive progress (the European Payments Union, the European Coal and Steel Community, the Rome treaties), Washington was obliged to accept London's reluctance to take part in the integration process, the failure of efforts to apply integration to defense (the European Defense Community [EDC] episode), the rather abject insistence of European (especially French Fourth Republic) governments on U.S. guarantees and physical presence in Europe (out of fear of the Germans as much as of the Russians), and the alarming possibility of a nuclear-armed Germany if U.S. troops were to withdraw. De Gaulle's across-the-board challenge to U.S. foreign policy after 1958 raised the possibility, finally, that a Europe based on a strong Franco-German axis might pursue its own agenda toward the international economic system, Russia, the Middle East, and the Far East.

In the 1960s a consensus emerged in the United States around several propositions. First, a considerable degree of European integration is positive (it fosters wealth, markets, and stability) and opposing unity would provoke an anti-American reaction. Second, the Europeans do not seem to be willing to coalesce except in the context of U.S. protection. Third, the breakup of the Atlantic community—the loosening of the U.S. political-military embrace—would lead to one of several possible results, each of which would be negative: Soviet domination of Europe; the return of internecine conflict; the emergence of a united but politically unreliable and/or protectionist entity. U.S. policy, therefore, sought to influence both the internal character and international orientation of the European Economic Community (EEC) with multilateral trade negotiations, bilateral "special relationships," and eventually direct ties with the Brussels bureaucracy, while striving to preserve NATO as the main instrument of U.S. influence and as the ceiling beyond which a purely European integration could not evolve.

In effect, this Achesonian consensus was a synthesis of Roosevelt's program to subordinate Europe and Kennan's and Eisenhower's desires to restore its strength and autonomy. Washington's approach was fundamentally ambivalent, reflecting the conviction that European unity entailed both benefits and risks for the United States. For their part, mainstream European leaders came to see the advantages of integration (with intra-European trade increasing dramatically after 1957), while they frequently resented the behavior of the United States. Indeed, there has always been a link between European perceptions of excessive U.S. power and/or U.S. unreliability and the will to pursue the Rome Treaty's aim of "ever closer union," and a more independent European role in the world. At the same time, few favored the surrender of sovereignty over defense and foreign policy, or believed that Europe could or should defend itself without U.S. backing. Throughout the Cold War, U.S. ambivalence toward European unity and autonomy was matched and reinforced by European ambivalence.

ACHESONIANISM'S SECOND LEASE ON LIFE

The collapse of the Berlin Wall, and of the Soviet Union itself, removed the most basic reason for NATO's existence and raised the possibility that the United States would return to a pre-1941 focus on domestic affairs and/or other parts of the world. The same events left the United States as the sole superpower. The sensation of a growing disparity in power between the United States and Europe was reinforced by the so-called Revolution in Military Affairs (RMA) on display in the Persian Gulf War in 1991 and during the Kosovo air campaign. Simultaneously, the end of the Cold War and the prospect of a U.S. withdrawal prompted the EC states to adopt plans for a more tightly integrated Europe able to house a reunified Germany. The Maastricht treaty creating the European Union (EU) committed Europe not only to Economic and Monetary Union (EMU), but a Common Foreign and Security Policy (CFSP) designed to enhance Europe's self-reliance and international influence. If the wars of the 1990s showed the unprecedented superiority of the United States, they prompted the Europeans to try to pursue Delors's ambitions in the realm of foreign policy and defense.

It fell to the George H. W. Bush administration to react to these dramatic developments and to answer the question of how important Europe would remain in the overall scheme of post–Cold War U.S. policy. In an address in 1989, Bush observed that "[t]here has been a historic ambivalence on the part of some Americans toward a more united Europe. To this ambivalence has been added apprehension at the prospect of the single market. But whatever others may think, this administration is of one mind. We believe a strong, united Europe means a strong America."[8] It would be an exaggeration to say that Bush's rhetoric masked a Rooseveltian hostility toward the idea of a strong Europe, but nor did his administration seriously consider reviving the Kennan-Eisenhower approach. One of the ironies of post–Cold War transatlantic relations is that while the EC was poised to begin its most dynamic decade since the 1950s, with the fading of the early postwar generation, there was no longer an influential segment of U.S. opinion supporting the idea of "a third great power bloc." Despite the president's pronouncements, Bush and his national security adviser later acknowledged that they *were* ambivalent toward the Maastricht project and concerned about a loss of U.S. control.[9]

If anything, their foreign policy was reflexively Achesonian, in both its Europe-first orientation and its basic aims. The administration rejected early the suggestion of a Rooseveltian or "Yalta II" approach—in effect, a continuation of two blocs with a Finlandized East-Central Europe. It decided instead to accommodate Germany's wish for rapid reunification and to pursue "a Europe whole and free." The fundamental aim was to ensure, in Secretary of State James Baker's words, that "the United States is and will remain a European power"—meaning the leading power—regardless of the events of 1989–1991.[10] The Clinton administration, reacting to what Secretary of State Warren Christopher called Bush's overly "Eurocentric" policy and fearing that the Balkans might become a Vietnam-like distraction from U.S. domestic priorities, initially seemed to adopt a more Kennanesque position and encourage the Europeans to manage their own security problems.[11] By the mid-1990s, Clinton too had adopted the Achesonian approach.

The Bush-Clinton policy was based on several widely held assumptions. First, the United States acting through NATO continued to be Europe's indispensable pacifier and organizer. Left to their own devices, the European states were unlikely to form an effective coalition. In trying to protect itself, Germany would create a "security dilemma," and old conflicts would reemerge.[12] A second, largely unspoken, assumption (though it lay behind the U.S. preference for a "broadening" of EU membership over a "deepening" of EU institutions and behind opposition to an EU bloc in NATO) was that the EU might coalesce to a point from which it could challenge the United States. Third, most European states wanted the United States to remain the leading European power as an insurance policy against Russia and preferred the United States as organizer-protector to the hypothetical alternatives of Germany or the EU.

Keeping NATO alive as the main instrument of U.S. political influence in Europe entailed giving it a new strategic concept, as well as new tasks to justify its existence in the eyes of U.S. public opinion: promoting stability in Central and Eastern Europe through the North Atlantic Cooperation Council, the Partnership for Peace, and eventually incorporating Poland, Hungary, and the Czech Republic into the alliance.[13] The motto of the neo-Achesonians became "out of [NATO] area, or out of business," an approach whose logical extension, once the pacification of the Continent was completed, would be to use NATO elsewhere, for example in the Middle East.

Keeping NATO alive also entailed dealing with the protracted controversy over the relationship between NATO and the EU's CFSP and eventually its European Security and Defense Policy (ESDP). The controversy began in the context of the Persian Gulf crisis. Europe's incoherent response reinforced Washington's view that, unless the United States took the lead, little or nothing would be done. In early 1991, the State Department warned the Europeans (through the so-called Bartholomew memorandum) against an EU "caucus" through which EU members of NATO would speak with a single voice in the alliance. In a move reminiscent of the Kennedy administration's démarche against the 1963 Franco-German treaty, Washington pressured the Germans not to accept a French proposal implying such a bloc.[14]

The United States was also concerned about a possible European entity that might act outside of NATO's integrated command. Bush's NATO ambassador warned that "undermining the alliance's integrated military structure . . . would be the height of folly." In trying to prepare for the day when the United States would no longer be in Europe, he said, the Europeans might actually accelerate U.S. withdrawal. Washington's policy was to circumscribe rather than openly oppose a "European Security and Defense Identity." Shortly before the signature of the Maastricht treaty, the United States persuaded its allies to endorse the Rome Declaration, which stated that NATO is the "essential forum for consultation and the locus of decision for agreements regarding the security commitments of the allies arising out of the North Atlantic Treaty."[15] In other words, whatever security policy the EU adopts must be compatible with the *existing* obligations of member states under the Atlantic pact.

In the mid-1990s, the Bosnia crisis reinforced Washington's already strong Achesonian predilections, namely, that the United States must embrace and lead Europe rather than allow it to fend for itself. The memoirs of Bosnia negotiator Richard Holbrooke (while acknowledging French president Jacques Chirac's role in forcing the Clinton administration to "fish or cut bait" in the Balkans) are laced with biting, patronizing commentary on the EU's incapacity to act. He approvingly quotes William Pfaff's analysis at the time of NATO's September 1995 bombing operation: "The United States today is again Europe's leader; there is no other. Both the Bush and Clinton administrations tried, and failed, to convince the European governments to take over European leadership." Europe's record was a sorry one, but in reality neither the Bush nor the Clinton administration had tried to convince European governments to assume main responsibility for the security of the Continent, and Clinton's had helped to undermine the UN-EU plan for Bosnia in 1993. Bosnia, in any case, was now the proof that it was "dangerous and unrealistic" to imagine that U.S. leadership in Europe was no longer needed. Like Baker, Holbrooke believed Europe was still an essential partner for the United States. And, echoing Baker, Holbrooke spoke of "America, still a European power."[16]

According to the old pattern, Europeans drew a rather different lesson—that they must be able to act more effectively on their own. At NATO's Berlin summit in 1996, an agreement was reached whereby the European Security and Defense Identity (ESDI) would rely on NATO assets in order to carry out a modest set of missions (the Petersberg Tasks). The next phase of the controversy began with the decision of the British government to agree to develop an autonomous EU defense capacity. The Europeans' perception of U.S. unilateralism and excessive power—combined with their sense of dismay at their own weakness— during the 1999 Kosovo campaign prompted them to accelerate plans for a 60,000-strong rapid reaction force, an EU military and security committee, and a military staff.

In the same breath as they criticized a lack of European will and capabilities, U.S. officials warned against an entity that might "decouple" U.S. and European security, lead to wasteful "duplication" of NATO assets, and "discriminate" against non-EU members of NATO, such as Turkey. Echoing the 1991 Rome Declaration, a U.S. congressman and a former supreme allied commander Europe (SACEUR) insisted after Kosovo that NATO must have "the right of first refusal" before the EU or other institutions became involved in decisionmaking on the handling of security problems on the Continent. In late 2000, almost exactly 10 years after the Bartholomew memorandum, the U.S. secretary of defense denounced the idea of an EU caucus in NATO. When the Republican administration took power in 2001, the question of whether the alliance would continue to serve as an instrument of U.S. leadership, and as a ceiling to purely European integration, was in doubt.[17]

American elites' skepticism extended to the EU's other ambitions. In a book called *Europe Adrift*, a prominent Europe watcher voiced doubts about EMU. The editor of an important foreign policy journal argued that EMU would be bad whether it failed or succeeded. Failure would mean the unraveling of European integration, while success would mean a more independent and defiant Europe. For an influential economist, "Instead of increasing intra-European harmony and global peace, the shift to EMU and the political integration that would follow it would be more likely to lead to increased conflicts within Europe and between Europe and the United States. . . ." A well-known commentator brilliantly, if inadvertently, expressed persistent American ambivalence toward European unity when he wrote, "The EU's progressive success in burying centuries-old European antagonisms would be well worth a gradual diminution of America's role as Europe's arbitrator." On an adjoining page of the same article, he noted,

> A larger Europe [an enlarged EU] will expand the range of American influence without simultaneously creating a Europe so politically integrated that it could challenge the United States on matters of geopolitical importance, particularly in the Middle East.[18]

THE REVIVAL OF ELITE EUROPHOBIA

A decade after Delors proclaimed "Europe's ambitions," the mainstream, psychologically reassuring, view in Washington continued to be that Europe was unlikely to "put its money where its mouth is." American observers tended to either deny or discount the EU's progress on the single market and EMU, for example, owing not only to the Balkans but also to the boom of the U.S. economy and stock markets (stoked by massive inflows of European capital), the lagging performance of the Continental economies, and the decline of the euro after its inception in 1999. But in instances where Europe did act, there was irritation with European pretensions and anxiety about the possible consequences. The latter cases included the European Commission's activism in the field of antitrust regulation (for example, the blocking of the Honeywell–General Electric merger) and plans to build Galileo, an alternative to the U.S. satellite-based global positioning system (GPS) that would break the U.S. commercial monopoly and portend greater European strategic independence from the United States.

Despite, or rather because of, its Euroskepticism, the Clinton administration's foreign policy proved in the end to be as Eurocentric as its predecessor's. Its triumphalist description of America as "the indispensable nation" was linked to Bosnia, Kosovo, and the enlargement of NATO. But even as the neo-Achesonians seemed to have confirmed their hold on U.S. European policy, a journalist commented: "Few Europeans have appreciated the extent to which, when the Cold War ended, their relevance to Washington ended too."[19]

The history of the 1990s indicates that this statement is an exaggeration, but there is no doubt that over the course of the decade older views of Europe had come into play. Although advanced mainly by conservatives, the chief competitor to the Achesonian view was strikingly Rooseveltian in some of its basic assumptions: as a geopolitical space Europe was not at the top of American priorities and should not be a drain on U.S. assets, and the United States was the force of the future and the countries of Europe were for the most part unhelpful or irrelevant to America's world mission. The United States' natural partners, starting with the Anglo-Saxon countries, were to be found beyond the confines of the European continent.

The reasons for the revival of a significant Rooseveltian, or Europhobic, strain in U.S. thinking are open to debate. In 1998, the political scientist, Stephen Walt, spoke of "deep structural forces" pulling Europe and America apart. "No matter how many new states join NATO, and no matter how many solemn reaffirmations emerge from the endless parade of NATO summits, the high-water mark of transatlantic security cooperation is past." He pointed to the erosion or disappearance of "three unifying factors": "America's economic stake in Europe," the Soviet threat, and a U.S. elite committed to the idea of an Atlantic community.[20] Historians are inclined to discount the importance of economic tensions, including the impact of the euro. These tensions, they argue, have been a permanent feature of transatlantic relations, and they have been coped with in the past. If, since 1983, U.S. trade with Asia has been greater in value than U.S. trade with Europe, trade with Europe has remained significant, and U.S. investment in Europe is several times higher than in Asia.[21] Walt's second factor was surely more significant: NATO's resilience notwithstanding, the demise of the Soviet Union inevitably brought a devaluation of Europe's relative importance in the eyes of many U.S. politicians and strategists. The change was reflected in the reduction of U.S. troop strength in Europe from about 300,000 to about 100,000 and in cuts in U.S. defense spending as a percentage of gross domestic product (GDP) to levels not seen since 1939.

In the context of downsizing and reduced spending, Washington adopted a strategy requiring the military to focus on preparing to win two simultaneous regional wars *outside* of Europe. Meanwhile, with Europe's defense spending and procurement falling even more rapidly than America's, the technological gap between the two sides and the feeling that European forces could no longer effectively operate alongside U.S. forces increased. These factors, along with the Vietnam-born fear of "mission creep," were evident in the reactions of the U.S. military and U.S. conservatives to the humanitarian interventions of the 1990s. The Defense Department stubbornly resisted the efforts of Holbrooke and his military adviser, General Wesley Clark, to impose a broad mandate on U.S. forces deployed to implement the Dayton agreement. Clark (appointed SACEUR after Dayton) observed that the Pentagon's refusal to countenance U.S. ground forces in Kosovo as a preventive measure in 1998 "reflected a reluctance in Washington to undertake another mission in the Balkans and a National Military Strategy obsessively oriented on fighting hypothetical conflicts in two other theaters." For the same reasons, the Pentagon strongly resisted planning for a ground offensive in Kosovo. "For some of my American colleagues and superiors in uniform [the Kosovo war] was at times a distant and troublesome distraction."[22] For others, the air operation, with its selection of targets by committee, was a deplorable example of how the United States had allowed others to tie its hands.

During the 2000 election campaign, Republicans charged that Clinton's combination of budget cuts and allegedly indiscriminate deployment of U.S. forces had been "devastating." George W. Bush's future national security adviser, Condoleezza Rice, indicated that escorting children to kindergarten in the Balkans would be left to others. More generally, she charged that the Clinton administration "had often been so anxious to find multilateral solutions to problems that it has signed agreements that are not in America's interest." Examples included the Kyoto protocol, the Comprehensive Test Ban Treaty, and the treaty creating the International Criminal Court (ICC). "Foreign policy in a

Republican administration will most certainly be internationalist . . . [b]ut it will also proceed from the firm ground of the national
interest, not from the interests of an *illusory international community*."
Rice and others laid out an ambitious program including "containing
Chinese power and security ambitions," developing national missile
defense (NMD) systems, and regime change in Iraq.[23] In contrast with
the ambivalent outlooks of the Bush Sr. and the Clinton administrations, the attitude of some in the George W. Bush circle toward Europe
was one of thinly veiled contempt.

This change begs consideration of the third of Walt's factors: the
evolving nature of public opinion. Walt invokes much-discussed trends
that include the fading of the World War II–Marshall Plan generation
("watching *Saving Private Ryan* is no substitute for having lived though
the real thing"), "a profound Westward shift in the U.S. population,"
and the changing ethnic makeup of the United States (the percentage of
U.S. citizens of European origin is expected to decline from 80 percent
in 1980 to 64 percent in 2020). Again, a historian is inclined to be skeptical. Recent polls indicate that most Americans have a favorable opinion of European countries and favor cooperation between the United
States and Europe. The appeal of the idea of a "Pacific Destiny" to the
popular imagination was probably stronger in 1900, or 1940, than it
was when Walt's article appeared in 1998. By the same token, American
popular hostility to European governments was deeper in the first decade of the twentieth century, or in the 1930s, when the ethnic composition of the United States was more solidly European, than it is today.
Nonetheless, there is truth in Walt's prediction that "instead of being
guided by an elite group of East coast internationalists committed to
Europe by family backgrounds, personal experiences, and professional
affiliations, U.S. foreign policy will be shaped by a more diverse collection of elites whose ethnic characteristics, geographic points of reference, and personal experiences will not grant Europe pride of place."[24]

Irving Kristol sheds useful light on the origins of these new elites. He
points to two significant developments of the 1960s and 1970s: the conversion of influential liberals like himself to a set of ideas known as neoconservatism and the rise of "religious conservatives, especially Protestant evangelical conservatives, as a force to be reckoned with." The new
conservatism's domestic enemy was not "statism in the abstract," but a
secular liberalism that undermined traditional values and fostered de-
pendency. "In a way, the symbol of the influence of neoconservative

thinking on the Republican party was the fact that Ronald Reagan could praise Franklin D. Roosevelt as a great American president." The party did not wish to destroy the welfare state but "to reconstruct it along more economical and more humane lines."[25]

In the realm of foreign policy, the galvanizing event for neoconservative Democrats and long-standing Republican conservatives was Vietnam. Kristol and others castigated "the liberal-internationalist foreign policy establishment, which brought the United States into the Vietnam War and then, through timidity and miscalculation, failed to win it." If that largely Protestant, Europhile establishment had thrown in the towel, the mainly Jewish neoconservatives viewed themselves as members of a legitimate successor elite. Before embracing Reagan they took as their political champion a Pacific coast Democrat of Polish Catholic origin, Henry Jackson. Another ambitious Polish Catholic with views similar to those of the neoconservatives declared in 1976 that the white Anglo-Saxon Protestant elite had met its Waterloo in Vietnam. In the wake of Vietnam, moreover, the moderate wing of the Republican Party fatally compromised its credibility in the eyes of conservatives by pursuing a strategy of "appeasement," Kissinger's détente.[26]

By contrast, Kristol wrote in 1985 that it was the view of the "new conservatism" that "we should aim to win this [Cold] war. . . . And, inevitably, as in any contest, if you aim to win rather than merely to tie, reasonable risks are to be taken." The United States, moreover, should be prepared to do this unilaterally:

> Abroad, an assertive American foreign policy meets with great resistance from our allies, most of whom are utterly risk-averse, and some of whom believe that a grudging appeasement of Soviet power will mollify its messianic appetite. *This is especially evident in Western Europe,* where under the American nuclear umbrella, national pride has softened into something that resembles national pique.[27]

NATO as currently structured was "an archaic institution." Anticipating Condoleezza Rice, Kristol asserted that there was no such thing as a "'community of nations' or any 'world community' that shares certain essential values." For Kristol it was "reasonable to foresee American foreign policy disengaging itself from all those 'foreign entanglements' our State Department has so assiduously contrived over the past forty years"—not just NATO but also the UN. "These turn out to be ineffectual barriers against 'aggression'—itself a murky concept—but very effective hindrances to American action. . . . In the years ahead, the United States will be far less inhibited in its use of military power, with or without the approval of its allies."[28]

Conservatives understandably saw the fall of the Berlin Wall as the vindication of their basic strategy. With the 1991 Gulf War and the unfolding of the much-vaunted RMA, they believed they had witnessed the coming of the "unipolar moment." America's allies during the campaign against Iraq had been mere window dressing. Charles Krauthammer dismissed the Bush administration's notion of a new world order based on a great-power concert working through the UN Security Council as needlessly multilateralist and wedded to the status quo. The United States could and would act to defend its interests unilaterally. In what must have been a spell of euphoria in the wake of liberal opposition to NAFTA and of the Republican victory in the 1994 congressional elections, Kristol stated, "one thing is clear: Multilateralism is dead so far as *both* parties are concerned. This is something our European allies seem not to understand."[29]

It is important to stress that in contrast with the 1980s, however, the 1990s were a decade of unfulfilled expectations and frustration for neoconservatives and their evangelical Christian allies. In their view, at the end of the Gulf War the Bush administration had let the strategic prize slip through its fingers out of deference to an international coalition. In general, U.S. foreign policy continued to be multilateralist and Achesonian in inspiration. Not only did Saddam Hussein survive; Bill Clinton—the man some considered to be the Antichrist—turned the tables on Newt Gingrich after 1994, crushed the Republican candidate in 1996, and beat back the crusade to drive him from office in 1998–1999. Conservative intellectuals charged that instead of "preserving and reinforcing America's benevolent global hegemony," the United States had "tended toward a course of gradual moral and of strategic disarmament." Instead of pressing for regime change in Baghdad, Pyongyang, and Beijing (!), American leaders had opted for "drift and evasion."[30] It is not difficult to see why, with the election of George W. Bush—a man lacking his father's multilateralist instincts and determined to retain the backing of the Republican Right—conservatives might believe that, twenty years after Reagan's victory, their day had once again arrived.

Early in the Bush presidency an influential analysis echoed Kristol's argument about the gulf in threat perceptions and "strategic cultures" between Europe and America. Robert Kagan's basic explanation was a discrepancy in the power and, consequently, in the psychologies of the two sides. As was only natural, U.S. military strength "produced a propensity to use that strength." Europe's military weakness produced "a perfectly understandable aversion to the exercise of military power." If the question was, "Can the United States handle the rest of the world without much help from Europe," Kagan's answer was that "it already does. . . . Europe has had little to offer the United States in strategic military terms since the end of the Cold War—except, of course, that most valuable of strategic assets, a Europe at peace." Europe, in other words, despite its combined GDP, despite the EU's accomplishments, despite the fact that military traditions flourished in several of its nations, was declared to be exactly what Roosevelt had wished it to be: retired from the game of power politics and basically irrelevant to the United States.[31]

GEORGE W. BUSH, EUROPE, AND SEPTEMBER 11, 2001

Once in power, no important Bush administration official openly challenged the United States' NATO commitment. The administration pursued Clinton's program of eastern enlargement of the alliance to its logical conclusion. On the Balkans, Secretary of State Colin Powell (following Baker, Holbrooke, Clark, and Albright, he became the custodian of Achesonian continuity in U.S. policy) assured the allies that Washington would not leave them in the lurch. Nonetheless, the administration "came into office with a chip on its shoulder. It was hostile to the new Europe."[32] The view that the Balkans, and the Continent in general, were distractions from more serious priorities, that the United States must not *and need not* allow the pursuit of its national interests to be conditioned by Europeans or by an "illusory international community," was tenaciously held in the National Security Council (NSC), the Pentagon, and the arms control bureau of the State Department.[33] The administration swiftly distinguished itself by its willingness to run roughshod over European sensibilities on climate change, national missile defense and the Anti-Ballistic Missile (ABM) Treaty, steel tariffs, agricultural subsidies, and the ICC.

Coming in this context, the events of September 11, 2001, had a contradictory impact on U.S.-European relations. Initial effects were deceptively positive. In Europe, September 11 produced genuine horror and feelings of solidarity, even if Europeans were quicker than

Americans to draw the connection between the attacks and America's hegemonic role in the Middle East.[34] Washington's relatively patient, focused, and successful conduct of the first phase of the war on terrorism suggested that it had rejected a unilateral crusade and recognized that it *did* need help to stabilize Afghanistan and crush Islamic terrorist networks—many of them located in Europe. In the aftermath of September 11, it appeared that some of the land mines in the path of U.S.-European relations might be sidestepped. With U.S.-Russian relations improving, the Bush administration's abrogation of the ABM Treaty and NATO's invitation to the Baltic states caused barely a ripple in transatlantic relations. China (Washington's designated "rogue," pre–September 11) seemed destined for a period of benign neglect—precisely when it needed calm in order to continue liberalization and carry out the transition to the "fourth generation" of party leaders. Given the U.S.-European divisions that a blowup in the Taiwan Strait would probably provoke, U.S. neglect of China had fringe benefits for the transatlantic relationship.

At the same time, the reaction of administration hard-liners to European offers of help was instructive: they viewed NATO's decision to aid the United States under Article V "less as a boon than as a booby trap." Deputy Secretary of Defense Paul Wolfowitz delivered Donald Rumsfeld's message that "the mission would define the coalition." A senior Pentagon official was quoted as saying with respect to NATO's post–September 11 relevance: "Preserve the myth, and laugh."[35]

A pair of key developments in the first half of 2002 further belied hopes for improved U.S.-European relations in the wake of 9/11. The Manichean ("either with us or against us") manner in which Bush defined the war against terrorism translated itself into what looked to Europeans like U.S. carte blanche toward Israeli leader Ariel Sharon's bid (predating September 11) to crush the Palestinian Authority. Europeans were appalled by Palestinian suicide bombings but also by what they considered Israel's brutal and strategically blind policy toward the occupied territories, implicitly backed by the United States. U.S. conservatives were appalled that Europeans were appalled.

The second development was Washington's deliberate conflation of the war against Al Qaeda with the objective of confronting "rogue states," announced without warning in President Bush's January 2002 State of the Union address, better known as the "axis of evil" speech. With Osama bin Laden still at large, and in the absence of proof linking

Iraq to Al Qaeda, the logic of this decision escaped most Europeans. It was a rude awakening to the reality that their views carried little weight.

Future historians will have an interesting time trying to reconstruct this decision. At least three factors appear to have been in play. The first was the climate of anger, fear, and vulnerability created in the United States by September 11, further widening the threat-perception gap between the two sides of the Atlantic. U.S. leaders reasoned that they would be derelict in their duty not to address the possibility, however unlikely, that states acquiring weapons of mass destruction might give them to terrorists to use against U.S. targets. Second, the abrupt fall of the Taliban not only put phase two on the agenda; it suggested that the United States was capable of taking down hostile regimes quickly and with a minimum of outside help. Third, and probably most important, September 11 created a golden opportunity for the hard-line elements of the administration to advance policies to which they had been committed long beforehand. The shared aim of old anti-détente Republicans like Rumsfeld and Cheney and neoconservatives like Wolfowitz and Richard Perle was to consolidate and prolong U.S. hegemony for an indefinite period; this meant the prevention of the emergence of peer rivals such as China or the EU. The same program foresaw exemplary preventive action—now easier to justify to the public than before September 11—against the most despised and most vulnerable of the rogues, Saddam Hussein.[36] Perhaps to counter the charge that the administration was anti-Islamic or Israel-centric, the neoconservatives advanced the dubious argument that transforming Iraq into a U.S. client would deliver a decisive blow to terrorism and lay the groundwork for a wave of democratization in the Middle East. Hard-liners were eager, in any event, to demonstrate what some had long been saying: the United States could and would act without interference from Europe or the UN.

Indeed it appeared to them, as it had to Roosevelt, that the natural partners of the United States in its pursuit of its global interests lay outside Europe: the British, the Russians, maybe even the Chinese. In the spirit of "out of area or out of business," former Clinton administration officials appealed for a NATO role in Iraq and, more grandiosely, for a "new transatlantic project" consisting of nation building in the Arab world.[37] But there were few takers on either side of the Atlantic. A prominent columnist argued that the core of "the new NATO" was now composed of "three like-minded, English-speaking allies—America,

Britain, and Australia." Another pontificated: "Equivocation and tink-ering—the heart and soul of Europe's current diplomacy—is [sic] rap-idly falling behind history's ever-accelerating curve."[38] Proponents of military action were indignant about Chancellor Gerhard Schroeder's antiwar position during the German elections, as if Schroeder had made Iraq an issue and as if U.S. Iraq policy was unconnected to U.S. domestic politics.

Administration officials lectured Europe about preserving the cred-ibility of the Security Council, as if the Bush administration had shown anything other than scorn for the UN before September 11, 2001. They were infuriated when France and Germany resisted U.S. efforts to in-voke NATO help for Turkey, as if the North Atlantic Treaty had to do with a situation in which a member state launched an unprovoked at-tack against a third party. Unable to believe that European resistance arose from legitimate concerns about the necessity and consequences of preventive war against Iraq and from doubts about U.S. motives, U.S. officials and their journalistic cheerleaders insisted that the French-German position arose from crass commercial motives and a congeni-tal tendency toward appeasement. Enamored of U.S. military prowess and of the neoconservative thesis about European weakness and irrele-vancy, they were unprepared for the reality that "old Europe" intended to try to contain U.S. power and that Washington might prove unable to execute its grand schemes on its own.[39]

Much depended after September 11 on the position of the sometimes cryptic president. From available evidence it appears that George W. Bush sanctioned a kind of unspoken agreement shortly after the attacks: Osama bin Laden would be the first target, but Saddam Hussein—whom Bush unaccountably believed was connected to 9/11—would be dealt with in due course.[40] In April 2002, with Afghanistan relatively quiet, Bush began to speak publicly of regime change in Iraq. From that moment on the credibility of Bush, and of the United States, were—or were seen to be—on the line. Temperament, ambition, and Bush's view of Europe placed him, in any case, closer to the hard-liners than to the Achesonians in his administration. In the fall of 2001, after a European leader had appealed for responsiveness to the view of others, Bush told his war cabinet, "that's very interesting. Because my belief is the best way that we hold this coalition together is to be clear on our objectives and to be clear that we are determined to achieve them. You hold a co-alition together by strong leadership." Rice paraphrased Bush's view of his presidency: "The country could sit on its unparalleled power and dispense it in small doses, or it could make big strategic power plays that would fundamentally alter the balance of power. Bush planted himself in the visionary camp." In August 2002, Bush observed that "action—confident action—that will yield positive results provides a kind of slipstream into which reluctant nations and leaders can get behind. . . . The vision thing matters." Bush's world was not his father's but one much closer to Ronald Reagan's. It was a world of bold colors and "moral clarity," in which allied doubts and fiscal deficits were secondary concerns, and the Middle East, the last ideological holdout to the "end of history," represented what the Soviet bloc had represented for Reagan twenty years before.[41]

How heavily did European reservations about war and the need for European peacekeepers, financial help, and legitimization weigh in Bush's decision—temporarily—to rein in Cheney and the unilateralists in September 2002 and accept Powell's advice to obtain what became Security Council Resolution 1441? Tony Blair's advice undoubtedly figured in Bush's thinking, but Powell's case, first made at a meeting with Bush and Rice on August 5, 2002, stressed factors other than Europe: the destabilizing effects of war (and of the specter of a U.S. general running Iraq) on the Middle East; the counterproductive effects on the war on terrorism; the impact on the economy; and the need for allies in the region. Perhaps the decisive factor pushing Bush toward the UN was U.S. public opinion. A poll published in the fall of 2002 showed that only 20 percent of Americans favored invading Iraq without UN and allied support. (A January 2003 poll indicated that a majority of Americans favored giving UN inspectors additional time before resorting to military action—essentially the Franco-German position.) In any event, Powell, though doubtful about the wisdom of an immediate military action, merely took the position that the UN should be given a last chance to prove itself—an experiment that the administration (for climatic and domestic political reasons) could not allow to continue beyond early 2003.[42]

CONCLUSION

These words are written after the end of combat operations in Iraq but at a time when it is still too early to draw up a balance sheet on the military intervention in that country. It seems reasonable to predict that if the U.S.-led occupiers guarantee stability, rising living standards, and the beginnings of self-government in Iraq within six months to a year, Old Europe will emerge chastened and discredited. Chirac's gamble—a coalition of France, Germany, and Russia—will look as illusory as de Gaulle's "Europe from the Atlantic to the Urals," and all three countries may have to come to Canossa and attempt to repair ties to the United States. (French and Russian support for a UN resolution ending sanctions and authorizing Anglo-American control over Iraq was a step in that direction.) Few tears would be shed in Washington, London, and Rome, just as few were shed there when de Gaulle's bid for a strong Franco-German pole faltered in 1963–1964.

Achesonians, meanwhile, will point to the possibility of a new lease on life for the Atlantic Alliance through cooperation in Iraq. But it is hard to imagine that NATO will recover its earlier identity and centrality. Rooseveltians have been confirmed in their anti-European (particularly anti-French) rancor and contempt. For U.S. conservatives, the Iraq episode has confirmed that the age of ad hoc coalitions and divide-and-rule tactics has arrived. To preserve a minimum of usefulness, in their view, NATO will have to be overhauled to allow the United States and its friends to outvote the Germans and/or the French.[43]

Still, the chastening of Old Europe might prove to be temporary. As of this writing, Iraq's weapons of mass destruction have yet to materialize. If the war leads or appears to lead to more terrorism, unleashes strife within Iraq, and/or accelerates—as logically it should—bids by other vulnerable states to obtain nuclear deterrents, European opponents of the war may find their position strengthened, and Washington hard-liners and their (fair-weather?) European backers could be discredited. It is difficult to see why a democratic domino effect should operate in the Middle East in the way it did in Eastern Europe, or why prospects for peace between Israelis and Palestinians will dramatically improve (Tony Blair's gamble) with the disappearance of Saddam Hussein. The occupiers' improvised, undermanned approach in April–May 2003 cast doubt on the possibility of a stable, united, democratic, and pro-Western Iraq. In the middle of a growing crisis in the United States and the administration's post-Vietnam leeriness with regard to nation building, will the U.S. public sustain a costly occupation? If not, Washington will have to come hat in hand to Europe, including France and Germany. The Rooseveltian conviction of Europe's weakness and irrelevancy to America's strategic fortunes would then look as hubristic and wishful as it did 60 years ago.

Does the moribund American vision of a united and self-reliant Europe look any less far-fetched under today's circumstances? Arguably it does not, but it is not inconceivable that Europeans, in the context of American unilateralism and ever greater Islamic anger, will take further steps to enable themselves to act autonomously from the United States in the Middle East. Certainly nothing has happened since September 11, 2001, to lead Europeans—including the British—to question their oft-stated view that the world is far too complicated a place to be run by Washington alone. Nor is it inconceivable that portions of the American elites, faced with the political and moral pitfalls of their empire and the prospect of an insolvent foreign policy, will begin to see again that the ambition of a united and self-reliant Europe, based on a strong Franco-German relationship and able to wield influence outside of Europe on behalf of the West, is not something to be treated with derision. In other words, that Monnet and Delors, and Eisenhower and Kennan, were right after all.

Notes

[1] Delors, "Europe's Ambitions," *Foreign Policy* 80 (Fall 1990): 14.

[2] John Lamberton Harper, *American Visions of Europe* (New York: Cambridge University Press, 1994).

[3] Ibid., p. 4.

[4] See the official notes of the conversation contained in *Foreign Relations of the United States (FRUS)*, 1942, vol. 3, pp. 568–569, 573. See also *American Visions of Europe*, chap. 3; and FDR to Queen Wilhelmina of the Netherlands, August 26, 1944, in Elliott Roosevelt, ed., *FDR: His Personal Letters, 1928–1945*, vol. 2 (New York: Duell, Sloan & Pearce, 1950), p. 1535.

[5] Charles Bohlen, *Witness to History, 1929–1969* (New York: Norton, 1973), p. 153.

[6] On Kennan, see *American Visions of Europe*, chap. 5.

[7] State-Defense Memo, September 8, 1950 (later NSC 82), *FRUS*, 1950, vol. 3, pp. 273–278. The memo refers to an integrated Western force, including U.S. and German troops. Eisenhower quoted in *FRUS*, 1955–57, vol. 4, p. 349.

[8] George Bush speech, May 21, 1989, cited in *Department of State Bulletin*, July 1989, pp. 18–19.

[9] See George Bush and Brent Scowcroft, *A World Transformed* (New York: Alfred A. Knopf, 1998), pp. 42–43.

[10] James Baker speech of December 12, 1989, to Berlin Press Club.

[11] The Bush administration was none too eager to become involved in the Balkans toward the end of its tenure in office.

[12] The basic rationale for continuing U.S. dominance of Europe (and elsewhere) was spelled out in the Pentagon's much-discussed "Defense Planning Guidance" document; see Patrick Tyler, "U.S. Strategy Plan Calls for Insuring No Rivals Develop," and "Excerpts From Pentagon's Plan: 'Prevent the Re-Emergence of a New Rival,'" *New York Times,* March 7, 1992.

[13] Adopted at the London NATO summit in 1990, the new concept was based on a reduced forward presence, new mobile formations, and the removal of ground-based nuclear weapons. Another of its rationales was to sweeten for Moscow the pill of accepting a reunified Germany within NATO.

[14] Fearing damage to NATO, Washington pressured Bonn to adopt the famous preamble to the treaty, stating that nothing in it was incompatible with Germany's prior commitment to the Atlantic Alliance.

[15] "Rome Declaration on Peace and Cooperation," Press Communique S-1 (91)86 (Brussels: NATO Press Service, November 8, 1991).

[16] Richard Holbrooke, *To End a War* (New York: Modern Library, 1999), pp. 65, 102–103, 242, 331, 368, 388.

[17] See press conference by Secretary of State Madeleine K. Albright, December 8, 1998, NATO Headquarters, Brussels; www.nato.int/docu/speech/1998/s981208x. htm. See also Rep. Douglas Bereuter, "The Creation of the ESDI within the European Union: A US Perspective," in *NATO Parliamentary Assembly: Defense and Security in the 21st Century* (July 2000), pp. 51–56. On the same point, see Wesley Clark, *Waging Modern War: Bosnia, Kosovo, and the Future of Combat* (New York: Public Affairs, 2001), p. 452. See also "Cohen Warns Europe That NATO Could Become 'Relic,'" *International Herald Tribune,* December 6, 2000.

[18] See John Newhouse, *Europe Adrift* (New York: Pantheon, 1997); Owen Harries, "America and the Euro Gamble," *National Interest* 53 (Fall 1998): 125–128; Martin Feldstein, "EMU and International Conflict," *Foreign Affairs* 76, no. 6 (November/December 1997): 61, 73; Zbigniew Brzezinski, "A Geostrategy for Eurasia," *Foreign Affairs* 76, no. 5 (September/October, 1997): 53–54.

[19] Michael Hirsh, "Bush and the World," *Foreign Affairs* 80, no. 5 (September/October 2002): 38.

[20] Stephen Walt, "The Ties That Fray: Why Europe and America are Drifting Apart," *National Interest* 54 (Winter 1998/99): 3–11.

[21] On the growing economic interdependence of the United States and Europe early in the twenty-first century, see Joseph P. Quinlan, *Drifting Apart or Growing Together? The Primacy of the Transatlantic Economy* (Washington, D.C.: Center for Transatlantic Relations, SAIS, Johns Hopkins University, 2003).

[22] Clark, *Waging Modern War,* pp. 425, 458, 460. Clark's Pentagon opponents

included not only his uniformed colleagues but also Secretary of Defense William Cohen. Together they engineered Clark's premature replacement as SACEUR immediately after the war.

[23] Condoleezza Rice, "Promoting the National Interest," *Foreign Affairs* 79, no. 1 (January/February 2000): 45–62 (emphasis added). For Rice's comment on the Balkans, see Michael R. Gordon, "The 2000 Campaign: The Military; Bush Would Stop U.S. Peacekeeping in Balkan Fights," *New York Times*, October 21, 2000, p. A1.

[24] Walt, "The Ties That Fray," 7–8; Craig Kennedy and Marshall M. Bouton, "The Real Trans-Atlantic Gap," *Foreign Policy* 133 (November/December 2002): 66–74.

[25] Irving Kristol, "America's 'Exceptional' Conservatism," in *Neoconservatism: The Autobiography of an Idea* (New York: Free Press, 1995), pp. 378, 380.

[26] Irving Kristol, "Foreign Policy in an Age of Ideology," *National Interest* 1 (Fall 1985): 12; Zbigniew Brzezinski, "America in a Hostile World," *Foreign Policy* 23 (Summer 1976): 65–96.

[27] Kristol, "Foreign Policy in an Age of Ideology," 13 (emphasis added).

[28] Ibid., 14.

[29] Charles Krauthammer, "The Unipolar Moment," *Foreign Affairs* 70, no. 1 (Special Issue: *America and the World*) (1990–1991): 23–33; Kristol, "America's 'Exceptional' Conservatism," pp. 384–385.

[30] Robert Kagan and William Kristol, "The Present Danger," *National Interest* 59 (Spring 2000): 58.

[31] Robert Kagan, "Power and Weakness," *Policy Review* 113 (June/July 2002): 3–28. Added to this was the cultural transformation wrought by the EU's postwar transcendence of power politics—allegedly making America's interventionism "a threat to Europe's new sense of mission." The article was written after September 11, 2001, but the trends analyzed by Kagan were visible long beforehand. To his credit, Kagan does not favor the continuation of a situation leading to further estrangement between the two sides.

[32] Ibid., 20.

[33] The reference is to the Under Secretary of State for Arms Control and International Security John R. Bolton.

[34] Osama bin Laden was on record as wanting to drive the U.S. infidels out of Saudi Arabia.

[35] Kagan, "Power and Weakness," 20. U.S. official quoted in Hirsh, "Bush and the World," 21.

[36] Iraq, after all, had suffered a crushing defeat in 1991, its army was half the size it had been before the war, and it controlled a mere one-third of its own airspace. No one claimed that it possessed nuclear weapons (though it was presumably trying to obtain them in order to deter the United States).

[37] Strobe Talbott, "From Prague to Baghdad, NATO at Risk," *Foreign Affairs* 80, no. 6 (November/December 2002): 49; Ronald D. Asmus and Kenneth M. Pollack, "The New Transatlantic Project," *Policy Review* 115 (October/November 2002): 3–17.

[38] Thomas Friedman, "A New Military Alliance, 'NASTY,' Already Works," *New York Times*, November 17, 2002; Jim Hoagland, "Europe Must Adapt to a Changing World," *Washington Post*, November 17, 2002.

[39] Keith B. Richburg, "NATO Blocked on Iraq Decision; France, Germany Lead Opposition to War," *Washington Post*, January 23, 2003, p. A1; and "'Old Europe' Reacts To Rumsfeld's Label," *Washington Post*, January 24, 2003, p. A20. Surprisingly, no one pointed out that Rumsfeld himself was a relic of the Cold War.

[40] Bob Woodward, *Bush at War* (New York: Simon & Schuster, 2002), pp. 83–84, 91, 167. Bush understandably did not share (or, at least, did not avow that he shared) the view that his father had been mistaken to leave Saddam Hussein in power in 1991.

[41] Ibid., pp. 281–282, 341. See also Bush's speech to the American Enterprise Institute on February 26, 2002; www.whitehouse.gov/news/releases/2003/02/print/20030226-11.html (June 4, 2003). During that speech, Bush stated that "A new regime in Iraq would serve as a dramatic and inspiring example of freedom for other nations in the region."

[42] Woodward, *Bush at War,* pp. 332–334. Kennedy and Bouton, "The Real Transatlantic Gap," 69; *Washington Post*-ABC News Poll, *Washington Post*, January 22, 2003.

[43] William Kristol has suggested "moving to a super-majority vote to authorize action, binding of course only on those who choose to contribute, but still under the NATO umbrella. In a sense this would institutionalize the coalition of the willing." See his testimony before the Senate Foreign Relations Committee, April 8, 2003; www.newamericancentury.org/nato-040803.htm (June 4, 2003).

THREE

IRAQ AND BEYOND

"OLD EUROPE" AND THE END OF THE U.S. HEGEMONY

Christopher Layne

The Iraq War may come to be seen as the high-water mark of American hegemony and as a watershed in transatlantic relations. Indeed, when future historians write about how American hegemony ended, they may well point to January 22, 2003, as a defining moment. On that day, French president Jacques Chirac and German chancellor Gerhard Schroeder jointly declared that Paris and Berlin would work together to oppose the Bush II administration's evident intent to resolve the Iraqi question by force of arms. Later that day, in a Pentagon briefing, Secretary of Defense Donald Rumsfeld responded to the Franco-German declaration by dismissing France and Germany contemptuously as representing the Old Europe and thereby ignited a transatlantic firestorm.

Although major combat in Iraq ended in April 2003, the transatlantic rift between the United States and the Old Europe has not healed visibly. The Bush administration continues to punish France and Germany for their opposition to its Iraq policy, both by ostracizing them diplomatically and, in Germany's case, by planning to shift U.S. military bases in that country to Poland, Romania, and Bulgaria. Contrary to the conventional wisdom that 9/11 "changed everything," geopolitically it did not. Before 9/11, for both policymakers and students of international relations theory and strategic studies, the main debates centered on the issue of American hegemony.[1] September 11—and the subsequent wars on terrorism and against Iraq—have had two important consequences: they have underscored the enormity of the United States' power and influence in international politics, and they have given fresh impetus to U.S. hegemonic ambitions.

This chapter looks at the future of American hegemony in the context of U.S.-Europe relations. The basic argument is twofold. First, the damage done to transatlantic and intra-European relations by the Iraq crisis is real and irreparable. Second, the Iraq War will prove to be catalyst for true counter-hegemonic balancing against the United States. France and Germany probably will lead a West European inner core as an emerging counterweight to U.S. power (and, ultimately, will find support from Russia and China). In its early stages, opposition to American hegemony is taking the form of soft balancing, but over time it will become more traditional hard balancing.[2]

The Iraq War's fallout on transatlantic relations also illustrates important continuities in U.S. grand strategy toward Europe. Since the end of World War II, the United States has been a global hegemon and has sought to maintain its geopolitical preponderance over Western Europe. Today, the United States and Western Europe are involved in the same game they have been playing for a half century: the United States is trying to prevent the emergence of competing poles of power in the international system—especially on the Continent—and Europe (or at least Old Europe) is looking to break free from American hegemony.

PASSING CRISIS OR PERFECT STORM?

The collision between the Bush administration and Europe was not a bolt from the blue. Tensions with Paris and Berlin had increased steadily in the wake of President George W. Bush's January 2002 State of the Union speech, when he indicated that the United States was prepared to act unilaterally to take out the "axis of evil." Throughout the run-up to the Iraq War, Old Europeans (and even public opinion in the United States' staunchest ally, Britain) became increasingly uneasy over the administration's predisposition to use military force unilaterally. Indeed, German foreign minister Joschka Fischer warned in February 2002 that Washington should not treat the European allies as "satellites."[3] The administration kept adding fuel to the fire, notably with its embrace of preemptive strike–preventive war options, and the September 2002 publication of its *National Security Strategy of the United States,* which boldly proclaimed the United States' intention to maintain its global hegemony by preventing any other power from surpassing, or even equaling, U.S. military capabilities.[4]

By early 2003, however, U.S.-European differences over Iraq had taken on an especially ugly tone, which largely emanated from conservative and neoconservative circles in the United States.[5] On both sides of the Atlantic, it became commonplace to claim that a growing divergence in values was fueling the transatlantic drift.[6] No doubt there is, and there has always been, a culture–values gap between the United States and Europe. The real question is, Does it matter? and, in terms of geopolitics, the answer is: Probably not. Notwithstanding transatlantic myth making (which extends back to the late 1940s), alliances are based on common *interests*, not on common values and a shared culture. So, in assessing the future of U.S.-European relations, the crucial issue is whether Europe and the United States still share enough common interests to hold them together in an alliance relationship.

So just how bad is the current rift in transatlantic relations? No matter how grave the crisis precipitated by the Iraq War and its aftermath, is it worse than Suez in 1956? Worse than Vietnam? Worse than the Gaullist challenge in the 1960s? Worse than the "Second Cold War" that followed the 1979 Soviet invasion of Afghanistan, when Western Europe declared itself an "island of détente" while the United States opted for renewed confrontation with the Soviet Union? Worse than the Euro-missile crisis during the early and mid 1980s? Time after time, as events have confounded predictions of an impending transatlantic breakup and NATO's demise, what is the case for arguing that maybe this time the sky really is falling with respect to U.S.-European relations? To answer, we need to recognize the nature of this recent crisis. The Iraq War is simply the proverbial tip of the iceberg. The causes of the coming train wreck in U.S.-European relations go much deeper. *This* transatlantic crisis is about American power. Specifically, it is about American *hegemony*. This is true for both Paris and Berlin, and, in the final analysis, for Washington, too. Herein is an interesting historical irony that cannot have escaped long-time students of U.S.-European relations. When they issued their joint declaration on January 22, Chirac and Schroeder used the occasion of the fortieth anniversary of the Franco-German treaty of Elysée to express their opposition to Washington. That treaty, negotiated by Charles de Gaulle and Konrad Adenauer, was itself intended as a bulwark against American hegemony. To grasp the full significance of the transatlantic collision between the United States and France and Germany, we need to understand its historical context.

THE UNITED STATES AND POST–COLD WAR EUROPE

Hegemony has been a major issue in U.S.-European relations since the United States emerged as a great power at the end of the nineteenth century. During the twentieth century, the United States fought two big wars in Europe out of fear that if a single power (in this case, Germany) attained hegemony in Europe, it would be able to mobilize the Continent's resources and threaten the United States in its own backyard, the Western Hemisphere. Conventional wisdom holds that U.S. post–World War II initiatives—the Marshall Plan, the North Atlantic Treaty—were driven by similar fears of possible Soviet hegemony in Europe. Indeed, many U.S. strategic thinkers, notably University of Chicago political scientist John Mearsheimer, describe this traditional European strategy of the United States as "offshore balancing."[7] As an offshore balancer, the United States supposedly remains on the sidelines with respect to European security affairs except when a single great power threatens to dominate Europe. U.S. grand strategy toward Europe, therefore, is said to be counter-hegemonic; the United States intervenes in Europe only when the European balance of power appears unable to thwart the rise of a would-be European hegemon.

This interpretation of U.S. intentions does not fit the facts, however. If U.S. strategy toward Europe indeed is one of offshore balancing and counter-hegemony, for the United States it should have been over, over there, when the Soviet Union collapsed. With no hegemonic threat to contain, U.S. military power should have been retracted from Europe, and NATO should have contracted into nonexistence rather than undergoing two rounds of expansion. Someday the Europeans may force the United States to leave the Continent, but the United States is unlikely to do so voluntarily anytime soon.

That more than a decade after the Cold War's end NATO is still in business and U.S. troops are still in Europe demands an explanation. After all, leading neorealist scholars have predicted that, as a consequence of the Soviet Union's demise, NATO would unravel, and U.S. troops would be withdrawn from Europe and East Asia. For those seeking to account for the continuing U.S. military presence in Europe, the past decade is an anomaly, not a predictor of U.S. strategy in the early twenty-first century. It is unrealistic, Mearsheimer argues, to have expected that with the Cold War's end the United States would walk away from Europe "overnight." Just give it a bit more time, and U.S. power soon will be retracted from Europe.[8]

A contrary view—and the central argument of this essay—holds that U.S. military withdrawal from Europe (or from East Asia) is not in the cards because the United States is, and has been since the early 1940s, pursuing a grand strategy of global hegemony, or preponderance.[9]

NATO, as the proverbial phrase has it, was created to "keep the Russians out, the Germans down, and the Americans in." It would be perhaps more accurate to say that the Atlantic Alliance's primary raison d'être, from a U.S. standpoint, was to keep America in—*and on top*—so that the Germans could be kept down and the Europeans could be kept from both being at each other's throats militarily and uniting as a counterweight to U.S. power. The attainment of U.S. postwar grand strategic objectives on the Continent required that the United States establish its own hegemony over Western Europe, something it would have done even if the Cold War had never happened. In other words, NATO is still in business because it serves to advance long-standing U.S. objectives that existed independently of the Cold War and, hence, were not invalidated by the Soviet Union's collapse.

Usually we look to history to help us understand the present and predict the future. Yet the reverse can be true as well: sometimes recent events serve to shed light on what happened in the past, and why it happened. Washington's post–Cold War behavior provides much support for the argument that U.S. postwar grand strategy with respect to Europe was driven at least as much—probably more—by non–Cold War factors as by the Soviet threat. As the Cold War wound down to its conclusion, U.S. policymakers faced a dilemma: without the Soviet threat, how could Washington keep NATO as a going concern and continue to justify the deployment of U.S. forces in Europe?

Following the Soviet Union's collapse, both the Bush I administration and the Clinton administration were determined to preserve NATO and to ensure that the United States remained a European power. To achieve its strategic objectives in the post–Cold War world, Washington determined it would have to reinvent NATO and invest the alliance with new roles and missions that would provide a convincing rationale for keeping it in business. Ronald D. Asmus, a former State Department official in charge of U.S. policy toward NATO, comments that the Clinton administration "wanted to update and modernize NATO to assume new roles that the American public could relate to and support, thereby ensuring its future relevance."[10] Above all, Washington was determined to refashion the alliance to maintain the transatlantic link with Europe and its preponderant voice in managing security in post–Cold War Europe.[11] Secretary of State Madeleine Albright's views on this subject encapsulated those of the Clinton administration and much of the U.S. foreign policy establishment. Asmus recounts that she believed that

> America was a European power. It had fought the Cold War not only to defeat communism but to win the peace as well. We had an historic opportunity to lay the foundation for a Europe whole and free in alliance with the United States—and we had to use it. Albright firmly believed that *America's interest and role in Europe transcended the Soviet threat*, but that the Alliance had to be reshaped if it was to survive.[12]

According to Albright herself, the United States had a window of opportunity to "recast the foundation of the Alliance." "If we get it right," she said, "NATO will last for another fifty years. . . . If we don't, the U.S. and Europe are likely to slowly drift apart and the Alliance will atrophy."[13]

U.S. policymakers' post–Cold War insistence on reaffirming NATO's continuing importance reveals a great deal about the nature of the interests that have shaped the United States' European grand strategy since the end of World War II. For the Bush I administration, the Soviet Union's collapse did not necessitate any reconsideration of the U.S. military commitment to Europe or of NATO. Philip Zelikow and Condoleezza Rice, both of whom served on the Bush I administration foreign policy team, observe:

> [The Bush I] administration believed strongly that, even if the immediate military threat from the Soviet Union diminished, the United States should maintain a significant military presence in Europe for the foreseeable future. . . . The American troop presence thus also served as the ante to ensure a central place for the United States as a player in European politics. The Bush administration placed a high value on retaining such influence, underscored by Bush's flat statement that the United States was and would remain "a European power." . . . *The Bush administration was determined to maintain crucial features of the NATO system for European security even if the Cold War ended.*[14]

The Clinton administration took a similar view. Post–Cold War NATO had to be revitalized because U.S. interests in Europe "transcended" the Soviet threat. Using phraseology reminiscent of Voltaire's comment about God, Secretary of State Albright added, "Clearly if an institution such as NATO did not exist today, we would want to create one."[15] Accordingly, given that the United States' perceived interests required it to assume the mantle of hegemon and stabilizer in post–World War II Europe, it is certain that had the Cold War not taken place U.S. policymakers in the late 1940s would have reached a similar conclusion to Albright's and acted upon it.

THE COLD WAR AND U.S. HEGEMONIAL DESIGNS

From its inception, the United States' postwar European grand strategy reflected a complex set of interlocking "Open Door" interests.[16] First, postwar U.S. officials believed that the United States had crucial economic interests in Europe. Even without a Communist threat to Western Europe, State Department Policy Planning Staff director George F. Kennan argued, the United States had a vital interest in facilitating Western Europe's economic recovery:

> The United States people have a very real economic interest in Europe. This stems from Europe's role in the past as a market and as a major source of supply for a variety of products and services.[17]

U.S. economic interests required that Europe's antiquated economic structure of small, national markets be fused into a large, integrated market. U.S. aims also required political and social stability in Western Europe in order to prevent far-Left parties (especially the Communists) from coming to power. Washington was less concerned about West European governments drifting into Moscow's political orbit than about them embracing the kinds of nationalist or autarkic economic policies that were anathema to the U.S. goal of an open international economy.

Second, U.S. strategists perceived that these economic interests would be jeopardized if postwar Europe relapsed into its bad habits of nationalism, great-power rivalries, and realpolitik. To ensure stability in postwar Europe, the United States sought to create a denationalized, integrated Europe in which Washington would assume primary responsibility for West European security and thereby preclude the re-emergence of the security dilemmas (especially that between France and Germany) that had sparked the two world wars. In turn, European economic integration and interdependence—under the umbrella of a U.S. military protectorate—also would contribute to building a peaceful and stable Western Europe. In this respect, U.S. economic and security objectives meshed with and reinforced each other.

U.S. strategy in postwar Europe has often been described as "double containment."[18] By containing and simultaneously integrating an economically revived Germany into a West European framework, the United States was said to have paved the way for the West Europeans to join the United States in containing the Soviet Union. While accurate, this description of U.S. strategy as double containment overlooks an important point: had there been no Cold War—had it not been necessary to contain the Soviet Union—the United States would still have been compelled to engage in "single containment" in Europe. Keeping the West Europeans from being at each other's throats was arguably even more important to U.S. interests than protecting them from the Soviet Union. The core assumption of U.S. postwar European grand strategy was that either a reversion to multipolarity within Europe (regional instability fueled by nationalism) or Western Europe's reemergence as an independent pole of power in international politics (a systemic change in the global distribution of power) would be inimical to U.S. interests.

To prevent these outcomes, the United States followed a sophisticated grand strategy of subordination, or denationalization, that established U.S. hegemony over Western Europe. One track of this grand strategy was to transform Western Europe into a U.S. protectorate and thereby negate West Europe's incentives to acquire the capabilities that would allow it to act autonomously in the defense and foreign policy realms. The second track of U.S. strategy was to dilute the sovereignty of the West European states by promoting integration. Although the framework of this strategy was in place before 1949–1951, NATO subsequently became the main instrument of U.S. hegemonic grand strategy in Europe.

Hegemony, of course, was not the only grand strategic option open to Washington with respect to postwar Europe. The obvious alternative to hegemony would have been an offshore balancing policy of restoring as quickly as possible Western Europe's capacity to act as an independent pole of power, thence passing to it the buck of containing the Soviet Union. No question, given Western Europe's only partial postwar recovery, the objective conditions to buck-pass did not exist in the 1940s. What is revealing, however, is that U.S. strategists were hostile to the very notion of adopting an offshore balancing strategy, as revealed by their firm rejection of the idea of Europe becoming an *independent* Third Force in international politics.[19]

Rejection of the Third Force reflected Washington's determination to prevent the emergence of new poles of power in the postwar international system. At the same time, U.S. policymakers also understood that U.S. interests required the United States to play the role of regional stabilizer in Western Europe. Postwar U.S. policymakers viewed Europe's traditional balance of power security architecture as a "fire trap" that had involved the United States in two world wars, and Under Secretary of State Robert Lovett said that Washington wanted to make certain that this firetrap was not rebuilt.[20] The kind of Western Europe that was central to postwar U.S. grand strategic objectives consisted of states whose freedom to act as sovereign national entities was severely constrained.

The United States pushed for European integration precisely to ensure that "divisive nationalist trends" would not re-reemerge. When American policymakers invoked, as they often did, the specter of European "disunity," they used the term as a code word to refer to the possibility that Europe would backslide into its traditional, multipolar pattern of security relations.[21] By persuading the West Europeans to pool their military and economic sovereignty, Washington aimed to strip them of the capacity to take unilateral national action. For the United States, institutions like NATO, the European Defense Community, the European Coal and Steel Community (ECSC), and the Common Market were the instruments it employed to contain the West Europeans. The U.S. aim was to create "institutional machinery to ensure that separate national interests are subordinated to the best interests of the community," and achieving this subordination was deemed essential if the United States was to accomplish its grand strategic purposes in Europe.[22]

NATO—and the Atlantic community concept to which it was central—became the linchpin of the U.S. strategy of preventing the reemergence of regional instability in Europe. Through NATO and the Atlantic community, Washington made certain that West European integration was harnessed to U.S. interests. The State Department Policy Planning Staff noted, "If there is to be an effective organization of Europe, it will have to be set in a framework which assures continuous and responsible leadership by the United States."[23] Referring to the link among NATO, the Atlantic community, and European integration, Secretary of State Dean Acheson stated:

> In all these fields basic criterion from US viewpoint is, of course, [the] extent to which any given action by Europeans promotes or prejudices US

security and basic interests. North Atlantic community, which finds increasingly concrete expression in NATO, is accordingly framework within which we seek maximum development of common action in pursuit of basic objectives common to North America and Western Europe.[24]

Since the 1940s, Washington has had to perform a delicate balancing act with respect to Europe. Certainly, for economic reasons, the United States encouraged Western Europe's integration into a single common market. At the same time, however, U.S. policymakers understood the reasons why their country had gone to war in 1917 and 1941. The last thing they wanted was to encourage the emergence of a new, *independent* pole of power on the European continent—whether in the guise of a resurgent Germany or of a politically united Europe. U.S. strategists always understood that in pushing for West European integration and unity, the danger of creating the geopolitical equivalent of Frankenstein's monster was ever present. Embedding West European integration in the U.S.-dominated Atlantic community would prevent the Europeans from veering off in the wrong direction. "An increased measure of Continental European integration," Acheson and Lovett told President Harry S. Truman, "can be secured *only* with the broader framework of the North Atlantic Community. This is entirely consistent with *our own desire to see a power arrangement on the Continent which does not threaten us* and with which we can work in close harmony."[25] Acheson stated U.S. strategic concerns bluntly when he spoke of the necessity of a "well-knit large grouping of Atlantic states within which [a] new [European] grouping can develop, thus ensuring unity of purpose within the entire group and precluding possibility of European Union becoming Third Force or opposing force."[26] Because the alliance was the main instrument of U.S. hegemony in Europe, U.S. policymakers never intended NATO to go out of business should the Cold War end. In the early 1950s, the United States already intended to remain in Europe permanently, irrespective of the threat of Soviet aggression.

Just as fear of a European hegemon led the United States to intervene in Europe's two great wars of the twentieth century, the West Europeans after World War II understood that the United States had established its own hegemony over them—and, as realist international relations theory would suggest, Western Europe tried to do something about it. In the five years or so after 1945, it was Britain that hoped to emerge as a Third Force in world politics to balance both the United States and the Soviet Union. The accelerating decline of Britain's relative world power demolished London's Third Force aspirations, but European Third Force aspirations did not vanish. In the late 1940s and 1950s, the founders of today's European Union (EU) hoped that the ECSC and then the Common Market would be the embryo of a united Europe that could act as a geopolitical and economic counterweight to the United States.

For sure, West European balancing against the United States was constrained. While fearful of U.S. power, the West Europeans feared the Soviet Union even more. Moreover, following World War II, Washington was able to use the carrot of economic assistance—mainly, the Marshall Plan—to keep Western Europe aligned (albeit very tenuously at times) with the United States. Yet by the early 1960s, French president Charles de Gaulle believed that Western Europe had recovered sufficiently from World War II's dislocations and was ready to reemerge as an independent pole of power in the international system.

Following Washington's successful facing down of the Soviet Union in the 1962 Cuban missile crisis, de Gaulle concluded that the world *already* had become unipolar—dominated by a hegemonic America. To balance U.S. hegemony, the general pushed for France to acquire its own independent nuclear capabilities. His efforts to build a West European pole of power around a Franco-German axis resulted, to Washington's clear apprehension, in the 1963 treaty—the one Chirac and Schroeder commemorated on January 22, 2003.

Washington recognized the Gaullist challenge for what it was—a direct assault on U.S. preponderance in Western Europe—and reacted by reasserting its hegemonic prerogatives on the Continent. President John F. Kennedy expressed the fear that Western Europe's emergence as an independent pole of power in the international system would be inimical to U.S. interests. Noting that "the European states are less subject to our influence," Kennedy went on to express the fear that, "If the French and other European powers acquire a nuclear capability they would be in a position to be entirely independent and we might be on the outside looking in."[27] By pushing for a multilateral nuclear force for Western Europe (in reality one that would keep Washington's finger firmly on the trigger), the United States sought—unsuccessfully—to derail France's nuclear ambitions. With considerably more success, however, the United States took the teeth out of the Franco-German treaty.

Given that Washington saw the Franco-German treaty as a dagger aimed at the heart of U.S. primacy in Europe, it is not surprising that the United States moved decisively to eviscerate the treaty. Washington pressured West Germany to renounce those treaty provisions that suggested Western Europe's defense could be based on a Franco-German alliance rather than on NATO.[28] Unless Bonn chose Washington over Paris, the United States threatened to withdraw from Europe militarily and wash its hands of any responsibility for West Germany's defense.[29] Rusk said:

> If Europe were ever to be organized so as to leave us outside, from the point of view of these great issues of policy and defense, it would become most difficult for us to sustain our present guarantee against Soviet aggression. We shall not hesitate to make this point to the Germans if they show signs of accepting any idea of a Bonn-Paris axis.[30]

Underscoring its alarm over the treaty, Washington intervened in West German domestic politics by collaborating with the "Atlanticist" wing of the ruling Christian Democratic–Christian Socialist coalition to undermine Adenauer's grip on the chancellorship and to secure passage by the Bundestag of a preamble to the treaty stating that it did not contravene West Germany's commitment to NATO.[31]

EU, NATO, AND U.S. STRATEGY TOWARD EUROPE

Forty years after the Franco-German treaty, Washington, Paris, and Berlin are still at it. Again, America is asserting its hegemony, and France and Germany are seeking (so far with much less success) to create a European counterweight. One related U.S. technique is to encourage European NATO members to concentrate individually on carving out niche capabilities that will complement U.S. power rather than potentially challenge it. A second U.S. tactic is to oppose the EU's attempts to build a transnational European defense industry and to withhold important technologies from the Europeans by opposing the proposed European defense procurement agency intended to facilitate the growth of an integrated European arms industry.[32] Even more important, however, Washington has attempted to derail EU plans to create, through the European Security and Defense Policy (ESDP), military capabilities outside NATO's aegis.

At their November 2000 meeting, EU defense ministers gave ESDP concrete expression by formally announcing plans to create a 60,000-

strong rapid reaction force (RRF). ESDP and the RRF fanned a sharp disagreement between the United States and the EU about how far the Europeanization of the Continent's defense should go. Immediately before the December 2000 EU summit in Nice, European Commission president Romano Prodi, French president Chirac, and French prime minister Lionel Jospin all indicated that, although it would draw on European military assets also earmarked for NATO, the RRF would be an autonomous European force—and the embryo of an EU army—with a chain of command, a headquarters, and planning staff separate from NATO.

The U.S. reaction to the RRF was swift and hostile. Speaking at a NATO defense ministers' meeting in Brussels just before the Nice summit, the outgoing secretary of defense, William Cohen, declared that if the EU created an independent defense capability outside the alliance's structure, NATO would become a "relic of the past." Cohen's comments were a toned-down version of reports from within the Pentagon that the United States would respond to the EU's approval of the RRF by withdrawing its own military presence from Europe. Foreshadowing the views of the Bush II administration, John Bolton, now an under secretary of state, several days after the Nice summit described the RRF as "a dagger pointed at NATO's heart."[33] Like its predecessor, the Bush II administration has tried to keep Europe's defense capabilities tightly bound to NATO by diverting European defense efforts away from the RRF and focusing them on building up a NATO response force.

Since the end of World War II, the United States has supported European integration for its own strategic, political, and economic reasons. However, U.S. support for European integration has always been conditioned on its taking place only within the framework of an overarching—and U.S.-dominated—Atlantic community, "a code phrase for overall American leadership."[34] In fact, the United States has never welcomed a truly equal Western Europe.

U.S. policymakers' reaction to ESDP and the RRF can be seen as the reflection of both long-standing U.S. fears that an equal and independent Europe would throw off Washington's tutelage and Washington's pervasive suspicion that, in this regard, ESDP and the RRF are the camel's nose in the tent—rivals to NATO's supremacy in European security affairs.[35] From Washington's perspective, ESDP can have only one acceptable purpose: creating a European pillar within NATO that will enable the Europeans to share more of the burdens of the Continent's defense. Secretary of State Madeleine Albright said in 1998 that ESDP is "a very useful way to think about *burden sharing*." Other senior Clinton administration officials made clear that, for the United States, ESDP must be based on "the principle that these institutions should be the European pillar of a strong trans-Atlantic alliance and not separate and competing entities."[36]

To block ESDP from undercutting NATO, the Clinton administration proclaimed the so-called Three D's: ESDP must not diminish NATO's role, duplicate NATO's capabilities, or discriminate against NATO members not belonging to the EU.[37] Of course, implementation of the Three D's—especially the nonduplication proscription—would foreclose the EU from ever achieving strategic autonomy, ensuring Europe's continuing security dependence on the United States. This is because the United States has a virtual monopoly on NATO military capabilities in key areas of intelligence, advanced surveillance and reconnaissance systems, power projection, and precision-guided munitions.

In addition to preventing Western Europe from becoming autonomous strategically, Washington has engaged in a game of divide-and-rule in a bid to thwart the EU's political unification process. For example, the United States is pushing hard for the EU's enlargement, and especially the admission of Turkey, with the expectation that a bigger EU will prove unmanageable and hence unable to emerge as a politically unified actor in international politics. Similarly, the United States has encouraged NATO expansion in the hope that the New Europe—Poland, Hungary, the Czech Republic, and Romania—which, with the exception of Romania, is set to join the EU in 2004, will side with Washington in both NATO and the EU against France and Germany. For the United States, a Europe that speaks with many voices is optimal, which is why the United States is trying to do what it can to ensure that the EU's state-building process fails, thereby also ensuring that a united Europe never emerges as an independent pole of power in the international system. Finally, the United States has continued to remind the rest of Europe—sometimes delicately, sometimes heavy-handedly (as in President George W. Bush's speech in Prague during the November 2002 NATO summit)—that it still needs American hegemony to keep the Germans down.

During the run-up to the Iraq War, Washington's aim of keeping Europe apart paid apparent dividends when, at the end of January 2003, the leaders of Britain, Spain, Italy, Portugal, Denmark, Poland,

Hungary, and the Czech Republic signed a letter implicitly rebuking Paris and Berlin and urging Europe and the international community to unite behind Washington's Iraq policy. Notably, the United States was able to use successfully the so-called New Europe to balance against the Franco-German core. Washington clearly hopes that states like Poland, Hungary, the Czech Republic, and Romania will represent Atlanticist interests over European ones within the EU and thereby form a counterweight to block French and German aspirations for a united Europe capable of counterbalancing American hegemony.

THE HEGEMON'S TEMPTATION

In the decade between the Soviet Union's collapse and 9/11, American hegemony (or, as some U.S. policymakers called it during the Clinton administration, America's "hegemony problem") was the central issue in debates about U.S. grand strategy. Since the Soviet Union's disappearance at the end of 1991, other states have expressed strong unease about the magnitude of U.S. power and the manner in which Washington exercises that power. Well before 9/11, Russia, China, India, and, of course, France and Germany feared that the United States unilaterally was seeking to maintain its global military dominance.

Why have France, Germany, and others worried about American hegemony? The simple answer is that international politics remains fundamentally what it always has been: a competitive arena in which states struggle for survival and security and to maintain their autonomy (not to mention to increase their relative power and also their prestige, that intangible indicia of power). When one state becomes overwhelmingly powerful, or hegemonic, others fear for their safety and their interests. Hegemony triggers what scholars of international relations call "balancing." In plain English, this means that other states will try to offset the hegemon's hard power (its military and economic capabilities) by forming counter-hegemonic alliances with other states and/or by building up their own hard-power capabilities.[38]

The historical record shows that sooner or later hegemons are defeated by other states' balancing behavior. Yet, often this has not been a smooth process, allowing would-be hegemons to believe that they can succeed where others before have failed. The risks involved in counter-hegemonic balancing give rise to collective-action problems—states prefer to pass the buck to others rather than bear the risks and costs of stopping the hegemon.

Each of the most recent three U.S. administrations has been determined to preserve U.S. post–Cold War hegemony (though without the current administration's sledgehammer diplomacy), convinced that the United States will escape the fate that invariably befalls hegemons. To explain why this is so, U.S. policymakers have constructed a number of (too) clever rationales. One such rationalization is to deny that the United States is a hegemon at all and assert that it acts instead as a mere offshore balancer in Europe. Another is to admit that the United States is a hegemon, but a hegemon of a different kind—one that is not threatening because it acts altruistically in international politics and because others are attracted to its soft power (its political institutions, values, and culture).[39] Yet another argument also acknowledges the reality of U.S. hegemony but concludes that the United States can do as it pleases because it is so far ahead in terms of hard power that no other state can possibly hope to catch up to America.[40] None of these arguments is compelling; they all overlook both European perceptions of U.S. power and attempts to counterbalance it and what might be called "the hegemon's temptation." For a hegemon, overwhelming power and lack of opposition create powerful incentives to expand the scope of its geopolitical interests.[41] Precisely because it is so unconstrained geopolitically, the United States will be tempted time and again to intervene promiscuously in conflicts abroad. The cumulative costs of fighting—or preparing to fight—asymmetric conflicts against terrorists (in the Philippines, Afghanistan, and possibly in a failed Pakistan), regional powers (Iraq, Iran, North Korea), and near-peer competitors could erode America's relative power (especially if the United States suffers setbacks in future conflicts, especially with China).

Hegemonic decline results from a combination of external and internal factors: overextension abroad (imperial overstretch) and domestic economic weakness.[42] As some scholars and analysts once again are noting, the imperial-overstretch debate of the late 1980s has reemerged with a vengeance. One reason is the disconnect between U.S. post–Cold War imperial ambitions (which have become even more extensive after 9/11) and its underlying economic vulnerabilities (endless budget deficits fueled, in part, by burgeoning military spending; and the persistent balance-of-payments deficit). For example, a recent report commissioned by the U.S. Department of the Treasury (but buried by the Bush administration) points out that the United States is facing huge chronic budget deficits and a fiscal crisis saddled with health care and pension commitments to the rapidly aging baby-boom gener-ation.[43] As Niall Ferguson and Laurence Kotlikoff suggest, facing the necessity of achieving fiscal solvency through a combination of painful tax increases and spending cuts, the United States may find that its im-perial ambitions are unaffordable.[44] Over time, the United States' fiscal troubles (and its chronic trade deficits) will erode its economic power, and, as the relative power gap with potential new great powers begins to shrink, the costs and risks of challenging the United States will also decrease.

Today other potential poles of power in the international system are eagerly waiting to emerge as counterweights to the United States. With the Bush II administration's Iraq policy, and its national security strat-egy, these new power centers have increasingly greater incentive to do so. During the run-up to the Iraq War, France and Germany—along with Russia and, in the background, China—engaged in soft balancing against the United States. After the war, these same countries have con-tinued to employ soft balancing in order to internationalize (or multi-lateralize) the postwar occupation and reconstruction of Iraq. This soft balancing has consisted of using international institutions (specif-ically the UN) and norms to delegitimize Washington's unilateral pol-icies. In the long term, however, the real significance of soft balancing lies in other states' ability to surmount the collective-action barrier to counter-hegemonic balancing by developing habits of diplomatic co-operation. In the future, we are bound to see more of this. More impor-tant, by facilitating soft balancing against the United States, the transatlantic crisis over the Iraq War may have paved the way for hard balancing as well.

For many European policymakers and analysts, the key lesson learned from the Iraq War is that Washington will pay little heed to European views on international political issues unless Europe can back up its voice with real military capabilities.[45] Will France and Ger-many serve as the motor force to unite Europe in opposition to the United States? Although only time will tell, today's Old Europe is not the Europe of the past. This is not 1956 during the Suez crisis when France and Britain caved in to U.S. pressure. In 2003, despite Washington's hardball tactics, France and Germany resolutely stuck to their guns in opposing Washington's Iraq policy. Nor is this 1963. The Cold War is over, and France and Germany are freer to challenge U.S. hegemony. The EU is in the midst of an important constitutional convention that is laying the foundation for a politically unified Europe. To be sure, this may prove to be an EU based on "variable geometry"—or even a rump EU organized around France and Germany—with European versus Atlanticist loyalties stirring latent divisions within the EU.

Whether the EU will split on the issue of balancing against U.S. pre-eminence is an open question, but any emerging European counter-weight to U.S. hegemony would certainly rest on the Franco-German axis, and, in the long run, such a counterweight would also be expected to begin acquiring hard-power capabilities. Indeed, as the Iraq War was winding down, France and Germany (along with Belgium and Luxembourg) met to lay the foundations for an independent European military capability, including a European military headquarters, built around the Franco-German core of Old Europe. Explaining this initia-tive, Chirac explicitly said the purpose was to enable a pole of power capable of playing its role in a multipolar system of balancing the Unit-ed States.[46]

U.S. policymakers should want to avoid the fate of hegemons. In the late 1890s, Great Britain, widely regarded at the zenith of its hegemonic power, had its own counterpart to U.S. unilateralism: splendid isola-tion. As speculation grew, however, that the other European great powers would form a coalition to balance against Britain, London re-alized its isolation was far from splendid. The British military analyst Spencer Wilkenson said at the time, "We have no friends, and no nation loves us." It's not much of a leap to suggest that by pursuing a hegemon-ic grand strategy, the United States is courting the nightmare scenario of the kind described by Wilkenson.

The Bush II administration seems blissfully unconcerned about this prospect. Flushed with triumph and an awesome display of military power, U.S. policymakers seem to believe that American hegemony is an unchallengeable fact of international life. It is not, if only because other states will draw the opposite conclusion—that the United States is too powerful and that its hegemony must be resisted. Although U.S. policymakers have convinced themselves that the United States is a be-nign hegemon, there is no such animal in international politics. The transatlantic split over Iraq underscores the self-defeating nature of U.S. hegemonic grand strategy. The costs and risks of this strategy are real, and growing, and it is time for a serious debate about alternatives, such as adopting an actual offshore balancing strategy.[47]

If the United States is not able to practice self-imposed restraint, others will impose that constraint on Washington. If that happens, the Bush administration will not be remembered for conquering Baghdad but instead for a policy that galvanized both soft and hard balancing against American hegemony. What the administration is trumpeting as "victory" in the Iraq War may prove, in reality, to have shattered the pillars of the international security framework that the United States established after World War II, pushed NATO into terminal decline, triggered a bitter transatlantic divorce, given the decisive boost to the political uniting of Europe (or at least the most important parts of it), and marked the beginning of the end of the United States' era of global preponderance.

Notes

[1]Stephen G. Brooks and William C. Wohlforth, "American Primacy in Perspective," *Foreign Affairs* 81, no. 4 (July/August 2002): 20–33; also Christopher Layne, "Rethinking American Grand Strategy," *World Policy Journal* 15, no. 2 (Summer 1998): 8–28.

[2] Similar arguments are presented in the author's "America as Hegemon," *National Interest* 72 (Summer 2003): 17–30; and "The European Counterweight," *Aspenia* 19–20 (2003): 52–68.

[3] Quoted in Steven Erlanger, "Germany Joins Europe's Cry That the U.S. Won't Consult," *New York Times*, February 13, 2002, p. 14.

[4] *The National Security Strategy of the United States of America* (Washington, D.C.: The White House, September 17, 2002), www.whitehouse.gov/nsc/nss.html.

[5] For a representative sampling, see Eric Alterman, "USA Oui! Bush Non!" *Nation*, February 10, 2003; Timothy Garton Ash, "Anti-Europeanism in America," *New York Review of Books*, February 13, 2003; and Stuart Reid, "The Anti-Europeans," *American Conservative*, January 27, 2003.

[6] In a much discussed article, the neoconservative foreign policy analyst Robert Kagan summed up his argument by claiming that Americans are from Mars and Europeans are from Venus. Robert Kagan, "Power and Weakness," *Policy Review* 113 (June/July 2002): 3–28.

[7] Mearsheimer argues that the United States is not a global hegemon. Instead, he claims, the United States is only a hegemon in its own region (the Western Hemisphere) and acts as an offshore balancer toward Europe, intervening only when the European balance of power has been unable to stop a continental hegemon. For elaboration, see John J. Mearsheimer, *The Tragedy of Great Power Politics* (New York: W.W. Norton, 2001). Although I believe that the United States

ought to be an offshore balancer with respect to Europe (and East Asia), I argue, unlike Mearsheimer, that, in fact, the United States is following a strategy of global hegemony, and, consequently, will remain in Europe as a regional stabilizer and pacifier. See Christopher Layne, "The 'Poster Child' for Offensive Realism: America as Global Hegemon," *Security Studies* 12, no. 2 (Winter 2002/2003): 120–164.

[8] Mearsheimer, *Tragedy of Great Power Politics*, pp. 390–392.

[9] See Melvyn P. Leffler, *A Preponderance of Power: National Security, the Truman Administration, and the Cold War* (Stanford, Calif.: Stanford University Press, 1992).

[10] Ronald D. Asmus, *Opening NATO's Door: How the Alliance Remade Itself for a New Era* (New York: Columbia University Press, 2002), p. 25.

[11] See Richard Holbrooke, "America, A European Power," *Foreign Affairs* 74, no. 2 (March/April 1995): 38–51. Asmus makes clear that Clinton administration officials were deeply concerned with keeping NATO "relevant" in order to preserve America's position as the major player in European security. See Asmus, *Opening NATO's Door*, pp. 118–119, 124–125, 132, 178–179, 260–261, 290–291.

[12] Asmus, *Opening NATO's Door,* p. 178 (emphasis added).

[13] Ibid., pp. 178–179.

[14] Philip Zelikow and Condoleezza Rice, *Germany Unified and Europe Transformed: A Study in Statecraft* (Cambridge: Harvard University Press, 1995), p. 169 (emphasis added).

[15] Asmus, *Opening NATO's Door,* pp. 290, 261.

[16] The seminal work of the Open Door school is William Appleman Williams, *Tragedy of American Diplomacy* (New York: Delta, 1962). When the Open Door literature is read as a whole, it clearly encompasses economics, ideology, national interest, and security as key factors of the Open Door, and it explores the interplay of these concerns in shaping U.S. grand strategy.

[17] PPS/4, "Certain Aspects of the European Recovery Problem from the United States Standpoint," July 23, 1947, in *The State Department Policy Planning Staff Papers*, vol. I, ed. Anna Kasten Nelson, p. 31.

[18] The term "double containment" is from Wolfram Hanreider, *Germany, Europe, and America* (New Haven: Yale University Press, 1989).

[19] To be sure, one can find statements by U.S. policymakers during 1947–1957 that seemingly embraced an independent European Third Force as an objective of U.S. strategy, but there is a lot less to those statements than meets the eye. For one example among others, in 1947 George F. Kennan said, "It should be a cardinal point of our policy to see to it that other elements of independent power are developed on the Eurasian land mass as rapidly as possible, in order to take off our shoulders some of the burden of 'bipolarity.'" (Wilson D. Miscamble, *George F. Kennan and the Making of American Foreign Policy, 1947–1950* [Princeton: Princ-

eton University Press, 1992], p. 74.) However, for Kennan, "independent power" meant power independent of Moscow but subservient to Washington. Similarly, President Dwight D. Eisenhower spoke from time to time in apparently approving terms about the prospect of Western Europe emerging as a Third Force; but rather than Western Europe being independent of the United States, he conceived of it as a factor that "would be to the benefit of the United States, the Atlantic Community..." (Memorandum of Conference, 2/6/57, *FRUS 1955–57*, IV:517.) Eisenhower also regarded the prospect of a European Third Force in terms of burden sharing, not burden shifting. A united Europe that did more for the common defense would enable the United States to "relax *somewhat.*" (Editorial Note: 267th Mtg of NSC, 11/21/55, *FRUS 1955–57*, IV:349 [emphasis added].) According to the diplomatic historian Geir Lundestad, "It is easy to go against dependence as such; *it is more difficult to do so when independence actually leads to opposition.* ... [A]ll American policymakers definitely wanted even a united Europe to cooperate closely with the United States within an Atlantic framework. Most policymakers probably assumed that Europe would come to do so. *Somehow Europe was to be independent and dependent on the United States at the same time.*" (Geir Lundestad, *"Empire" by Integration: The United States and European Integration, 1945–1997* [New York: Oxford University Press, 1998], p. 18 [emphasis added].)

[20] Minutes of the First Meeting of the Washington Exploratory Talks on Security, July 6, 1948, *FRUS 1948*, III:151; Minutes of the Fourth Meeting of the Washington Exploratory Talks on Security, July 8, 1948, *FRUS 1948*, III:167–168.

[21] Acheson to Bruce, October 19, 1949, *FRUS 1949*, IV:471. For representative warnings about European "disunity," see Minutes of the Seventh Meeting of the Policy Planning Staff, 1/24/50, *FRUS 1950*, III:620; Luce to Dept. of State, 5/4/54, *FRUS 1952–54*, V:954.

[22] Paper [n.d.] prepared in the Department of State, "Economic Benefits of European Integration," *FRUS 1949*, III:133.

[23] Paper prepared by the Policy Planning Staff, "The Current Position in the Cold War," 4/14/50, *FRUS 1950*, III:859.

[24] Acheson to Certain Diplomatic Offices, January 29, 1951, *FRUS 1951*, III:761.

[25] Acheson and Lovett to Truman, July 30, 1951, *FRUS 1951*, III:850 (emphasis added).

[26] Acheson to Bruce, September 19, 1952, *FRUS 1952–54*, V:324.

[27] Remarks of President Kennedy to the National Security Council, 1/22/63, *FRUS 1961–63*, XIII:486.

[28] Memorandum from Rusk to Kennedy, February 26, 1963, JFKL, POF 117a, German Security (January 1963–March 1963).

[29] Summary Record of NSC Executive Committee Meeting no. 40, 2/5/63, *FRUS 1961–63*, XIII:175, 178–179; Memorandum of Conversation, 2/5/63, *FRUS 1961–*

63, XIII:182–187. See also Rusk to the Embassy in France, 5/18/63, *FRUS 1961–63*, XIII:704.

[30] Rusk to the Embassy in France, 5/18/63, *FRUS 1961–63*, XIII:704. U.S. talking points prepared in connection with German foreign minister von Bretano's early 1963 visit to Washington stressed that "We . . . should leave von Bretano with no illusions about our views on a bilateral Franco-German relationship which might be divisive in NATO and form the basis for a closed, autarchic Continental system. . . ." Talking Points, n.d., JFKL, POF 117a, German Security (January 1963– March 1963).

[31] See Marc Trachtenberg, *A Constructed Peace: The Making of the European Settlement, 1945–1963* (Princeton: Princeton University Press, 1999), p. 377; Roger Morgan, "Kennedy and Adenauer," in *John F. Kennedy and Europe*, ed. Douglas Brinkley and Richard T. Griffiths (Baton Rouge: Louisiana State University Press, 1999), p. 27.

[32] Judy Dempsey, "Italians in Vanguard of Push for EU Arms Industry, Despite US Misgivings," *Financial Times*, July 11, 2003.

[33] Douglas Hamilton and Charles Aldinger, "EU Force Could Spell NATO's End, Cohen Says," *Washington Post*, December 6, 2000; Robert Fox, "US to Pull out of NATO if EU Force Goes Ahead," *Sunday Telegraph*, October 29, 2000; Matthew Campbell and Stephen Grey, "Bush Aides Launch Assault on Euro Army," *Sunday Times*, December 17, 2000.

[34] Lundestad, *"Empire" by Integration*, p. 40.

[35] See Joseph Fitchett, "EU Takes Steps to Create a Military Force, Without Treading on NATO," *International Herald Tribune,* March 1, 2000; James Kitfield, "European Doughboys," *National Journal* 32, no. 9 (February 26, 2000): 610–615; Carol J. Williams, "Conference Highlights Flaws of NATO's Kosovo Campaign," *Los Angeles Times*, February 6, 2000.

[36] Secretary of State Madeleine K. Albright, "Press Conference at NATO Headquarters," December 8, 1998, Office of the Spokesman, U.S. Department of State (emphasis added); Under Secretary of Defense for Policy Walter Slocombe, "Partnership for Peace and NATO-Russian Relations," CSIS, Washington, D.C., March 2, 1995, cited in *Defense Issues* 10, no. 28; www.defenselink.mil/speeches/1995/s19950302-slocombe.html (March 3, 2003).

[37] Albright, "Press Conference at NATO Headquarters."

[38] On this point, see Christopher Layne, "The Unipolar Illusion: Why New Great Powers Will Rise," *International Security* 17, no. 4 (Spring 1993): 5–51.

[39] For representative arguments, see Joseph S. Nye Jr., *Bound to Lead: The Changing Nature of American Power* (New York: Basic Books, 1990); G. John Ikenberry, "Institutions, Strategic Restraint, and the Persistence of Postwar Order," *International Security* 23, no. 3 (Winter 1998/99): 76–77; G. John Ikenberry and

Charles A. Kupchan, "The Legitimation of Hegemonic Power," in *World Leadership and Hegemony*, ed. David P. Rapkin (Boulder, Colo.: L. Reinner, 1990).

[40] Brooks and Wohlforth, "American Primacy in Perspective," 21.

[41] This is the core insight of offensive realism. Key works on offensive realism include Robert Gilpin, *War and Change in World Politics* (Cambridge: Cambridge University Press, 1981); Christopher Layne, *The Peace of Illusions: America's Pursuit of Global Hegemony since 1945* (Ithaca, N.Y.: Cornell University Press, forthcoming); Mearsheimer, *Tragedy of Great Power Politics*; and Fareed Zakaria, *From Wealth to Power: The Unusual Origins of America's World Role* (Princeton: Princeton University Press, 1998).

[42] Gilpin, *War and Change*; Paul Kennedy, *The Rise and Fall of the Great Powers: Economic Change and Military Conflict from 1500 to 2000* (New York: Random House, 1987).

[43] Peronet Despeignes, "Report Warns of Chronic US Deficits," *Financial Times*, May 29, 2003, p. 1.

[44] Niall Ferguson and Laurence Kotlikoff, "The Fiscal Overstretch That Will Undermine an Empire," *Financial Times*, July 15, 2003, p. 15.

[45] Kirsty Hughes, "Europe Will Not Be Subservient," *Financial Times*, July 16, 2003; Gordon Adams, "Europe Should Learn to Fend for Itself," *Financial Times*, July 2, 2003.

[46] Judy Dempsey, "EU Leaders Unveil Plan for Central Military HQ," *Financial Times*, April 30, 2003.

[47] For arguments in support of offshore balancing as an alternative U.S. grand strategy to hegemony, see Benjamin Schwarz and Christopher Layne, "A New Grand Strategy," *Atlantic Monthly* 289, no. 1 (January 2002): 36–42; Christopher Layne, "From Preponderance to Offshore Balancing: America's Future Grand Strategy," *International Security* 22, no. 1 (Summer 1997): 86–124; Layne, "American Grand Strategy after the Cold War: Primacy or Blue Water?" in *American Defense Annual 1994*, ed. Charles F. Hermann (New York: Lexington, 1994), pp. 19–43.

FOUR

RECONCILING NOVEMBER 9 AND SEPTEMBER 11

Daniel S. Hamilton

The transatlantic partnership was a key casualty of the Iraq War, and the wounds were self-inflicted. It is not an exaggeration to say that differences over Iraq produced the gravest crisis in transatlantic relations since the birth of the Atlantic Alliance. Of course, there have been many transatlantic squabbles during past decades, but the not-so-friendly fire over Iraq contained new and troubling elements.

First, the degree of transatlantic recrimination and bitterness was unprecedented. Second, the disunity that emerged was unparalleled, both across the Atlantic and throughout Europe itself. Third, arguably for the first time since the end of World War II, a U.S. administration actively, even eagerly, encouraged and exploited divisions that set Europeans against one another.[1] Fourth, for the first time since the founding of the Federal Republic of Germany, a German chancellor abandoned his traditional role of mediating between Paris and Washington, tied German fortunes to Gallic ambition, and in fact went beyond specific policy differences with Washington to encourage deeper currents of criticism in Germany—and elsewhere—that consider the United States to be a greater threat to world peace than those who would threaten the Atlantic community.

Policy differences over a host of other issues beyond Iraq have exacerbated matters. Even before the eruption of the Iraq crisis, European concerns had been fueled by the Bush administration's refusal to participate in international agreements ranging from the International Criminal Court and the Kyoto Protocol on climate change to a worldwide ban on antipersonnel land mines, a global treaty to protect biodiversity, a verification mechanism for the Biological Weapons

Convention, and the Comprehensive Test Ban Treaty. Europeans have been critical of the Bush administration's treatment of suspect individuals in the United States and suspect terrorist fighters being held at Guantánamo Bay naval station in Cuba, its pullout from the Anti-Ballistic Missile Treaty, its neglect of the Arab-Israeli peace process, and its embrace of preemptive military action as a foreign policy doctrine.

Americans often retort that their European friends seem eager to lecture Americans about U.S. failings but are unwilling to spend the money necessary to make European troops effective. Europeans are said to be too absorbed with the details of deeper and wider European integration to recognize the dangers posed by terrorists wielding weapons of mass destruction (WMD). Europeans are eager to trumpet "noble" multilateralist instincts in contrast to America's "retrograde" unilateralism (except when it comes to international rules that do not support EU preferences),[2] and have failed to advance economic reforms that could sustain European prosperity or anchor world growth in the New Economy. Some accuse Europeans of using antagonism toward the United States as a way of defining their own identity. These quarrels on international issues are exacerbated by a series of transatlantic spats over such traditionally domestic issues as food safety, corporate governance, the death penalty, data privacy, freedom of speech and religion, and a range of other civil liberties.

In short, Iraq was a real transatlantic brawl, but differences on that issue alone do not explain the emotional or broad-based nature of transatlantic tensions. That is because much of the debate both within and between Europe and the United States has been less about Iraq itself and more about what our approaches to Iraq may say about how Europeans and Americans may be approaching international relations in the twenty-first century as well as the nature of our future partnership. Transatlantic squabbles may be nothing new; however, they are taking place in a new context and, in this debate, personalities, policies, catalytic events, and deeper structural changes of world politics all play a role.

THE NOVEMBER 9 AND SEPTEMBER 11 VIEWS OF THE WORLD

One's view of one's partner is, in large part, derived from one's view of oneself. Europeans and Americans are each presently engaged in a rather fluid debate about the future direction of their roles in the world and increasingly appear to be viewing international issues through different foreign policy lenses. Each view is framed by a separate catalytic event, and, depending on the outcome of our respective debates, each of us may come to view the other in a new light.[3]

For most Europeans the catalytic event framing much of their foreign and security policy remains the fall of the Berlin Wall on November 9, 1989, and the accompanying collapse of the Soviet Union and European Communism. When the people on the streets of Central and Eastern Europe brought down the Iron Curtain with their collective cry of "We want to return to Europe," they unleashed an earthquake that is still shaking the Continent and its institutions. Europeans are engaged in a period of fundamental transformation of their continent, marked by the introduction of a single currency, the euro; enlargement to ten new members within the next year; serious debates about reforming post-Communist economies and retooling social welfare economies that have been the mainstay of Europe for a half century; and a constitutional convention and an intergovernmental conference intended to transform Europe's basic institutions and define a role for Europe in this new century. Together, these developments represent a historic opportunity to build a continent that is truly whole, free, and at peace with itself.[4] It is a goal that Americans share and to which the United States has contributed significantly. Yet it continues to absorb—almost overwhelm—European energy and attention.

For most Americans, November 9 also played a catalytic role and informed much U.S. foreign policy in the ensuing decade. In the American public consciousness, however, the horrific events of September 11, 2001, transformed November 9, 1989, into a bookend to an era of transition to a new and newly dangerous century. September 11 has unleashed a very fundamental debate in this country about the nature and purpose of the United States' role in the world.

In many ways, the current debate is analogous to the period of the late 1940s and early 1950s, when America had won a war but not yet found a role. In that period, the notion of containment emerged as an organizing principle of U.S. foreign policy. Events of November 9, 1989, represented the logical conclusion—and the triumph—of that policy.

Today, the debate is how the threat of terrorism, coupled with the proliferation of WMD, should lead the United States to reframe its foreign and security policy. As Americans engage in this debate, some differences with the containment debate of the late 1940s are instructive for transatlantic relations. Americans believed then that one part of Europe was the front line and another part of it posed grave dangers. As a consequence, the central premise and preoccupation of U.S. foreign policy was the need for European stability.

Today, Americans believe they themselves are on the front line, and the danger no longer emanates from Europe but from beyond it. Europe, as a consequence, having already been "won," is seen increasingly by some in the Bush administration more as a platform than as a partner in its new global campaign.

These lenses explain somewhat the differing U.S. and European approaches to current issues. The November 9 world is one of promise, of new possibilities; the September 11 world is one of tragedy, of new dangers. The November 9 perspective says the worst is over; the September 11 perspective says the worst is yet to come. November 9 tells Europeans that, if they work together, they jointly may be able to manage the security of their continent for the first time in their history. September 11 tells Americans that they alone may not be able to ensure the security of their homeland for the first time in the nation's history. The November 9 view says the management of global dangers, while important, is a less-immediate priority than the historic opportunity to transform intra-European relations. The September 11 view says that in its basic contours a Europe whole and free is already here; the priority challenge now is to transform global relations to meet new threats.

As each of these debates proceeds, there is a lazy temptation to use the other—or, more typically, a caricature of the other—as an instrument with which to bash one's domestic opponents and to advance one's own political agenda with gratuitous insults and cartoon images, the self-righteous triumphalism or the hollow posturing. Style and tone matter, and the eagerness with which so many on each side of the Atlantic have been willing to sweep away facts and interests for the sake of a good stereotype should give us pause. They point to differing perspectives that are serious and should thus be taken seriously.

Yet are these views irreconcilable? Is transatlantic divorce inevitable?

The short answer is no, and for a simple reason: neither side can afford it.

DRIFTING APART, OR GROWING TOGETHER?

A weaker transatlantic bond would render Americans and Europeans less prosperous, less secure, and less able to advance either our ideals or our interests in the wider world.

Promoting prosperity

It is fashionable to suggest that Europeans and Americans are drifting apart. Yet our citizens tell us a different story. Every single indicator of societal interaction—whether flows of money, services, investments, people, or ideas—underscores a startling fact: our societies are not drifting apart; they are growing closer together. The years since the Cold War—the years when the eroding glue of the Cold War partnership supposedly loosened transatlantic ties—marked, in fact, one of the most intense periods of transatlantic integration ever.

One of the most dangerous deficits affecting transatlantic relations today is not one of trade, payments, or military capabilities, but instead a deficit among opinion leaders—in and out of government—in their understanding of the vital stake Americans and Europeans have developed in the health of our respective economies. The political, economic, and media errors that result from this deficit are shortchanging U.S. and European consumers, producers, workers, and their families.

The facts are straightforward yet rarely acknowledged. Despite the perennial hype about the significance of the North American Free Trade Agreement (NAFTA), the rise of Asia, or big emerging markets, the United States and Europe remain by far each other's most important commercial partners. The $2.5 trillion transatlantic economy employs more than 12 million workers on both sides of the Atlantic, workers who enjoy high wages, high labor and environmental standards, and open, largely nondiscriminatory access to each other's markets. The economic relationship between the United States and Europe is, by a wide margin, the deepest and broadest between any two continents in history—and those ties are accelerating.[5]

Lost in headline stories about banana, beef, or steel disputes are two critical facts. First, these squabbles represent less than 1 percent of overall transatlantic economic activity. Second, trade rows themselves are a misleading benchmark of transatlantic economic interaction, since trade itself accounts for less than 20 percent of transatlantic commerce. Foreign investment, not trade, is the backbone of the transatlantic economy, and, contrary to common wisdom, most U.S. and European investments flow across the Atlantic rather than to lower-wage developing nations. Our companies invest more in each other's economies than they do in the entire rest of the world put together. Such investments are creating jobs for U.S. and European workers, profits for U.S. companies, and better choices for U.S. consumers. They bind our societies together far more tightly than the shallow form of integration represented by trade flows.

Over only the past eight years U.S. investment in the tiny Netherlands alone was twice what it was in Mexico and ten times what it was in China. Europe, not Asia or Latin America, is the most profitable place in the world for U.S. businesses: U.S. companies rely on Europe for more than *half* of their total annual foreign profits. The United States' asset base in the United Kingdom alone is roughly equivalent to the combined overseas U.S. affiliate asset base in Asia, Latin America, Africa, and the Middle East. Two-thirds of U.S. corporate international R&D is in Europe, and two-thirds of the world's industrial R&D is concentrated in Europe and the United States. Moreover, European companies account for a significant percentage of all U.S. portfolio inflows—not insignificant for the world's largest debtor nation, which has to borrow more than $1 billion a day to finance its record current account deficits.

By the same token, Europeans have never been as dependent on U.S. prosperity as they are today. In fact, Europe's investment stake in the United States is one-quarter larger than the United States' stake in Europe. There is more European investment in Texas than there is total U.S. investment in Japan. German affiliate sales in the U.S. market are more than four times greater than German exports to that same market—a dramatic disproportion given Germany's traditional image as a classic trading nation. The bulk of corporate America's overseas workforce does not toil in low-wage nations like Mexico and China. Rather, they are employed in relatively well-paying jobs in Europe. The manufacturing workforce of U.S. affiliates in Germany is double the number of manufacturing workers employed by U.S. foreign affiliates in China. The number in the UK is five times what it is in China.

Of course, companies on each side of the Atlantic are economic rivals, but so many have fused that it is difficult to tell whether they are "European" or "American." If the U.S. Congress wants to punish "German" or "French" companies because of their government's policies toward Iraq, they are likely to put U.S. workers in Illinois, Texas, South Carolina, or California out of a job.

For workers and consumers, economics is not a zero-sum game. If Europe grows, Americans prosper. If Europe builds a larger single market without barriers to commerce, Americans profit. Because the European market is so large, a 2 percent growth rate there would create a new world market bigger than Taiwan itself. Unfortunately, the Congress and the Bush administration, together with their EU counterparts, have become trapped by mercantilist trade rhetoric. Trade competition between the United States and Europe is not war by other means. Yet officials and politicians on both sides of the Atlantic find it politically attractive to portray the other as a relentless foe in a struggle for global market share. This makes it increasingly difficult to focus on our much more fundamental common interests in advancing multilateral trade liberalization through the Doha Round, or to build policies that address our growing interdependence. Over time, such posturing creates a public impression, reinforced in the media, that the transatlantic relationship is more adversarial than complementary— and for that, we are all poorer.[6]

If one uses Tom Friedman's definition of globalization as farther, faster, deeper, and cheaper integration at intercontinental distances, then globalization is advancing farthest, fastest, deepest, and cheapest between the continents of Europe and North America.[7] The networks of interdependence that are being created across the Atlantic have become so dense, in fact, that they have attained a quality far superior to those either continent has developed with any other part of the world. Thus, many transatlantic tensions result less from the fashionable notion that our societies are drifting apart, and more from the growing evidence that they are in fact drawing closer together. Often these frictions are so severe precisely because they are not traditional, at-the-border trade disputes, but reach beyond the border, affecting such fundamental domestic issues as the ways Americans and Europeans are taxed, how their societies are governed, or how their economies are regulated.

These issues go to the heart of globalization. If globalization is going to proceed in ways that make Americans, Europeans, and others more prosperous and secure, the United States and Europe will have to show that they can deal with the challenges generated by the deep integration of our economies. If the United States cannot resolve such differences with Europe, it is unlikely to resolve them with economies much less like its own. The possibilities—and potential limits—of globalization are likely to be defined, first and foremost, by the successes or failures of the transatlantic relationship.

Enhancing security

In the post-post–Cold War world, Americans share a strange sense that they are uniquely powerful and uniquely vulnerable at the same time, and that the former may not prove sufficient to guard against the latter—vulnerabilities that may derive as much from who Americans are as a society as from what the United States does as a government. On September 11, 2001, in fact, the United States learned that perhaps its greatest strength—a free society—could be used against its own people. The attack on the World Trade Center was not only an attack on freedom; it was, as the *Economist* noted, "an attack through freedom." Al Qaeda used the very instruments of a free society to achieve its murderous aims.[8]

In short, power is relative to influence. The mere fact of power does not necessarily mean it can be wielded effectively to maintain order or to enhance stability. This is why the prevailing caricature of "American power and European weakness" is so fatally flawed.[9]

First, by any standard, Europeans *are* powerful: they boast a multi-trillion-euro economy, generate a tremendous amount of innovation and technology for the world, possess the second largest concentration of sophisticated military power on Earth, are leagues ahead of all others except the United States in their ability to project and deploy their military capacity, are represented strongly in international organizations, and are the only other grouping of nations with a history of leadership, a tradition of advocating universal values based on democracy and the rule of law, and a sense of global responsibility. Together with the United States, Europe is the core of a robust, largely democratic, market-oriented zone of peace and prosperity that encompasses more than two-thirds of the world economy.

Second, those who advance the proposition of American power and European weakness reduce the concept of power to its purely military component—a simplistic, unidimensional view of power in a complex, multidimensional world. It is as if you were forced to watch a black-and-white, reel-to-reel movie on the wall of your basement when you know the full-color, digital surround-sound version is playing in the theater next door. Of course, there is no substitute for effective military power when it comes to certain dangers. But in the post–September 11 world, power is distributed differently on different issues and, as Joseph Nye has written, it resembles a three-dimensional chessboard. On military issues, the world certainly is unipolar. On economic issues, however, as described above, the world is multipolar, and on the third level of play—transnational issues outside the control of governments—power is too chaotically organized to speak of a unipolar moment. "Those who focus on only one board in a three-dimensional game are likely to lose in the long run," Nye cautions.[10] Inordinate attention to one dimension of power deprives you of other tools in your toolbox and blinds you to problems for which military power may not be the answer—WMD terrorism, or peaceful reconstruction and rehabilitation of failed or rogue states such as Afghanistan or Iraq, for example.

Few great goals in this world can be reached without the United States, but few can be reached by the United States alone. Americans are unlikely to support an approach to the world that makes every problem their problem and then sends their warriors to conduct the nation's foreign policy. In this era of shadowy networks and bioterrorists, failed states and recession, the only way we can share our burdens, extend our influence, and achieve our goals will often be by banding together with others, particularly our core allies.

U.S. military capabilities are vast. Firepower is not staying power, however. The United States can win wars without allies, but it can only secure peace with allies, and the most essential allies for winning the peace are its European partners, because the tools of peace-winning—trade, aid, peacekeeping, monitoring, and policing—are a European strength. Europe delivers 70 percent of global civilian development assistance—four times more than the United States. Of international aid to Afghanistan, 90 percent flows from Europe. European troops are keeping the peace in trouble spots ranging from Afghanistan to Cyprus to Macedonia to Guatemala to Eritrea to the Congo. In fact, EU members and applicants contribute 10 times as many police forces and peacekeeping troops as the United States.

Third, we are most likely to both win the wars and secure the peace if our power is perceived to be legitimate. The genius of the U.S.-led system constructed after the collapse of Europe, following two world wars, was that it was perceived as legitimate by those within its ambit. A 60-year-old peace in the West has not been enjoyed merely by virtue of our democratic style of governance (although democracy is a major contributor), but because of a dense network of security, economy, and society that was successfully built among partners who came to believe that, by and large, they had a voice in the overall direction of this community.[11] This U.S.-led framework has made it possible to avoid older, more tragic approaches to international relations, such as balancing or containing latent rivals, by giving others a stake in our success and thus undercutting any motive or opportunity for confrontation by other powers.

The effective use of power includes the ability not just to twist arms but to shape preferences and frame choices—to get others to conceive of their interests and goals in ways compatible with ours. As the EU's foreign policy representative (and former NATO secretary general) Javier Solana put it, "Getting others to want what you want can be much more efficient than getting others to do what you want."[12]

In short, the widely perceived legitimacy of U.S. leadership was key to U.S. success in the past century. It remains essential if we are to wield our unprecedented power effectively today. Legitimacy, in turn, depends on creating a wide international consensus on controversial issues. Previous U.S. engagement on difficult issues—from the Persian Gulf War to wars in Bosnia, Kosovo, and Afghanistan—enjoyed considerable international support. U.S. engagement in Iraq did not. In a matter of only 18 months, the Bush administration squandered the tremendous political capital it had amassed following the September 11 attacks. The huge resentments generated by the U.S.-led preemptive war, including in such closely allied countries as Britain, Spain, and Italy, are acting as a cancer on the relationship.

As a result, the global legitimacy of U.S. leadership has become a defining issue for transatlantic relations and the measure of the Bush presidency well beyond Iraq. The United States cannot lead unless others choose to follow, and they will not make that choice over and over again unless they perceive it to be in their own best interests to do so. This depends on the degree of confidence they have in Washington's capacity to cope with core challenges, and whether the way in which we do so is perceived to be legitimate. The best evidence is North Korea, where the Bush administration seems to be stymied. We cannot antagonize the international community on one issue and then expect it to accommodate us on another.

A United States without the umbilical links to its core partners in Europe, provided through a revamped NATO alliance and more effective U.S.-EU channels, is an isolated America adrift in a hostile world, a power without peers but also a power without reliable partners.[13] Posses may be a last resort if the "sheriff" is desperate and alone, but they tend to be rather motley, unreliable affairs. Outlaws armed with WMD are more likely to be subdued by organized forces of law and order that employ their power through the consent and prescription of their communities. Any approach that willfully seeks to disparage or diminish those forces in favor of whatever international posse we can rustle up shortchanges American security, American prosperity, and American freedom.

Similarly, U.S. efforts to pit some parts of Europe against others are a reversal of American support, over six decades, of an ever-closer European Union, and threaten to return that continent to the very pattern of history that in the past century brought untold tragedy, not only to Europe but to the United States and the wider world. Such efforts are as inept as they are dangerous, and must be rejected.

A NEW ATLANTICISM

A new Atlanticism begins by resisting the easy temptation to cast one's partner as the Ugly Other. It also means rejecting lazy division-of-labor arguments. These come in two guises. The first says that we should simply stop trying to reconcile our efforts: Europeans should manage European security and Americans should manage global security. This would be a disaster of the first magnitude, for it would leave the United States with the by far more demanding and dangerous assignment, relieve Europeans of any broader sense of responsibility, and place Europe's broader global security interests in Washington's hands. It would reinforce European inwardness, diminish U.S. influence in Europe, generate new resentments, and corrode our partnership.

The second version says, since Europe will never catch up to the United States in terms of military capabilities, it should not even try. Likewise, since the United States will never allocate the resources or develop the inclination for post-conflict civilian peacekeeping, monitoring, or rehabilitation, it should not pretend that it can. Instead of each partner working fruitlessly on its relative weakness, let each partner play to its strength: the Americans do the dirty military work and the Europeans do the post-conflict cleanup. This is a seductive idea, but it again endangers U.S. soldiers primarily, generating resentment in the United States, while it forces Europeans to pick up the leftovers from interventions about which they had little voice, thus reinforcing European resentments. Ultimately, such a division of labor would lead to a division of perspective and ultimately divorce, by reinforcing European tendencies to think all conflicts can be managed through civilian power and reinforcing U.S. tendencies to apply military solutions to nonmilitary problems.

These are false choices. A real choice calls for a complementary sense of risk and responsibility that aligns our respective strengths (and minimizes our respective weaknesses) to respond to the challenges that face our community. Viewing the world primarily from a November 9 or a September 11 perspective is like trying to see though prescription glasses with one lens missing. Much is sharp, much is blurred, and the result is a headache. Our common challenge is to see through both lenses, to reconcile the promise offered by November 9 with the challenges posed by September 11—to reconcile Europe's grand experiment of integration with a reorientation and strategic transformation of transatlantic relations to create a new model, and a new focus, for our partnership.

Taken together, November 9 and September 11 convey a single message. We should trade in our old transatlantic barometer, which measured the health of the transatlantic partnership by the degree of American engagement on the European continent, for a new measuring stick, which gauges the ability of the United States and Europe to cope—together—with the promises and dangers of globalization. If the fall of the Berlin Wall was the triumph of globalization's positive elements, the fall of the World Trade Towers was the shuddering response by its darker forces. Seen in this way, November 9 and September 11 convey both opportunity and obligation to recast our partnership, and, with it, the international system.[14] In fact, two major results of the post–November 9 world—peace among the great powers and the potential for a strong, united Europe at peace with itself—can be major assets in the campaign to confront the challenges of the post–September 11 world.

The greatest security threats to the United States and Europe today stem from problems that defy borders: terrorism and WMD proliferation, pandemics, and environmental scarcities. They stem from challenges that have traditionally been marginal, but contentious, in the transatlantic security dialogue: peacekeeping outside the traditional NATO area; post-conflict reconstruction and rehabilitation; rogue states, failed states, and states hijacked by illegal groups or networks. Moreover, these threats come from places, such as Africa or

Southwest and Central Asia, that the transatlantic agenda has often ignored.

On many of these issues, there is often disagreement within as well as between Europe and the United States. Yet unless Europeans and Americans find a way to focus together on them, these challenges will surely drive us apart. A first step in this direction is to remember that the relationship between the United States and Europe remains distinctive from any other relationship either side has in the world. When Americans and Europeans agree, they form the core of any effective global coalition. When they disagree, no global coalition is likely to be effective. More than with any other part of the world, the United States' relationship with Europe is what one might call an enabling or empowering relationship. When it works, it enables each side of the Atlantic to achieve common goals that neither could achieve alone. The Bush administration failed to put this premise to the test in Iraq, and the post-Iraq situation is troubling. The EU failed to put this premise to the test on climate change, and the result is a climate regime in disarray.

A new Atlanticism must build on this fact through three new strategic bargains. First, while Americans must be clear that they support a strong, coherent Europe, Europeans must also be clear that they are building Europe as a partner, not a rival, to the United States. A second bargain is for both sides of the Atlantic to supplement their traditional focus on European stability with more effective ways to engage together on the global stage. That means, as a matter of priority, a Europe that can act and an America that can listen. Finally, a third bargain requires that Europeans, who believe that robust international norms and enforcement mechanisms are needed to tackle these challenges, must focus equally on the effective enforcement of such regimes and be more forthright about the necessity to act when these regimes fail. Conversely, however, Americans, who tend to see these treaties and regimes at best as ineffective and at worst as an unacceptable constraint on U.S. freedom of action, should heed the costs of unilateral action in terms of less legitimacy, greater burdens, and ultimately the ability to achieve one's goals.

Taken together, these bargains underpin a new Atlanticism. The old Atlanticism was equated with the institution of NATO. The new Atlanticism must include a stronger, larger NATO able to engage wherever alliance interests are threatened.[15] Given the nature of our world, however, such a NATO must be seen as the densest weave in a larger, multidimensional fabric of inner-European and transatlantic mechanisms and networks that can enhance our ability to work better together in fast-breaking crises, manage our differences before they impair our ability to cooperate, and improve joint efforts to address emerging threats and global issues.

The real question, in fact, is less one of institutions than of complementary perspectives and determination. Are Europe and the United States prepared to work together on the broader challenges their community faces in this new century as they did during the past century? If they are not, their common future is diminished. Life without the other will be less prosperous, less safe, and less free.

The post–November 9 world offers us an unprecedented strategic window to use the United States' preeminent position to harness positive forces of integration with its key partners, lock in the gains offered by great-power peace, and use these to address the challenges posed by the post–September 11 challenges of WMD terrorism and its causes. It is decidedly in the United States' interests to seek a more effective global partnership with a Europe that can act in real time on pressing international matters.

FOUR PRIORITIES FOR A NEW ATLANTICISM

Transforming the Greater Middle East

A most immediate task, of course, is reaching agreement on post-conflict reconstruction and rehabilitation in Iraq, and on the role of the international community. This goal remains difficult and contentious, but we must also frame the continuing transatlantic debate over Iraq with a wider perspective if we are to pick up the pieces of this broader relationship.

To be successful, efforts to transform Iraq must be part of more comprehensive transatlantic strategies aimed at the modernization and transformation of the Greater Middle East itself. A circle—with its center in Tehran—that has a diameter roughly matching the length of the continental United States covers a region that encompasses 75 percent of the world's population, 60 percent of its GNP, and 75 percent of its energy resources. The Greater Middle East is the region of the world where unsettled relationships, religious and territorial conflicts, fragile and failed regimes, and deadly combinations of technology and terror brew and bubble on top of one vast, relatively contiguous energy field upon which Western prosperity depends. Transformation of this region is the strategic challenge of our time and a key to winning the campaign against terrorism. Choices made there could determine the shape of the twenty-first century—whether WMD will be unleashed upon mass populations, whether the oil and gas fields of the Caucasus and Central Asia will become reliable sources of energy, whether the Arab world will meet the challenges of modernization and globalization, whether Russia's borderlands will become stable and secure democracies, whether Israel and its neighbors can live together in peace, and whether the great religions of the world can coexist peacefully.

This is a long-term effort: this turbulent region will not soon be transformed into an area of democratic stability and prosperity. But we can act more successfully together to defend common interests, to dampen the negative trends that are gaining momentum, and to work with those in the region who seek to carve out areas of civil society where the totalitarian state cannot intrude. Such an effort is far more likely to succeed if the United States and Europe were to pool their energies and resources and pursue it together.

New approaches to strategic stability

A second, related priority is to generate a new understanding of strategic stability. During the Cold War the two superpowers preserved stability, despite their animosity, because they felt equally at risk. They shared the view that the prospect of suicide would deter anyone from actually using WMD, and they were willing to negotiate certain rules of the road together with other nations. Today, all three of these premises have vanished. Other nuclear powers have emerged—and their rules of the road are unclear. Terrorists are not deterred by suicide, and they are not at the negotiating table. They have nothing to protect and nothing to lose. In short, Cold War deterrence will not work as it once did, and in some cases it may not even work at all.

A new conception of strategic stability must weave what have been separate strands—the fight against terrorism, nuclear force posture, nonproliferation, and defense efforts—into a comprehensive defense against WMD. These strands must be considered jointly, and discussion of the Bush administration's doctrine of preemption should be incorporated into a broader discussion of what is likely to constitute security and stability in the new century.

Transatlantic homeland security

Third, we must develop *transatlantic* approaches to homeland security and societal protection. When the United States was attacked, allies in Europe immediately invoked the North Atlantic Treaty's mutual defense clause, in essence stating that the September 11 attack was an attack on a common security space—a common "homeland." It is unlikely that a successful effort to strengthen homeland security can be conducted in isolation from one's allies. The United States may be a primary target for Al Qaeda, but that group is known to have also planned major operations in Europe.

A terrorist WMD attack on Europe would immediately affect U.S. civilians, U.S. forces, and U.S. interests. If such an attack involved contagious disease, it could threaten the U.S. homeland itself in a matter of hours. The SARS epidemic, while deadly, is simply a mild portent of what may be to come. Bioterrorism, in particular, is a first-order strategic threat to the Euro-Atlantic community. A bioterrorist attack in Europe or North America is more likely and could be as consequential as a nuclear attack, but it requires a different set of national and international responses. Europeans and Americans alike are woefully ill-prepared for such challenges.

In the aftermath of the September 11 attacks, it has become clear that controlling borders, operating ports, and managing airports and train stations in the age of globalization involves a delicate balance of identifying and intercepting weapons and terrorists without excessively hindering trade, legal migration, travel, and tourism—all aspects upon which European and U.S. prosperity increasingly depend. Efforts to protect the U.S. homeland against cyberattack, for example, can hardly be conducted in isolation from key allies whose economies and information networks are so intertwined with ours.

Unless there is systematic trans-European and transatlantic coordination in the area of preparedness, each side of the Atlantic is at greater risk of attack. Uneven homeland security coordination and preparedness within Europe renders North America more vulnerable, particularly since North America's security is organically linked to Europe's vulnerability to terrorist infiltration. Similarly, if U.S. and Canadian efforts render the North American homeland less vulnerable to terrorist attack, terrorists may target Europe.[16] Just because the Cold War has faded does not mean that Europeans and North Americans are less dependent on one another.

Current efforts are a good start but still tend to be ad hoc and uneven. Complementary, sustained, and well-institutionalized efforts are needed in areas ranging from intelligence, counterterrorism, financial coordination, and law enforcement to customs, air and seaport security, and other activities.

New models of transatlantic governance

A fourth priority is the development of new models of transatlantic governance. Among the nations of the European Union, the policies of European integration reach so deep that it is common to hear that European policies have become domestic policies, and that EU countries have entered a new realm of "European domestic policy." This is true, but it does not begin to capture the real dynamic of what is happening. A similar, if largely unnoticed, process has been under way for some time across the Atlantic. Our economies and societies have become so intertwined that in a number of specific areas Europeans and Americans have transcended "foreign" relations.

We have moved into a new arena of "transatlantic domestic policy" —a new frontier in which specific social and economic concerns and transnational actors often jump formal borders, override national policies, and challenge traditional forms of governance throughout the Euro-Atlantic world. Many of the issues confronting European and U.S. policymakers today are those of deep integration, a new closeness that strikes at core issues of domestic governance. That is of a qualitatively different nature than the shallow-integration model of the Bretton Woods–GATT system established at the end of World War II. Deep integration is generating new transatlantic networks and connections. However, because it reaches into traditionally domestic areas, it can also generate social dislocation, anxiety, and friction in issues such as food safety or competition policy. At the same time, European and American scientists and entrepreneurs are pushing the frontiers of human discovery in such fields as genetics, nanotechnology, and electronic commerce, where there are neither global rules nor transatlantic mechanisms to sort out the complex legal, ethical, and commercial trade-offs posed by such innovation.

Neither the framework for our relationship nor the way our governments are currently organized adequately captures these new realities. Across the Atlantic such quasi-domestic issues need to be managed through new and more effective forms of transatlantic regulatory and parliamentary consultation and coordination as well as more innovative diplomacy that takes account of the growing role of private actors. If we are serious about a transatlantic marketplace, then the United States and the EU must work systematically together to develop joint or complementary approaches to such areas as financial services and capital markets, aviation, the digital economy, competition policy, and performance of our regulatory systems.

Iraq was a loud wake-up call to transatlantic partnership. The question is whether, in the wake of this episode, Europeans and Americans will be led astray by false choices or the lazy caricature of the Ugly Other, or whether we will assume the global obligations our partnership demands. For history will ultimately judge us not only in terms of how well or badly we managed a particular crisis, but also how well we used such crises to shape our relationship for the future.

Notes

[1] For an incisive reflection on the Iraq crisis and transatlantic relations, see Timothy Garton Ash, "Are You With Us? Are We Against You?" *New York Times*, May 30, 2003.

[2] For a critique of European approaches to multilateralism, see John van Oudenaren, "What is Multilateral?" *Policy Review* 117 (February/March 2003): 33–47.

[3] For an early interpretation of these differing perspectives, see Daniel S. Hamilton, *Die Zukunft ist nicht mehr, was sie war: Europa, Amerika und die neue weltpolitische Lage* (Stuttgart: Robert Bosch Stiftung, December 2002); also Martin Walker, "Post 9/11: The European Dimension," *World Policy Journal* 18, no. 4 (Winter 2001/2002): 1–10.

[4] For the dilemmas facing this new Europe, see Robert Cooper, "Europe, The Post-Modern State and World Order," *New Perspectives Quarterly* 14, no. 3 (Summer 1997): 46–57.

[5] For details on deeper transatlantic integration, see Joseph Quinlan, *Drifting Apart or Growing Together? The Primacy of the Transatlantic Economy* (Washington, D.C.: Center for Transatlantic Relations, SAIS, Johns Hopkins University, 2003).

[6] For further details on transatlantic economic challenges, see David L. Aaron, John D. Macomber, and Peter W. Smith, *Changing Terms of Trade: Managing the New Transatlantic Economy* (Washington, D.C.: Atlantic Council of the United States, April 2001); www.acus.org/Publications/policypapers/energy/trade%20 report.pdf (June 9, 2003).

[7] Thomas L. Friedman, *The Lexus and the Olive Tree: Understanding Globalization* (New York: Farrar, Straus & Giroux, 2000).

[8] "Liberty vs. Security," *Economist*, September 29, 2001.

[9] Robert Kagan, "Power and Weakness," *Policy Review* 113 (June/July 2002): 3–28.

[10] "Europe Is Too Powerful to Be Ignored," *Financial Times*, March 11, 2003, p. 13. Also Joseph S. Nye Jr., *The Paradox of American Power: Why the World's Only Superpower Can't Go It Alone* (New York: Oxford University Press, 2002).

[11] For an extended analysis of this system, see works by Daniel Deudney and G. John Ikenberry, including "The Logic of the West," *World Policy Journal* 10, no. 4 (Winter 1993/94): 17–25; "Structural Liberalism: The Nature and Sources of Postwar Western Political Order," working paper, Christopher H. Browne Center for International Politics, University of Pennsylvania, May 1996.

[12] Javier Solana, "Mars and Venus Reconciled: A New Era for Transatlantic Relations" (Albert H. Gordon lecture, Kennedy School of Government, Harvard University, April 7, 2003); www.useu.be/TransAtlantic/030407SolanaHarvard.htm (June 9, 2003).

[13] For a more detailed call for a "global" transatlantic partnership, see David C. Gompert and F. Stephen Larrabee, eds., *America and Europe: A Partnership for a New Era* (New York: Cambridge University Press, 1997).

[14] For further treatment of this theme, see Hamilton, *Die Zukunft ist nicht mehr, was sie war.*

[15] See the debate between Daniel S. Hamilton and Timothy Garden, "Debate: Should NATO's New Function Be Counter-Terrorism?" *NATO Review* 50, no. 2 (Summer 2002): 16–20; available at www.nato.int/docu/review/2002/issue2/english/debate.html (June 9, 2003).

[16] See Jonathan Stevenson, "How Europe and America Defend Themselves," *Foreign Affairs* 82, no. 2 (March/April 2003): 75–90.

PART THREE

EUROPEAN VISIONS OF AMERICA

FIVE

DILEMMAS OF A SEMI-INSIDER

BLAIRITE BRITAIN AND THE UNITED STATES

Christopher Hill

Neither the passage of time nor a succession of gloomy predictions over more than half a century has destroyed the alliance between Britain and the United States, which is formalized in NATO and in various bilateral defense agreements. However much the analysis of objective trends in international relations may suggest reasons for an inexorable divergence, a major military crisis usually finds the two countries "shoulder to shoulder," in Tony Blair's phrase of September 11, 2001. The operative phrase here is "major military crisis," for just as it is commonplace to assert that the "special relationship" has shrunk back to little more than its defense and intelligence dimensions, so it can be argued that only on the highest of high-politics issues do London and Washington continue to hold firmly together—that is, when their very survival seems at stake and the memory of having made common cause in 1944, 1982, 1986, and 1991 is evoked.

These very dates raise questions about instances when even crisis was not enough to ensure solidarity. If, instead of D-Day, the Falklands, Libya, and Kuwait, we cite Korea (1950), Suez (1956), the October War and Year of Europe (1973–1974), and Bosnia (1992–1995), it will be seen that the two states have often been at odds over the purpose and the uses of force. Disagreements, however, have never been cumulative, unlike common actions, which have created trust by steady accretion. Arguably, once modern institutional alliances become established, especially at the bilateral level, they constitute a form of learned behavior, which unravels only with great difficulty. The weight of supposition and organizational procedure is all in favor of continuation, not of schism, just as much in the Anglo-American relationship as it is in the Franco-

German couple.[1] Disputes become insulated and managed within the core structure of trust and cooperation.

Nevertheless, the projection of a past trend into the future can never be taken for granted, since each new issue has the potential to spin out of control, with transformational effects. The current environment illustrates the dangers clearly. The atrocities of September 11 may or may not have led to fundamental changes in international politics. What they did in the short term was to precipitate a prolonged crisis over Iraq in which the intramural consequences for NATO and for EU foreign policy came close to being fatal. Even if the Republican foreign policy team had been planning to unseat Saddam Hussein since the late 1990s, it seems highly unlikely that it would have come to this without the events of 9/11 and the subsequent sense of the world having been turned upside down. Neither Britain nor the United States, therefore, despite their governments having held together under intense political pressure during this crisis, can assume that their alliance is unbreakable. The very notion of crisis implies the possibility of a parting of the ways, of some irrevocable choices having to be made; and when tensions between governments and publics are added to the strains of diplomatic conflict, it is only to be expected that some adjustment to the new realities will have to be made eventually.

The argument of this paper, therefore, is that the current solidarity masks significant difficulties that, even without the catalytic fallout from the Iraq crisis, would still have come to the fore eventually. Moreover, some of these difficulties are caused by what, counterintuitively, can be termed the "Europeanization" of British culture and politics. George Ball once dismissed the "emotional baggage" of the special relationship, but it may now be the case that, because the baggage weighs less heavily, there is space on the British side for the formation of new attachments, despite ourselves and even unconsciously. The "cousins" coexist at second or third remove, while new family ties have been forming through 30 years of EU membership and 40 years of domestic multiculturalism. These trends cannot be controlled by patriarchal elites.

PRECEDENTS

The Iraq War is far from being the first occasion in the post-1945 era when a British government has supported the United States in the face of doubts from its own domestic opinion. Notably over the possession of nuclear weapons, Labour governments have been prepared to risk internal splits to go along with U.S. strategy. In the case of Polaris and Trident it may have been Her Majesty's government who were the *demandeurs* of the two sides, but during the Intermediate-Range Nuclear Force (INF) debate of the late 1970s the argument that "it was the Europeans who asked for Cruise and Pershing" wore thin in the case of Britain. James Callaghan, Denis Healey, and David Owen had shown themselves to be good Atlanticists, when, along with Harold Wilson, they chose to support Washington during the Vietnam War despite clear British public opposition against such support.[2] Despite the spirit of '68 (and the rebuff of their efforts at mediation), Wilson's Labour government largely refused to join France in explicit criticism of the policies of Lyndon Johnson and Richard Nixon.

It was less difficult for Margaret Thatcher's ensuing government to ride out opposition to her support for President Reagan in the "second Cold War." Floating voters were not going to change their allegiance over a foreign policy matter—at least, not so long as they felt the safety of the realm was not at stake. After her departure, the tortuous years of John Major's wrestling with his own party over Europe plus the optimism of the new post–Cold War era prevented even the serious disagreements over the Balkans from turning UK-U.S. relations into a cause célèbre. When Tony Blair then proclaimed his fraternity with Bill Clinton, and later even with the latter's Republican successor, the odds against U.S. foreign policy becoming a serious source of friction in British politics seemed long indeed.

The story of the 45 years after the traumatic blow dealt by the United States to Britain over Suez is thus one of both intermittent disagreement between the two states—albeit contained within a rock-solid alliance structure—and the gradually shrinking scope of the "special relationship," as the defeated powers of 1939–1945 regained their bona fides in Washington and established their own privileged partnerships. Britain's membership in the European Community (EC) also inevitably reoriented the country's trade and political cooperation, not least at the U.S. behest. It would be inaccurate to talk of the steady disintegration of what has been (ironically) an entente cordiale of remarkable durability. Sentiment, language, culture, and investment have provided some of the glue that has preserved the structure of this enduring bilateral relationship. Even more important has been the sense of fundamentally shared strategic interests, as U.S. antagonism to colonialism necessarily faded and Britain settled into a self-image of a power in reduced circumstances but still important enough to have the ear of the White House, particularly on matters of declared vital interest.

Yet the humiliation of Suez has never been forgotten in London, and sentiment has not blinded British decisionmakers to the reality that the United States could easily leave Britain exposed or vulnerable simply by following its own needs. Not surprisingly perhaps, given that Suez destroyed one of their number, Tory prime ministers have learned this lesson most sharply, though with varying conclusions: Harold Macmillan sought membership in the EC; Edward Heath wanted to make a full-hearted commitment to European integration to give Britain an alternative power base to the special relationship; Margaret Thatcher had to remind Ronald Reagan, post-Reykjavik, that nuclear disarmament might present serious disadvantages for the United Kingdom. For Tony Blair's part, it is likely that his decision to associate himself with George W. Bush (before September 11, over nuclear missile defense, let it not be forgotten) was based less on instinctive pro-Americanism than on anxiety about what the new administration might do (or not do, as it seemed at the time) and a wish to help moderate its approach to international relations. There was, of course, no perceived incompatibility at the time between closeness to the United States and a more proactive European policy. If not seeking the by now redundant role of bridge builder, New Labour certainly saw itself as a leader in the creation of a new transatlantic partnership, made possible by French softening on NATO and the long-held U.S. wish for greater transatlantic burden sharing.

CURRENT DILEMMAS

Transatlantic solidarity

The attacks on Washington and New York did not, therefore, require any volte-face in Blair's attitude to the United States. It was natural, both emotionally and politically, for him to offer total solidarity to President Bush, as indeed did most other European leaders. It was also natural and logical to extend this support to the campaign in Afghanistan, which swiftly followed. What seemed less necessary, in the eyes of many of his supporters, was the willingness to follow when the United States decided to target Saddam Hussein, sometime in the spring of 2002. There does not seem even to have been a serious pause for thought on the part of the British government, despite the fact that this was the moment when dissociation might have been achieved with relatively little loss of face on both sides. As events moved on, it became increasingly more difficult—and ultimately impossible—for Britain to take an independent line on Iraq. Blair seems to have been sucked into making Iraq the strategic priority almost as part of a "coordination reflex" with the White House—a phrase that is, in fact, supposed to describe the interaction among the participants in the EU's Common Foreign and Security Policy (CFSP). Indeed, Downing Street and the Foreign and Commonwealth Office consciously became players in the United States' own foreign policy making process through their attempts to bolster the position of the embattled secretary of state, Colin Powell.

It would be interesting to know how far war aims on Iraq were also discussed between Britain and its European allies, and at how early a stage.[3] The public record, for what it is worth, is clear. The European Council in Barcelona in March 2002 was preoccupied with Israel/Palestine, and the conclusions of the summit did not mention Iraq. The EU summit in Seville, on June 21–22, focused on the Treaty of Nice (and the implications of the "no" vote of the June 2001 Irish referendum on ratification of the treaty), handling all external relations cursorily. The subsequent Brussels European Council of October 24–25 moved on EU-NATO relations but again did not mention Iraq. Only by the Copenhagen European Council of December 12–13, 2002, called to deal with enlargement, do we see concern with Iraq creeping in, with a declaration giving full support to UN Security Council Resolution 1441, both in its call for "full and immediate compliance by Iraq" and in its stress on the importance of the UN and the role of the inspectors.

By this time, the issues—and the tensions within the EU—were becoming obvious, even as it was too late either to head off the United States from its decision for war or to ensure European cohesion around a position that stood at a suitable distance from the position of Washington. The conclusion has to be that Tony Blair either neglected to consult properly with his European partners or had assumed that they would come round to his position in the end. This approach was to leave him, and the UK, dangerously exposed. What is more, although the other European states must share the responsibility for a lack of joint planning, it does seem that the CFSP was barely relevant to the day-to-day conduct of UK foreign policy, with a concern for European solidarity being merely an empty phrase of New Labour rhetoric.

These two conclusions seem to imply that the Blair cabinet sees little reason to worry about the political consequences of Britain becoming isolated in Europe as the main supporter of a hard-line U.S. policy in Iraq. If a close relationship with Washington is Britain's main foreign policy priority, as Blair has stated it to be, then his display of loyalty and firmness under pressure should have made it even more secure. Arguably, public opposition can be contained in the British context, given the prime minister's continuing large parliamentary majority, which makes it almost impossible for him, in normal circumstances, to lose the next election. The Labour Party, even if unhappy, will see the crisis as a one-time trauma. All this would seem reassuring if the wider context, and in particular that of the EU, could be discounted.

Of course, the latter cannot be so discounted, and that is why there has been so much unease about the future, not just among the Labour Party faithful, but also among the officials responsible for the professional conduct of British policy. Moreover, the three consecutive ministerial resignations that followed Britain's decision to support the United States in waging war against Iraq without UN authorization—by Foreign Secretary Robin Cook, Health Minister Lord Hunt, and Home Office Minister John Denham—have not seen their parallel since the Korean War, when Prime Minister Clement Attlee faced two almost simultaneous resignations from his cabinet over foreign policy.[4]

This unease continues for a number of reasons. First, Britain's importance to the United States partly resides in it being a European power and a key player in the EU. Outside a particular kind of military crisis, its usefulness as a bilateral partner is limited. This means that any notion of an Atlantic versus Continental choice is misplaced. Britain would be foolish to alienate its partners in either quarter. Equally, it is narcissistic and self-deceiving to imagine that the UK can act as a bridge or balancer between the two sides, when Washington has so many diverse conduits into European politics, and vice versa. Even if the UK did wish to become the indispensable partner of the United States and were willing to both pay the costs of client status and close off alternatives, such a policy would be difficult to sustain for long. Why should the United States forgo an eclectic diplomacy for an ally with limited assets and nowhere else to go?

Embedded Europeanism

Britain has been a member of the European Union and its predecessors for more than 30 years (an anniversary not, by the way, celebrated on either side of the channel in 2003) and has participated in European efforts at foreign policy coordination since the creation of the European Political Cooperation (EPC) process in 1970. With EPC and CFSP as central to the European project, indeed as an area in which many believe Britain should lead, Whitehall and Westminster (in that order) have become committed both to the processes of diplomatic coordination through the EU and to various substantive European initiatives. A Europe that is hopelessly divided as a result of Iraq is not just a humiliation for the CFSP; it also reflects on Britain's capacity to lead and to sustain consensus in the EU.

What is more, if France is likely to suffer the consequences of having opposed the United States, nothing is more certain than that Britain will find everyday life in the EU more difficult for having once more "taken the American side" in opposition to France and Germany—although, at least this time, London has Madrid and Rome to share the ignominy.

Most particularly, the grand Anglo-French European Security and Defense Policy (ESDP) project, launched with startling velocity in 1998–1999, appears also in jeopardy. It is hard to imagine how the two EU states most capable of projecting military power beyond the "near abroad" can move ahead on the basis of intensive cooperation after signally failing to do so in harness over Iraq (just as they could not even harmonize diplomacy over Zimbabwe). The one-hundredth anniversary of the entente cordiale in 2004 may turn out to be a hollow affair.

Yet diplomatic rows and personal antagonisms between leaders have a way of proving ephemeral. Only historians now remember "l'affaire Soames" of 1969,[5] while the row over BSE (mad-cow disease) and beef has quickly come to seem remote and relatively trivial. Britain is going to have to work with its European allies on a whole range of problems —domestic, "inter-mestic," and international—on a day-to-day basis, inside a highly structured environment consisting of meetings, texts, and the EU's *acquis*, both *communautaire* and *politique*. However close the Anglo-American relationship, it does not match this day-to-day familiarity except in certain areas of military and intelligence cooperation— not least because as a relationship it is so asymmetrical.

One does not have to be a neofunctionalist to understand that this continual *engrenage* among the various European states breeds not only familiarity, but also some convergence of attitudes and expectations. It is revealing that the setbacks of CFSP, devastating as they sometimes are, do not lead to demands for its abandonment, least of all in Britain and France, which see it as a platform for their particular national contributions to international politics. What is more, the populations of Europe, perhaps as a result of the failures of collective foreign policy as much as its successes, are gradually learning what they want the EU to do on their behalf in relation to outsiders, and what, indeed, they think they stand for in comparison with others outside their continent.

First among the EU's "others," inevitably, stands the United States, seen as friendly yet different, relatively benign but still a superpower. It should perhaps be admitted that most Europeans, including the British, are apprehensive about the impact the United States can have on the world, and know that only the EU has some hope of balancing/persuading Washington into policies with which they feel comfortable. This explains why some states, namely Italy, Spain, and the candidate countries as well as Britain, seek security through closeness to the United States, while others prefer to let Washington know clearly what their concerns are—as exemplified most recently by the Iraq crisis. The strategies are different, but the concerns they reflect are common. It would be an illusion to assume that the former group clusters around the United States simply because of a shared ideology. Even Italy's prime minister, Silvio Berlusconi, has shown, through his talk of peace and his enthusiasm for Russian president Vladimir Putin, that a shared enthusiasm for capitalism does not translate into the same view of international relations, or assertive foreign policy goals, as those of Bush administration officials.

The Iraq crisis offers, therefore, hardly any clues as to its likely long-term impact on British policy and the latter's evolving relationship with the United States. In his decision to identify himself fully with the Bush policy, Blair elevated tactics over deeper currents of policy and also over his own concerns about the Republican turn in the conduct of U.S. foreign policy. The undoubted strain of pro-Americanism in New Labour (indeed in most quarters of British life) does not mean that there is an identity of interests or views of the world. In accepting the "with us or against us" choice posed by George W. Bush, the current government in London accepted a Procrustean bed, causing problems for existing commitments in the European sphere.

Since 1945, British policy has always sought to avoid having to choose between the extremes of bandwagoning and balancing the United States. Rather, the aim has been to position the country as the one best able to convince Washington of the value of friendly criticism, as well as of the importance of not abandoning Europe in favor of hemispheric or Asian-Pacific priorities. Such a policy has involved an increasing British immersion in Europe and in its common institutions. Over the past decade this has taken the form of both an enthusiastic support for EU enlargement (in order to promote a larger, looser system of European governance) and a courting of the Franco-German leadership couple in the hope of creating a ménage à trois.

This rather contradictory policy has only been possible because of Germany's own support for enlargement. It has been now weakened by at least two further developments: the quarrel with French president Jacques Chirac and German chancellor Gerhard Schroeder; and Britain's perceived connection to U.S. interference in the EU's internal affairs, both in pressuring the 2002 Copenhagen European Council to give Turkey a starting date for accession negotiations and through the Letter of Eight, by which candidate states were drawn in to support the London-Madrid-Rome triangle against Paris and Berlin over Iraq. With the European Convention on the Future of Europe and the Inter-Governmental Conference (IGC) to concentrate minds, Britain is going to have to focus on some strategic choices in these matters in the near future.

Such choices are never made in a vacuum. The United States is always a factor in British calculations about Europe, even if only implicitly. The more Euroskeptical elements have always been baffled by U.S. pressure on Britain to accept the logic of European integration; they may now be relieved by what appears to be a U.S. turning away from the Franco-German project, and a sharper awareness of the dangers of possible rivalry. If the United States comes to believe that a deeper Europe does not in fact serve its interests well, some of the ambiguity in the context of British decisionmaking would be removed. On the other hand, U.S. antagonism toward political integration might, paradoxically, lead to more reflection in the UK as to whether an EU reduced to little more than a highfalutin customs union would truly be in British interests.

The political aspect of the EU has always caused Britain trouble. Instinctively hostile to any notion of a political union that might imply single statehood, the British are not at all unhappy about the alternative interpretation that has come to dominate in recent years, namely that of intergovernmental supremacy over the Brussels institutions, with the bigger countries forming an informal *directoire*. They have always been supportive of the EU having an external political role, precisely because intergovernmentalism always seemed set in stone as the preferred method of decisionmaking in the EPC and CFSP—and for largely practical reasons. Who could imagine national foreign policies being subject in practice to the discipline of qualified majority voting, whatever the theoretical possibilities opened up by the treaties of Maastricht and Amsterdam?

Beyond this instrumental reasoning, British governments of both parties have found that operating in the external world through the framework of European foreign policy coordination confers substantive advantages. At the lowest level, they can draw on a wider range of information and expertise on any given problem, both in the central political committees and working groups and in third-country capitals. More significantly, even the more powerful member states like Britain benefit from the cover or alibi function of the CFSP, which essentially amounts to safety in numbers. The Europeans have, for example, taken a view of the Israel-Palestine dispute that is markedly different from that of the United States, one that, therefore, causes them regular transatlantic discomfort. It would be much worse were Washington able to pick them off individually over this policy issue, just as it has done with the bilateral immunity agreements over the International Criminal Court. Indeed, on the Middle East, EU members have for 30 years now forged a common policy, which is settled in its basic components even though the leverage to implement it is lacking. Consequently, they have been able to spare themselves the divisions characteristic of other areas of European foreign policy. Common convictions and a diplomatic *acquis* ensure a degree of resilience. Britain, revealingly, has preferred to stick with this policy despite pressure and blandishments from Washington and Tel Aviv.

At a structural level, Britain's foreign policy instruments are also entwined with the resources of the EU. Any economic sanctions have to be consistent with the common commercial policy, implemented through Article 301 of the European Union treaties. For any use of diplomatic carrots, the formidable resources of the EU, whether through preferential agreements or the Union's extensive system of aid to developing countries, are a first port of call. If stabilization and peacekeeping in Europe are the issue, then coordination within the EU and the

Organization for Security and Cooperation in Europe (OSCE) is necessary. It was the weakness of British and French national positions in the Balkans that led to the St. Malô initiative for an EU rapid reaction force, while the project of rebuilding Central and Eastern Europe could never have been attempted without the collective options of EU enlargement and the coordination of economic assistance through the European Commission. To be sure, Britain plans over the next three years to claw back a good deal of the money it currently funnels through the EU for overseas development assistance, but this is more because of the elephantine procedures of the latter than any inherent desire to go it alone or to coordinate more closely with the United States on a number of foreign policy issues.

Thus Britain cannot at will opt in and out of its Europeanism in foreign policy without paying significant costs. Partly this is related to limitations posed by formal commitments and procedures; and partly it is the result of a socialization process, more subtle and long term than the fiercest Euroskeptics could dream of, leading to positions that imply convergence around a distinctive European view of the world, and, therefore, to some extent also divergence from that of the United States. Both values and interests are in the process of being articulated by the historical and, no doubt, bumbling process of European foreign policy cooperation. Although most such values and interests can be expected to overlap strongly with those of the United States, they cannot be identical. In the medium term, that overlap in transatlantic approaches and the limits of the CFSP mean that Britain's only realistic option—other than accepting subservience to Washington—is to fall back on variable geometry and coalitions of the willing.

VIEWS OF INTERNATIONAL RELATIONS

It would be foolish to assert that "Europe" holds to one coherent philosophy of international relations. The split over Iraq was more than just a matter of tactics; it also reflected the divide between two notions of an "ethical foreign policy" extant inside the EU. These include the British-led belief in a new right of intervention, expressed in Tony Blair's Chicago speech of April 1999, and the concern of others for pacific methods of conflict resolution. The first implies the necessity to confront gross human rights abuses and rogue regimes; the second sees the greater evil in the resort to organized violence, whether within or between states.[6] The interventionist view is superficially close to the current American outlook, but in practice the world's only superpower places much more emphasis on security and the preservation of its dominant world position—a matter on which the Europeans are ambivalent.

Britain's dilemma here is twofold. First, there is a need to decide whether to continue to hold to the Blairite wish to consign the Westphalian international system to history, or whether to fall back on a more prudential tradition of only entering the lists against states that are demonstrable threats to British security and/or to the general stability of the system. (British governments have been traditionally willing to recognize unpleasant new regimes so long as they were in effective control of their country.) Second, the UK must decide whether a U.S. hegemony is essentially also in British interests, or whether it should work subtly toward a system of checks and balances as part of a multi-cleavage, multipolar world. This will require some detachment from events and a degree of conceptualization that most pragmatic politicians are impatient with. Yet unless the fundamentals are addressed the drift of events will decide for us.[7]

The rub comes with the doctrine of preemption. Tony Blair may have implicitly subscribed to this notion through his solidarity over Iraq, but as a general guide to international conduct it poses serious problems for any British decisionmaker. As was evident during the bitter divisions in the UN Security Council over Iraq, it is most unlikely that the international community will agree to a systematic campaign to rid the world of rogue states. The doctrine of preemption is a hegemonic design because only a hegemon has the capability (and possibly the interest) in pursuing it. It follows that, as an independent state with more limited capabilities and interests, Britain has a lot to lose—in terms of money, lives, and political goodwill around the world—by signing up to a strategy of multiple interventions. In particular, it is almost impossible to imagine any British government being willing to participate in a campaign of pressure against Iran or North Korea of the kind that has been conducted against Iraq. It is much more likely that the Europeans in general would oppose such moves, with Britain being drawn back into a common European position.

At bottom, British foreign policy elites (and even more so general opinion) believe in an international system that accepts and institutionalizes diversity—a Grotian international society where law seeks to protect the rights of individual societies to pursue their own political paths so long as they do not threaten their neighbors. This involves an idea of international community based on consensus; it is not just a synonym for what the leading states are convinced is in the general interest. Blair's actions in dealing with difficult allies and domestic opinion suggest the latter view, and thus put him at odds with the majority in the British system who take the former position. In a way, the consensus model is logical for a state that, even at the height of its power, always relied on checks, balances, and cooperation to preserve the status quo. As a postcolonial, upper-middle-ranking power, Britain more than ever requires a system that legitimizes mutual respect among the competing political tendencies in the world.[8] If, by contrast, Britain becomes indelibly associated with an attempt to remake the world in a particular image, it risks being exposed to huge antagonisms while being almost wholly dependent on the power of its patron for protection against them.

Military capability

Military hardware, and the extent to which it can be produced at home, has been a major source of difficulty in British foreign policy since 1945—from the U.S. McMahon Act of 1946, which denied the UK access to nuclear technology, through the Skybolt debacle of 1962, to the domestic divisions over the acquisition of the Polaris and then Trident submarine-launched ballistic missile systems. The United States has been at the heart of all these issues, and when one adds dilemmas over bases, dual-key operations, and nuclear missile defense Washington comes out as more than a significant outside actor. The United States is deeply implicated in the very making of British defense policy.[9] This puts, however, a particular gloss on the problems affecting any modern government in this area, namely, of how far the technological tail wags the defense dog, and, more fundamentally, how to reconcile the Clausewitzian insistence on the primacy of politics with the almost irresistible temptation to accept the cut-price hardware deals offered from Washington. Rather than setting the parameters of foreign policy and adjusting defense procurement to fit that policy, Britain follows the path of falling back on both U.S. protection and equipment, and accepting the political implications that flow from it.

The United Kingdom is unusual in world politics in that it has been active in both peace enforcement and peacekeeping operations despite being only a middle-range power, having been forced as long ago as the 1960s to relinquish its empire, its global ring of military bases, and much of its strategic arms industry. Bigger and potentially more powerful states, such as Russia, China and India, may have the mass, but they possess neither the reputation for technical military competence nor the same will as Britain to engage in so many operations far from home. The list of British involvement in major operations *since* its withdrawal from east of Suez in 1968 is striking, given economic constraints and the continued presence of troops in Northern Ireland. These operations include the Falklands war of 1982, the Persian Gulf War of 1991, ongoing operations in Sierra Leone and the Balkans (Bosnia and Kosovo), and the intervention in Iraq in 2003. Only in the cases of the Turkish invasion of Cyprus in 1974 and the crisis in Albania in 1997 did Britain refuse to intervene—despite being a guarantor power in the case of Cyprus.

Should we conclude, then, that the UK just "does war," rather like Japan "does cars and cameras," and that military capability is a comparative advantage for Britain and an important means of leverage in the world? If so, hard questions need to be answered for the future. First, how much of this capability can Britain afford, in terms of both men under arms and state-of-the-art equipment? The history of defense policy over the past half century has been one of steady retrenchment and rationalization, with even the spending increases authorized by Prime Ministers Thatcher and Blair limited and vulnerable to treasury clawbacks. It is thus hardly surprising to find recurrent transatlantic rows over equipment levels and suppliers of goods from rifles to aircraft carriers. Even during the Falklands war, Britain was probably the loss of a few Harrier jets away from either defeat or total dependence on U.S. decisions. In an era in which public expenditure is deemed inimical to economic growth and the health of the currency (to say nothing of entry into the eurozone), it is difficult to see any London government embarking on a program of (pro rata) military spending like that of the United States.

The second difficult issue for Britain relates to what the country actually gets out of its high military profile. There is a risk that the justifications here are merely circular, with military activism satisfying the United States and the elites who believe in the importance of global responsibilities, without identifying the payoffs for or to the wider domestic constituency. Historical reflexes, what Lord Franks called in 1950 "the habit and furniture of our minds," make it difficult to think outside an established set of assumptions and envisage, for example,

Britain behaving in the more cautious mold of a Sweden or a Germany. A cost-benefit analysis might lead to skeptical conclusions about both whether military actions were justified in a given situation and whether it need always be Britain on the front line offering to conduct these operations. In either case, there is certainly a loss on the financial account.

Perhaps it is Britain's place as a permanent member of the UN Security Council that leads it—like France to some degree—to assume responsibilities that are at the very edge of its capacity to deliver. But the Security Council seat is itself the source of further hard questions about circularity. Does Britain need to be internationally active in order to justify and retain its seat, or does it wish to hold onto the veto power—yielding seat in order to be involved at the highest levels of international politics? Furthermore, the possession of nuclear weapons is a crucial dimension of the problem and one becoming more tricky as the U.S. determination to limit other states' access to weapons of mass destruction becomes apparent. Without nuclear weapons Britain's claim to a permanent seat could come to be seen as much more flimsy (although the same absence of a nuclear power status has not stopped the candidatures of Germany and Japan). To obtain the next generation of strategic nuclear forces, however, London is now almost wholly dependent on decisions in Washington about procurement and price.

It is always difficult to disagree with an ally capable of supplying this apparently indispensable capability, alongside nuclear missile defense, satellite intelligence, and other relevant capabilities. Many critics of official policy, however, would say that the logic should be reversed: if the UK ceased to see the need for maintaining strategic nuclear forces, it would be able to take a more clear-sighted view of foreign policy pressures exerted by the United States. If, by contrast, the UK decided that it needed the insurance of a serious military capability but did not want the dependence on the United States that currently goes with it, then the only serious option would be to build up the ESDP within the EU. Here, too, the financial costs would be high and the political uncertainty serious, given that, as David Owen has said, "the EU does not yet know how to exercise power."[10] The ESDP cannot be achieved without Britain and France being prepared to lead, by political risk taking as well as by increasing the resources they devote to defense. It would also take a long time and cause inevitable crises in Anglo-American relations, however skillful the diplomacy on both sides. It may seem that the post-Iraq condition of Anglo-French relations rules out such a choice. This may be less important, however, than structural trends toward transatlantic rivalry. The real dilemma for Britain is its wish to resist apparently teleological trends in world politics and to square the three traditional circles of its diplomacy.[11] Since the Atlantic circle provides more substantial collective goods for foreign and defense policy than do the EU and the Commonwealth, the default setting for the UK is likely to continue to be that of reliance on the United States. The political consequences of being pulled in different directions, however, are likely to be ever more uncomfortable.

Globalism and globalization

For a period in the 1980s it looked as if Britain was willing to accept Henry Kissinger's assessment of the European powers as being reduced to a regional role. Resource problems, post-colonial inhibitions, and domestic preoccupations combined to make the prospect of intervention outside the European theater remote. The end of the Cold War, the relative economic recovery in the UK, and the arrival of human rights as a central theme in international politics have turned the situation on its head. Despite (or perhaps because of) the loss of Simonstown, Diego Garcia, and Hong Kong, Britain is now less defensive about various forms of involvement in distant locations such as Sierra Leone, Zimbabwe, East Timor, South Africa, and Afghanistan. The potential reach or scope of British foreign policy must, therefore, be counted once again as global, not least because the country has as many far-flung interests as ever—in terms of diasporas, trade, investment, and diplomatic missions.

This is not to say that there is a great deal of substance behind Britain's politico-military global role, or that it could act independently of its various groups of partners and allies. A crisis in Hong Kong, to say nothing of Korea or the Taiwan Strait, would soon expose British vulnerability, while even the Falklands has been made secure only by virtue of Argentina's chronic weakness. The high-profile role that Britain enjoyed in the Pinochet case in 1998 was due to the pure accident of the Chilean general preferring to shop and seek medical attention in London rather than in New York or Madrid. The likely regime crises in the Persian Gulf monarchies in the next few decades will expose the vulnerability of British investments in the region and their dependence on local conditions. Kashmir, where London has a historical responsibility (and would be under competing pressures from ethnic groups at home to act in case of a renewed crisis), will be even more immune to the kind of hand-wringing mediation that Britain tends to fall back on in such circumstances.

It is evident that Britain has global interests, but it does not follow that these can be furthered or protected by global activism, especially when military action or other kinds of major resource commitments would be at stake. "Globalization" is the latest version of the idea—always important to Britain—that world markets, trade routes, and communications should be as open as possible. Now that Britain no longer has imperial preferences to worry about and domestic protectionism is ruled out by EU rules, the commitment can be more unqualified than at any time in the past. It is true that some new preferences have to be protected as a result of the EU's pyramid of privileges, but this has not stopped Britain from developing its own more flexible economic model, influenced by the U.S. labor market, or from playing to its strengths in the provision of international services.

The dilemma here, however, goes far beyond ideology or economic theory. It relates back to our discussion of embedded Europeanism. Committed to global free trade and without the luxury of either the huge home market or the natural resources of the United States, Britain can no longer entertain seriously the question of cutting itself free from the EU. Given that the U.S. domestic market is also protected in various ways from foreign competition, the NAFTA option is just as unattractive. The UK is both dependent on the global economy and insufficiently strong to do without the shelter of the EU's large internal market, especially now that the latter absorbs more than 60 percent of British trade. Britain is never going to be hostile to globalization as such, and, as the largest foreign investor in the United States, it must often resist the criticism that globalization equals Americanization equals cultural imperialism. It needs to keep both the United States and its European partners committed to economic liberalism at the global level, and away from each other's throats. Although Britain is not alone in its commitment to free trade, succeeding in such a balancing act remains a Herculean task.

Public opinion

Foreign policy used to be an area where British governments did not have to worry much about public opinion. This situation had started to change long before the eruption of the crisis over Iraq—a period during which citizens (exceptionally) had the time to inform themselves. Consequently, attention built up to a crescendo.[12] Yet an increasing public interest in foreign policy matters does not imply a better informed public attitude toward generalities such as "anti-Americanism" or "Europhobia." Most statements about public opinion are meaningful only in the context of particular policy debates. There exists a large fund of goodwill in the United Kingdom toward the United States and its people, expressed in frequent exchanges between the two countries and the popularity of many aspects of American culture, from Florida to Frasier Crane. Equally this does not prevent the emergence of strong trends of contrary opinion, or currents of distrust, over specific issues, ranging from U.S. gun culture to military detention camps in Guantánamo Bay.

Public opinion is both expressed through and influenced by the various institutions of political society. Of these the parties are the principal conduits. Both the Labour Party and the Conservative Party have long traditions of close cooperation with the United States and of support for the main planks of its foreign policy. The Liberal Democrats have always been the most enthusiastic supporters of European integration and are, therefore, more willing than the other political parties to consider some fundamental changes in Britain's foreign policy orientation, but they too have a long record of support for the Atlantic Alliance. There have been some recent changes since the Bush administration came to power, and in particular since the early days of the Iraq crisis. Yet there is no particular reason to suppose that these will be any more permanent than similar periods of cooling have been in the past.

The press also continues to be Atlanticist. To be sure, since September 11 there has been some polarization, with the *Daily Mirror* and the *Independent* showing increasing concern about the tendency to use force, especially over Iraq, while the traditionally liberal *Observer* joined the Murdoch papers in supporting a war against Saddam Hussein. Even that notice board of the progressive classes, the *Guardian*, was torn between its critical instincts toward U.S. foreign policy and its concern about the human rights of those living under dictatorships. For their part, the conservative newspapers, in their rush to get on the anti-appeasement bandwagon, forgot old attachments to isolationism or the rights of states.

It is at the level of civil society and electoral politics where the supporters of the special relationship find most cause for anxiety. The various intermediary organizations promoting Western solidarity during the Cold War have either died or lost their impetus, while the burgeoning NGOs of the contemporary scene tend to focus on environmental, developmental, and human rights issues, all of which tend to foster critical perspectives of U.S. foreign policy and multinational companies. At the purely cultural level, although the freewheeling vibrancy of American lifestyles continues to influence all Europeans, with special reference to music and film, it is also evident that young Europeans have a strong sense of the value of their own, shared culture. A form of Euronationalism is becoming evident in sport, notably golf and football, while the Slow Food movement, started in Italy in 1986 as a conscious reaction against U.S. fast food, has grown substantially.[13] The explosion of cheap short-haul flights (ironically on the model of the U.S. carrier Southwest Airlines) has enabled many more Europeans to purchase holiday properties in other states, while large numbers of young, Continental Europeans are flocking to the UK and Ireland for their higher education—with exposure to native English and yet still inside the EU being part of the attraction. The institutions of the EU and associated bodies provide jobs for thousands of members of the transnationally educated classes.

All this means that gradually, and almost unnoticed, a more confident "domestic" Euroculture is finally loosening the United States' powerful hold over the imagination of European societies' most active members. This does not translate, in some simplistic way, into a certain public opinion on foreign policy, but it does help to explain why, when many governments were supporting President Bush over Iraq, public opinion—as expressed through polls and demonstrations—was hostile. Citizens are not dependent on their politicians or media to form their opinions, or even for most of their information; they interact transnationally and are subject to influences similar to those on their counterparts in other countries. To the extent that they do not appreciate their leaders lining up with a U.S. president who causes widespread nervousness in Europe, politicians like Blair and Aznar can expect to suffer electoral punishment at some point.

The polls are interesting in that they have shown British opinion to be not so very far out of line with its continental European equivalents. On the general question of whether the partnership between Western Europe and the United States should remain as close as ever or whether Europe should be more independent, British respondents appear divided.

In an April 2002 survey by the Pew Research Center, 48 percent of British respondents favored the first proposition, as against 47 percent in favor of the second. By contrast, the responses for France and Italy were 33/60 and 36/59 in favor of more independence. Even here, the German figures, at 44/51, come close to those from the UK. One year later, following the conclusion of military operations in Iraq, the responses revealed significant changes only in the case of France and Germany. The British were still divided at 51 percent in favor of remaining close to the United States against 45 percent supporting a more independent approach. (In France, Italy, and Germany, the updated figures were 23/76, 37/61, and 42/57, respectively.)[14]

Likewise, when we focus on more detailed issues relating to the United States, British opinion does not take a sharply contrasting path, being only slightly less critical than public opinion elsewhere in Europe. For example, as part of the April 2002 survey, UK respondents gave a 40 percent approval rating to President Bush's international policy (against 17 percent in August 2001), in comparison with 44 percent for Italy (29 percent), 35 percent for Germany (23 percent), and 32 percent for France (16 percent). Two further tables below make a similar point:[15]

Do you disapprove of . . .

	France	Germany	Italy	UK
Axis-of-evil rhetoric	62	74	60	55
U.S. steel import tariff	81	74	58	65
U.S. Middle East policies	63	63	51	39

With whom do you sympathize?

	France	Germany	Italy	UK
Israel	19	24	14	17
Palestinians	36	26	30	28
Both	8	4	15	11
Neither	25	33	32	23
Don't know	12	13	9	21

A further extensive survey, conducted more than two months later, confirmed these findings. To the MORI (Market & Opinion Research International) organization's question "How do you rate the George W. Bush administration's handling of overall foreign policy," the following replies (in percentages) were given:[16]

	France	Germany	Italy	UK	Netherlands	Poland
Excellent	1	3	10	3	1	7
Good	20	33	47	7	27	55
Fair	53	50	28	44	58	22
Poor	21	12	9	22	12	4
Don't know	4	3	5	4	3	12

If anything, these data suggest that UK citizens, while not the most critical of U.S. policies, are not the most sympathetic either. Adding the "excellent" to the "good" ratings, the percentage figures favoring Bush amount to 21 for France, 36 for Germany, 57 for Italy, 28 for the Netherlands, 62 for Poland, and 30 for the UK.[17] In short, British opinion on foreign policy, if not British policy per se, may now have become Europeanized and, to a degree, predictable on that basis.

CONCLUSIONS

The present transatlantic crisis is passing, as will the Bush and Blair eras in due course. The issues underlying the United Kingdom's relationship with the United States, however, will remain, even if they are bound to be of decreasing importance to the latter. Iraq will leave scars despite the apparent Anglo-American solidarity during the prewar and early postwar phases of that crisis. This is because the only actors that have made common cause here are the two governments, with serious divides opening up within the British polity. Vietnam provides some precedents. The polarization of that period is only now working its way through, as the experiences of those who were students or soldiers 35 years ago come to affect elite attitudes and policies.

Unless there are some very unpleasant surprises in store in terms of domestic developments on either side of the Atlantic, we can expect continued routine cooperation in the old alliance in the years to come, just as we can expect further noisy disputes. The UK will find itself, perhaps increasingly, arguing on the European side—to the extent that the geopolitical divide between Atlanticists and Europeans remains clear in an enlarged EU—because the EU represents its only feasible framework for foreign policy cooperation and burden sharing. The London-Washington partnership is simply too asymmetrical and no longer exclusive. Closer UK cooperation with the EU will be particularly true for issues that do not involve the specter of war and its associated diplomatic dramas—that is, when EU resources, peacekeeping, sanctions, mediation, and other forms of soft power take precedence over hard security issues. On these matters the UK will want to agree with the United States, but it will also be working more closely with its European partners—albeit not with all at once, given the practical constraints within an EU of 25-plus members. There may even come a time when London decides not to heed a U.S. call to arms.

The European system of external relations is, in the public eye, at its lowest ebb. Yet that does not mean that it is on the verge of disintegration or that it does not perform important functions. Indeed, if it did not exist, the UK and the other bigger European states would have to invent it as a means of self-protection against benign domineering on the part of the United States, and as an insurance against the possibility of Washington losing interest in European security altogether. Now that this system of external relations has shown some signs of substance, through the ESDP and Franco-German defiance of U.S. policy on Iraq, it will attract venom and scorn in equal measure, from both U.S. and some British critics. This means that Blair and his successors will have some keen dilemmas to face. They will find it less possible to compartmentalize disputes with the United States than in the past, when chicken wars or bitterness over extraterritoriality did not usually spill over into strategic matters.

Britain is now locked into a European foreign policy process in which numerical unity is actually less important than the range of issues discussed and instruments disposed of. British governments need a European foreign policy as much as they contribute to it. Even more important, British governments and their publics are subject to a slow process of external socialization owing to their particular geopolitical position and participation in common European institutions, defined rather more in contradistinction to the United States than to the more familiar candidates for "othering." For all the talk of "public diplomacy" and "branding," identity formation is a process that governments cannot easily shape.[18]

Even if U.S. policy is conducted with wisdom and in a just cause, it is bound to make those living in societies that do not enjoy the same level of power nervous about the consequences of general destabilization. This outcome is even more likely to come about if the United States, angered by the nihilistic hatreds that have been turned against it, throws aside all self-restraint and disregards any notion of international society. Public opinion in Britain, no less than in other states, will find it difficult to relate to such policies, forcing it to seek various forms of European self-protection. Furthermore, even where they may not actually wish to sound antagonistic, Europeans will feel ever more detached from U.S. concerns in the Asia Pacific or Latin America, not least because of their own lack of projecting power outside their "near abroad"—the definition of which remains, in an era of enlargement, admittedly diffuse. Whereas the crises over Cuba in 1962 or Haiphong in 1972 could have led to a major conflict being fought out on European soil, in the post–Cold War environment Europeans feel that they can detach themselves from U.S. policies on the other side of the world—whether they approve of them or not—more easily than in the past.

Britain used to have distinctive concerns, whether in the Far East or in the conduct of great-power relations, that marked it out from other European states. Despite the present divisions, it no longer has either significant interests or values that set it seriously apart from its European partners, even if it does not always recognize that reality. Conversely, and largely at the level of public opinion, Britain is beginning to display some systematic differences from the United States and to identify with widely shared European positions. These may not amount to Robert Kagan's Europeans-from-Venus thesis or validate Robert Cooper's postmodern-Europe claim,[19] but they do represent a significant trend, in which foreign policy becomes more closely related to domestic values. Europeanization is a more subtle, long-term, and multifaceted process than it is given credit for, and even Britain is subject to it at home and abroad.

Notes

[1] It is interesting that neither of the adjectives "Anglo" and "American" is an accurate description of the state involved, revealing perhaps the rhetorical and emotional, more than functional, character of this particular alliance.

[2] Harold Wilson served twice as Labour prime minister (1964–1971 and 1974–1976), followed by James Callaghan in 1976–1979. Denis Healey served as chancellor of the exchequer under both Wilson and Callaghan (1974–1979). David Owen was Labour secretary for foreign and commonwealth affairs between 1977 and 1979.

[3] The general background of EU attitudes to Iraq can be found in Christopher Hill and Karen E. Smith, eds., *European Foreign Policy: Key Documents* (London: Routledge, 2000), pp. 330–342.

[4] International Development Secretary Clare Short eventually resigned from Tony Blair's cabinet, too, although her resignation—coming almost two months after that of her three other colleagues—was more directly related to the postwar administration of Iraq. In 1951, the resignations of Harold Wilson and Aneurin Bevan—as well as of John Freeman (the latter though not as member of the cabinet but as parliamentary secretary to the ministry of supply)—were over the introduction of national health service charges to finance rearmament for the Korean War. For an example of two resignations over a straight foreign policy issue, we have to go back to John Burns's and John Morley's decisions to leave Herbert Asquith's cabinet upon Britain's entry into the war in August 1914.

[5] The Soames affair—secret talks with de Gaulle over British entry to the European Economic Community (EEC), which the UK then revealed to Germany—caused a furor at the time. See P. M. H. Bell, *France and Britain 1940–1994: The Long Separation* (Harlow: Longman, 1997), pp. 215–217.

[6] For a development of these issues see Christopher Hill, "Foreign Policy," in *The Blair Effect: The Blair Government 1997–2001*, ed. Anthony Seldon (London: Little, Brown, 2001); Richard Little and Mark Wickham-Jones, eds., *New Labour's Foreign Policy: A New Moral Crusade?* (Manchester: Manchester University Press, 2000); Tim Dunne and Nicholas J. Wheeler, "Blair's Britain: A Force for Good in the World?' in *Ethics and Foreign Policy*, ed. Margot Light and Karen E. Smith (Cambridge: Cambridge University Press, 2001).

[7] William Wallace, "American Hegemony: European Dilemmas," in *Superterrorism: Policy Responses*, ed. Lawrence Freedman (Oxford: Blackwell, 2002).

[8] Michel Girard argues that transatlantic differences are due to the different kinds of world the United States and the Europeans inhabit, with the latter having become used to a more domesticated external environment. (Michel Girard, "Malentendus transatlantiques ou divergences épistémiques?" *Revue Politique et Parlementaire* 1022 [January/February 2003].)

[9] John Baylis, *Anglo-American Defence Relations, 1939–1984,* 2nd ed. (London: Macmillan, 1984).

[10] David Owen, *Balkan Odyssey* (London: Indigo, 1995), p. 402.

[11] Anne Deighton, "The Past in the Present: British Imperial Memories and the European Question," in *Memory and Power in Post-War Europe*, ed. Jan-Werner Müller (Cambridge: Cambridge University Press, 2002), pp. 116–120.

[12] For a discussion of the increased importance of public opinion to foreign policy making (and vice versa), see Christopher Hill, *The Changing Politics of Foreign Policy* (Basingstoke: Palgrave, 2003), pp. 250–282.

[13] Slow Food now has 30,000 members in Italy and another 30,000 worldwide (www.slowfood.com).

[14] *Americans and Europeans Differ Widely on Foreign Policy Issues* (Washington,

D.C.: Pew Research Center for the People and the Press, April 17, 2002), http://people-press.org/reports/display.php3?ReportID=153; and *Views of A Changing World 2003* (Washington, D.C.: Pew Research Center for the People and the Press, June 3, 2003), http://people-press.org/reports/display.php3?ReportID=185.

[15] *Americans and Europeans*, April 2002.

[16] The German Marshall Fund and the Chicago Council on Foreign Relations, *Worldviews 2002* (Transatlantic Key Findings Topline Data, Question 10a); released on September 4, 2002; available at www.worldviews.org/key_findings/transatlantic_report.htm (June 3, 2003).

[17] On page 30 of the Pew Research Center's June 2003 public opinion survey, *Views of a Changing World 2003*, 51 percent of British respondents said they had "a lot" or "some" confidence in Bush's ability to do the right thing regarding world affairs, ranking him fourth after Annan (72 percent), Blair (71 percent), and Putin (53 percent).

[18] See Jarol B. Mannheim, *Strategic Public Diplomacy and American Foreign Policy: the Evolution of Influence* (New York: Oxford University Press, 1994), and Michael Kunczik, *Images of Nations and International Public Relations* (Mahwah, N.J.: Lawrence Erlbaum Associates, 1997).

[19] Robert Kagan, "Power and Weakness," *Policy Review* 113 (June/July 2002): 3–28, and *Of Paradise and Power: America and Europe in the New World Order* (New York: Alfred A. Knopf, 2003). See also Robert Cooper, *The Post-Modern State and the World Order* (London: Demos, 1996).

SIX

DIVERGING VISIONS

FRANCE AND THE UNITED STATES AFTER SEPTEMBER 11

Guillaume Parmentier

The attacks against New York and the Pentagon on September 11, 2001, gave rise in France to a wave of sympathy for the United States unseen since the Liberation of Paris in 1945. It has become trite to quote the headline in *Le Monde* two days later—"*Nous sommes tous Américains*" [We are all Americans]—but this phrase truly reflected the way most French citizens felt about the events as they carried signs in the streets of Paris and elsewhere in the country to show their emotion and confirm their solidarity with the nation that had been targeted by these horrific actions.

Given that they, too, had suffered mightily at the hands of Middle Eastern terrorists, the French could easily identify with the Americans on this occasion. Over the course of the past decade, French department stores and the Paris métro were bombed, among many other less spectacular attacks, most of which took an inevitable toll in human casualties. Clearly, the events of 9/11 were of a different dimension, but the causes were seen as being the same; in their intentions, if not in their scope, the terrorist attacks bore an eerie resemblance to the average French citizen's personal experience. After all, it was only in 1995 that a plane hijacked by terrorists aiming to destroy the Eiffel Tower was stopped and overwhelmed by the French antiterrorist squad on the tarmac of Orly airport near Paris. The solidarity bred by identification was apparent on the streets, where many in France wore signs demonstrating their sympathy with the victims and the American people. The U.S. embassy in Paris and American consulates elsewhere in France were overwhelmed by demonstrations of support coming from high and low. At the highest official level, President Jacques Chirac captured the nation's mood by flying the French flag at half-mast over the Elysée palace, an act as unprecedented as the level of solidarity it meant to convey.

Nor was the French reaction merely symbolic. On September 12, under French presidency and at France's behest, the UN Security Council passed a resolution expressing support for the United States and authorizing retaliation by the attacked country in the name of self-defense under Chapter 7 of the Charter, thus making it impossible for members of the UN in the future to be equivocal in their support for U.S. action against terrorists associated with the attacks. Furthermore, France joined Canada and its European allies in invoking Article 5 of the NATO treaty in favor of the United States. Offers of military support on a bilateral basis were made to the Bush administration within a few days of the September 11 events.

To be sure, some voices soon started questioning the "innocence" of the United States. Some analysts suggested that the Americans were the victims of their own policies, much along the lines of the argument made by Noam Chomsky in the United States. Still, these voices remained isolated. Late in the year, the military campaign against Afghanistan stirred little criticism in France, and whatever criticism there was raised questions of effectiveness rather than strategic legitimacy. Critics in France argued that the U.S. policy was not effective enough, not that it was ill suited to the circumstances of the time. It is only when disappointment set in, for reasons given below, that the wisdom of U.S. policy started to be challenged in wider, if still minority, circles.

Unfortunately, France's spontaneous identification with the injured Americans laid the basis for future misunderstandings. Like most Europeans, the French believed that this newly shared experience would naturally lead to closer bilateral relations. This belief, however, underestimated the trauma suffered by Americans, including its psychological and political consequences for U.S. attitudes toward the rest of the world. The French, again like most Europeans, wrongly believed that the United States would react in ways similar to the Europeans under comparable circumstances. While the United States was expected, and even entitled, to strike more forcefully and, if necessary, more brutally than the Europeans had done during earlier instances of domestic terrorism, 9/11 was not perceived, in France and elsewhere in Europe, as significant or revolutionary enough to justify the beginning of a new era in international relations.

This was not the U.S. view of these events, which President Bush quickly described as having placed the nation "at war." Unlike what most Europeans understood this phrase to mean, this was not a mere hyperbole. The U.S. president was articulating the mood of an entire nation while seizing the opportunity to place his administration, which had hitherto been searching for a message and a direction, firmly in control of events. Constitutionally, the word "war" has significant ramifications in the United States; when the country is at war, the executive power is allowed a much greater measure of discretion by the legislative branch than is normally the case. Thus the executive saw this as a chance to redefine itself in the new circumstances as a bulwark for the bereaved nation. This instrumentalization of public feelings by the Bush administration only added to what, in American eyes, was the unique, extraordinary, and unprecedented character of the era inaugurated by September 11.

The outburst of solidarity in Europe after September 11 set the stage for future disappointments. In the weeks following the attacks, the United States became increasingly self-centered, giving the impression that the nation was losing interest in international support. The reaction of the U.S. Department of Defense to the NATO invocation of Article 5 was especially disappointing. After all, this had been a significant gesture of allied support for the United States, including a commitment to participate in the U.S. retaliation against the September 11 attackers. It was also a considerable demonstration of solidarity toward the American people. Given the still-vivid memory of the 1999 NATO war on Kosovo, however, when the interference of NATO's political bodies was a repeated source of irritation for U.S. military planners, Washington's reaction to the invocation of Article 5 was distinctly unenthusiastic and, arguably, contemptuous of the allies' ability to contribute significantly to a U.S. retaliatory operation against Al Qaeda.[1] This attitude, embraced especially by the civilian leadership at the Pentagon, had a negative reception in Europe in general and in France in particular, a country that takes pride in its military capability.

Thus, America missed an opportunity to engage its allies not only in the military operations against Afghanistan but also in the broader fight against international terrorism. In a way, the latter was even more significant, as became clear later on. The considerable experience of the Europeans, including the French, in the management and legal pursuit of counterterrorist activities could offer valuable assistance to U.S. efforts. Even during the war in Afghanistan, low-flying French Mirage aircraft, armed with temperature-guided bombs, played a significant role in clearing out the caves occupied by Al Qaeda forces. Indeed, 18 months later, with U.S. priorities shifted to Iraq, the Europeans were already in command of the stabilization force in Afghanistan.

All this strengthened lingering feelings in Europe that the Americans were only interested in their allies' contributions on an à la carte basis. In France, it also reawakened a long-held skepticism of U.S. motivations in general, dating back to the United States' taciturn attitude toward Vichy and the Free French during World War II; the successful U.S. effort to thwart Britain, France, and Israel during the Suez crisis in 1956; the subsequent U.S. opposition to French policies in Algeria; and, more recently, the questionable pre-9/11 U.S. support for some Islamic fundamentalist groups fighting the Soviet occupation of Afghanistan. Thus, the French mood rapidly turned against the United States, perceiving the reaction of the latter as reaffirmation of past U.S. practices. While French disappointment with the United States was less acute than in more Atlanticist countries, the opportunity was lost to move beyond the ingrained negative reaction to U.S. foreign policy.

FRANCE AND THE TRANSATLANTIC RELATIONSHIP: A RELUCTANT ALLY

France attaches great importance to its relations with the United States: It is America's oldest ally, and the only large European country never to have been at war against the United States. Exchanges between the two countries, especially in the economic and cultural fields, have traditionally been strong and have expanded considerably in recent years.[2] History, especially in the twentieth century, has nonetheless taught the French to be cautious of absolute reliance on alliances. Furthermore, there has always been some skepticism in France over the ability of the United States to fulfill its promises—from the Senate's rejection of the 1919 Treaty of Versailles to Congress's refusal to ratify the 1999 Comprehensive Test Ban Treaty (CTBT).

France is, therefore, unique among West European countries in its unwillingness, at least since de Gaulle, to pay a heavy price for maintaining a U.S. presence in Europe. Traditionally, however, the French position has been that this presence was due to a well-founded perception of U.S. interests, and that whatever the Europeans did, it would not alter this perception. Admittedly, there was no point in weakening the transatlantic relationship, but it was similarly naive to expect that subservience would induce the United States to listen more to its allies. This judgment has shaped French foreign policy since the 1950s, and nothing in the aftermath of September 11 has induced French leaders to modify this judgment. Quite the contrary. Furthermore, because of the unease that the United States' use of its military power inspires abroad, the French tend to be wary of U.S.-led foreign ventures in which they might not be in a position to influence subsequent decisions sufficiently.

In this respect, the French attitude has changed considerably since the war in Kosovo. Previously, France's suspicion of NATO meant that preference was given to ad hoc arrangements under a UN Security Council mandate. This attitude prevailed during the conflicts in the Balkans. In 1994–1995, even France's reluctant acknowledgment of the indispensability of U.S. involvement for resolving the crisis in Bosnia did not translate into a full-hearted endorsement of NATO over ad hoc arrangements. It is only when France came to the same conclusion as the United States about NATO as a potential tool for multilateral action—and, in France's view, one that can be used to contain U.S. unilateral power—that the French government expressed its preference for handling peacemaking and peacekeeping operations through the alliance's structures. Once again, an identical French and U.S. diagnosis of a situation led the two countries to draw opposite policy conclusions.

This traditional French unwillingness to be entangled in foreign operations led and devised by another nation was much in evidence in the months leading to the 2003 war against Iraq. The French insistence on UN primacy in Iraq recognized that France alone could not contain U.S. power. By virtue of its permanent seat on the UN Security Council, however, France could more readily ensure that agreed standards of behavior could be enforced with regard to U.S. actions in Iraq. This, as well as a strong legalistic tradition, explains French support for multilateral institutions and multilateral processes, which President Jacques Chirac and his government expressed so prominently, so vehemently, and even so effectively during the Iraq crisis of 2002–2003.

Contrary to some Americans' belief, France does not see unchecked U.S. power as the most serious problem in the world. Structural and historical reasons are mostly responsible for the present U.S.-French dissonance. Historically, France has always resisted the concentration of power on the international scene. The French state's traditional role has been to ward off aggression and domination by other empires. In some ways, this stance resembles Americans' own perceptions of their country as having been built by the Founders to defend against the concentration of power on the domestic scene. France has built its own identity upon opposition to the overwhelming power of the secular (Holy Roman) Empire on the one hand and the papacy's spiritual one on the other. In short, France is fundamentally suspicious of unchecked international power.

For France, like for the United States, a concentration of power is predictably easier to bear when it happens to be in one's own hands. It is, therefore, absurd to describe French criticism of U.S. policy or power as anti-Americanism. The notion of anti-Americanism suggests hostility toward the U.S. society, its constitution, and way of life.[3] Yet, the vast majority of the French people and all French leaders admire the U.S. Constitution and the country's economic, cultural, and international achievements. France applies to the international community the same rules that the United States devised when it was still a lesser power. After all, it was the United States that invented multilateralism in order to contain European powers. The reversal in the power relationship between the two countries has also led to an unsurprising reversal in their respective positions on the management of the international system.

This means that now as before France remains reluctant to accept or follow U.S. directions blindly. Rather, the French government will follow the United States when it perceives U.S. positions to coincide with or to sustain France's own interests and what it believes are those of the wider international community. In other cases, it will have no qualms about opposing them, even as its opposition need not always be as vocal and as prominent as it was over Iraq. This does not mean that France's position is that U.S. power represents the most dangerous problem in today's world, as some Americans seem to believe. For example, in addition to its long-standing concern over terrorism and its related commitment to confronting forcefully violent displays of Islamic fundamentalism, France is equally serious about the need to confront the threat represented by the proliferation of weapons of mass destruction (WMD), a central item in the European Union strategic document signed by the EU foreign ministers in late June 2003. As a leading architect of this document, France has also been especially sensitive to keeping its arms exports procedures as tight as possible and specifically in adherence with the norms defined by the international treaties and agreements to which the French government is a signatory.

Thus portraying the French as being bent on opposing the United States on every issue is profoundly wrong. That the French will never accept a transatlantic relationship based on blind followership is well understood. In French eyes, Europe needs to become an international player because it has legitimate interests that it needs to pursue. It is obviously better when these interests coincide with those of the United States. When they do not, the emphasis should be on reconciliation of differences rather than on confrontation, but there will be times when opposition will be inevitable. After all, this is true in a democracy, and it should be true also in an alliance of democracies.

The above illustrates why moves toward unilateralism in the United States are of such concern to French leaders. In this respect, the extraordinary resonance that Robert Kagan's article in *Policy Review* has had in the United States—a resonance that goes beyond the ideas contained in the article itself—is cause for concern.[4] To be sure, 9/11 has been instrumental in explaining this interest in Kagan's ideas, particularly the considerable emphasis on the military dimension of power to the detriment of all other forms of international power. Yet, Kagan points to an evolution in U.S. attitudes that could prove worrisome for the future of transatlantic relations.

Other elements have also played a part in the evolution of the transatlantic relationship in recent years. Before September 11, a growing gap in social values had been the focus of an increasingly bitter debate. The main issues discussed at the time were the death penalty, criminal punishment, and the detention of prisoners as well as the Kyoto Protocol on climate change. Diverging views on treaty commitments and the use of international institutions were also the focus of much discussion although in a general and more philosophical way rather than in strictly security terms. September 11 changed the tone of this entire debate as security issues came back to the fore, where they seem bound to remain.

Significantly enough, the debate among policy experts now goes beyond the trite confrontation between multilateralism and unilateralism, which concentrated on what is essentially a mere consequence of the international power configuration. More significant are the reasons for the difference in attitudes between the United States and Europe with regard to the international system. Apart from the fact that no policy can ever be 100 percent unilateral or 100 percent multilateral, the distinction between unilateralism and multilateralism only relates to the means employed in conducting foreign policy. Clearly, Europeans and Americans would not differ on the means if their respective visions of the international system and the direction it should take were fundamentally similar. Rather than focus on the manifestation of this transatlantic divergence, in other words on the symptoms of the recent drift, Europeans and Americans need to go back to what triggered that drift in the first place. Thus, it is perhaps to Kagan's greatest credit that he has placed the debate on more useful ground, emphasizing the divergent visions of international society that prevail on each side of the Atlantic—or, more precisely, between the United States and continental Europe, since British policy is often closer to U.S. positions even as British public opinion rarely differs significantly from public opinion in the rest of the European Union.[5]

THE UNITED STATES AND THE TRANSATLANTIC RELATIONSHIP: CLASHING CONCEPTS OF POWER

Kagan's thesis, by virtue of its success, has had a real impact on the judgment of a large number of Americans about Europe. More specifically, because it was crafted in such a way as to appear easily applicable to numerous situations, Kagan's vision of Europe will be repeated and recycled in a host of different cases, including some where the concoction may not always be to anyone's taste, including its author. The effects were already discernible in the context of the Iraq debate, where many Americans believed they could detect a "European" pacifist attitude in the French position, even though the latter was inspired by a real concern to disarm Saddam Hussein and a preference to use military force only as a last resort. This position is quite distinct from the German position, but it is also distinct from a European attitude that seems only too happy to wallow in lamentations about the weaknesses of Europe, even without the requisite reservations. The main failing in Kagan's argument about power and weakness is that he tends to amplify a given trait in order to render his demonstration of that trait more spectacular. This reduces his argument at times to the level of a caricature. There is much in the U.S. behavior in the world that tends to deny U.S. policy a clear "martial" appearance, but there is also more to Europe than a "Venusian" image viewed through community-tinted glasses and painted with a Brussels-soaked brush.

Undoubtedly, the divergence in attitudes between Europeans and Americans is largely a function of structural differences resulting from contrasting conceptions of power on both sides. U.S. primacy in the majority of spheres that confer international power endows the United States with a much larger degree of freedom of action on the world stage than that enjoyed by the Europeans. As described above in the context of U.S. bilateral relations with France, U.S. leaders are anxious to retain their autonomy of action, and their European counterparts seek to strengthen control mechanisms designed to channel international power, including, first and foremost, U.S. power.

The U.S. preference for freedom of action is neither surprising nor reason for condemnation. There is also no doubt that the United States has traditionally applied moderation in its use of power. Because of the system of checks and balances, the United States can never rely on a brutal use of its international power for more than brief periods. Any imperialist or headstrong venture would inevitably end in a backlash, reducing in turn the capacity of the executive branch to use the full panoply of means that would be at the disposal of its counterparts in a less balanced institutional order—except, of course, when the country is at war. This is why the use and abuse of the phrase "war on terrorism" has such significant implications.

From this point of view, the attack upon Iraq is epoch making. It marks the first time in U.S. history that an attack against a foreign country cannot convincingly be presented as a response to an attack or as a way to thwart a potential act of aggression against the United States or one of its allies. It actually goes beyond the accepted definition of preemption that the administration adopted as a central feature of its new strategic doctrine. As all public opinion polls show, the new policy receives shallow support and is in deep contradiction with traditional U.S. thinking, which has always insisted on adding instruments of persuasion to its means of coercion.

The most remarkable achievements of U.S. power have not been on account of its military instruments, although at least since World War I these have been formidable by any standard. Rather, the real trump card of United States' foreign policy has been the country's ability to convince foreign governments—and, often, the people in foreign lands despite their governments—that its vision of the world has been not only in the U.S. interest but also in the interest of those governments. This is what has traditionally made U.S. policies so effective and, in many cases, so irresistible. Indeed, whenever the United States strayed from that course, often with the best of motives as during the Vietnam war, the effectiveness of its policy was compromised.

An equally important issue relates to the means that Europeans and Americans have at their disposal in the face of international crises—means that, in many regards, dictate the behavior of each of the partners. The problem posed by Europe's relative military weakness is real and justifies calls for an increase in European capabilities to avoid a widening of the gap between Europe's capacity to wage war and that of the United States. Yet levels of defense spending are not the only, or even the most important, transatlantic issue. Although the French defense budget for 2003, based on a 15 percent annual increase, and the five-year defense review (2003–2007), with an overall increase of a further 30 percent in equipment spending, might justify a certain degree of optimism, the problem of compatibility of military equipment among transatlantic partners, particularly compatibility of their operational concepts, will demand a far more sustained effort from the Europeans.

This is certainly not the time—although some Americans are keen to do it—to make the military capacity of U.S. forces the primary point of reference with regard to the Europeans. Is it sensible, for example, for the United States to spend almost 50 percent of global military expenditures and to increase spending in all armament categories, including those where the likelihood of their ever being used is extremely slim—either because the threats they are intended to counter are so infinitesimally small, or their use in the actual theater against unsophisticated enemies would render prohibitive the cost of their possible loss?[6] Only in the context of a case-to-case analysis of potential threats should a given military effort be evaluated. In sum, while the need for Europeans to increase the quantity and quality of defense expenditures is an uncontested prerequisite if the Atlantic Alliance is to be maintained as an effective and balanced force, the focus should be on how to move closer together the transatlantic partners' views of the actual threats and challenges to their security, and thus also the definition of responses to those threats and challenges.

This groundwork, which should be conducted in the context of the alliance or, more convincingly, among the major allies, is not being completed satisfactorily at present. It is, however, an important priority if there is to be any sort of convergence of views on international security within the alliance. On this point, U.S. reticence is at least as great as that of its main partners in Europe, though this may simply indicate that true consultation on these points would actually have the effect of restraining, at least marginally, the United States' decision-making freedom. On topics such as the Middle East or nation building, it is hardly surprising that a U.S. administration, of whichever ilk, does not wish to find itself trapped between Congress and U.S. public opinion on the one hand and its allies on the other. However, that is often the price to be paid for transatlantic cooperation.

A more problematic issue, because of its structural nature, involves the different comparative advantages of the transatlantic allies in addressing various international problems. This best explains the choices made on each side of the Atlantic over the past few years. It is not simply because the United States is stronger that it chose after the Cold War to revert to a traditional concept of power and thus place greater emphasis on the use of military power. Since the beginning of the twentieth century, Americans have attempted to extend to Europe a concept of international relations according to which a threat against the legitimate security interests of a country is a threat not solely to that country but to all other countries with a stake in preserving the foundations of international order and, thus, peace itself. This "post-nationalism," dubbed "internationalism" in the United States (and known as "Wilsonianism" in Europe), helps transcend crass conflicts of interests between states. It is therefore remarkable that this attitude should now be termed "European" by American observers when it took nothing less than two world wars and 50 years of continued U.S. presence for it to prevail on the Old Continent.

The reason why the United States has turned its back, at least in part, on this concept in recent years relates largely to the fact that the United States currently dominates the international system without the presence of a true counterweight to restrain it. That this change of course also appears contrary to the U.S. tradition of checks and balances may be seen—preceding the war and the usual rallying-round-the-flag phenomenon—in the widespread U.S. public opposition to military intervention in Iraq without a UN mandate or an international coalition.[7]

The document on national security strategy adopted by the Bush administration in September 2002 exemplifies the narrow vision that now seems to inspire U.S. policymakers. Much has already been written about the document's emphasis on preemption. Certainly, the formulation of an entire doctrine on the mere basis of an anticipated act of aggression carries significant risks, but U.S. constitutional checks and balances make it highly unlikely that preemption will become a systematic U.S. policy doctrine. Besides, acting against an anticipated attack (through prevention rather than preemption) is sometimes legitimate against a forthcoming attack or the use of weapons of mass destruction, even if it is highly preferable to seek a clear UN Security Council mandate beforehand. On the other hand, less ink has been spilled over another aspect of the new doctrine that is far more symptomatic of the U.S. international attitude early in the twenty-first century: the stated determination to prevent the emergence of any potential strategic competitor to the United States. Certainly, the emergence of a strategic competitor to the United States is not an issue today and there is no prospect of it becoming one in the foreseeable future. Still, it is surprising that the United States of America, a country that has always defined itself as an active player in the international community of nations with the same rights and obligations as all other countries, should in 2002 endorse a vision that introduces radical inequality between itself and everyone else.

Has the United States, traditionally suspicious of all power, thus become a classic nation-state, on the model of European nation-states of the nineteenth century? Or, to put it more bluntly, has the United States turned into a nationalist power—be it as a result of September 11, 2001; the election of George W. Bush; or, long before that, following the nation's rise to unprecedented heights of world power? Indeed, it would be most ironic if the country that once sought to immunize Europe against the nationalist disease, and succeeded beyond all expectations, should itself succumb to that same temptation. A comparison, however imperfect, between the United States of today and the major European states of the nineteenth century can yield a great deal by way of historical understanding. The (mostly) unilateral attack on Iraq in March 2003 may bring about either a fundamental shift in U.S. attitudes toward the world community or a domestic backlash that would restore the United States to the inclusive, open conception of its national interest that the country pursued with such success throughout most of the twentieth century and that it so successfully applied in Europe.

Another reason, no less compelling, for the increasing concentration of U.S. power in the military sphere is that it is in this sphere that the United States enjoys the greatest comparative advantage vis-à-vis its partners and competitors. Not only is its military primacy unchallenged and growing, not only are the chances of any competition emerging extremely slight, the United States does not hold such a comparative advantage in any other sector of international action. It is powerful in the economic realm, but the European Union and, perhaps tomorrow, the Asian powers are equal to the challenge. In addition, Washington often finds itself lacking the funds and resources for the equally important nonmilitary components of its international activities.[8]

In a way, Europe's difficulty in engaging the funds that would provide access to a significant military role is matched by the problems encountered at the U.S. federal level in mobilizing sufficient means to carry out international tasks that do not rely on the effective use of military force. Whereas U.S. military capabilities grew rapidly after a swift reduction at the end of the Cold War up until 1994, diplomacy and nonmilitary resources at the disposal of the federal government fell in real terms at a regular and worrying pace. Consistent with this pattern is the unilateral reduction of U.S. contributions to United Nations budgets, which was only partially settled as a result of the solidarity the UN showed to the United States in the wake of September 11. All U.S. secretaries of state since the mid-1990s have had cause to complain about the weakening of the United States' diplomatic resources. Official U.S. development assistance had fallen dramatically up until the Monterrey summit in March 2002, while a large part of the remaining funding has been traditionally allocated to Israel, a country whose standard of living hardly qualifies it to receive development aid. Moreover, the increase in U.S. international aid announced at Monterrey in the wake of the September 11 attacks still awaits implementation.

Wherever one looks, the resources of the United States for international action are dwindling over the long term, with the exception of the military domain. It is, therefore, not at all surprising that U.S. policy values and enhances that dimension of international policy where its comparative advantage is greatest. There is no shortage, however, of examples of the inadequacy of a principally military approach. In the Balkans, it was fortunate that the United States took the initiative in 1995 to use military force to allow the Dayton talks to go ahead.[9] That the European approach had remained too hesitant to make any impression on Slobodan Milosevic is beyond doubt, but, as Richard Holbrooke notes in his memoirs, the U.S. involvement in the resolution of the crisis would not have happened if the French, British, and Dutch had not changed strategy after May 1995.[10] In the case of Kosovo, the U.S. will to impose a solution by military means may be said to have undermined the international community by bypassing the UN Security Council and prompting Russia's opposition as a matter of principle. Even so, without the U.S. threat of force, the international community, and primarily the Europeans, would have been deprived of an essential instrument of pressure against the Serb leader. The same was true of the decisive support given to the UN inspectors by the U.S. military build-up in the Persian Gulf between November 2002 and March 2003, which provided the conditions under which Saddam Hussein had to make concession after concession to the international community.

There is no need, therefore, to set up some artificial divide between the military approach and the civil or diplomatic approach. Foreign policy today needs to include both of these dimensions, along with a capacity to define the right policy mix in each case. In the Balkans, the European military presence now greatly exceeds that of the United States, with Europeans making up the essential forces on the ground in both Bosnia and Kosovo and helping to not only maintain peace but also facilitate reconstruction and reconciliation. In these two areas, economic and political, the combined European contribution easily exceeds that of the United States. The same is true in Afghanistan where, in the wake of September 11, the stakes remain high for the United States and where the disastrous experience of neglect at the end of the 1980s should incite Washington to display greater patience this time around.

As a result, the United States might be tempted to confine itself to the military aspects of crisis management. Congress is often hostile to the idea of nation building, and the vast majority of U.S. military personnel still oppose it. It is this mind-set Condoleezza Rice was conveying when she affirmed during the summer 2000 presidential campaign that U.S. soldiers would not be reduced to helping children cross the street in countries where they were stationed. This attitude, coupled with a strong resistance to funding civil reconstruction efforts, leads U.S. policymakers to put more emphasis on the military tasks, leaving the responsibility for civilian reconstruction to their allies. The lesson learned in the 1991 U.S. war with Iraq, which nonfighting countries essentially financed, has been extended into the postwar phase of most U.S.-led operations. As a result of the 2003 experience in Iraq, this attitude may be about to change, but not without some potentially grave consequences for Iraq and for U.S. and allied forces deployed on its soil.

EUROPEAN CONSTRUCTION AND
THE TRANSATLANTIC RELATIONSHIP

The Europeans are, of course, the first allies to whom the Americans turn in these postconflict situations. This was also the case in Iraq in early summer 2003, when the United States hoped for significant contributions of European troops, including troops from countries that had earlier opposed the war and were now reluctant to rush into a potential U.S.-led quagmire. Europe's readiness to support civil operations rather than military ones mirrors the inverse problem of the United States: as difficult as it is for Europeans to fund a military endeavor, it is politically quite easy for them to contribute, either directly or via the European Union, to the reconstruction of countries where crisis management operations have just been completed. This situation can have disastrous consequences in terms of the use of international power. The spectacle of Israeli planes and missiles, funded by U.S. assistance, destroying Palestinian civilian and police installations, financed largely through European contributions, is an extreme but telling example of Europe's frustrating inability to influence the course of events in which it has significant stakes.

The evolution of events in the Balkans, where the contrasts are less pronounced, nonetheless provides much food for thought. In both Bosnia and Kosovo, European funds are financing a situation that is largely the result of plans imposed by U.S. force. The division of labor between Europeans and Americans, with the former providing support for reconstruction in the widest sense of the term while the latter bask in the glory of military prowess, puts Europe in an awkward situation politically because there is usually little appreciation to be found for the task of always cleaning up the mess left behind by the departing military forces of the world's only superpower. On the other hand, the medium-term consequences of rebuilding shattered societies can also work to Europe's advantage.

The problem posed by these interventions is as much a problem of influence, or perhaps soft power, as of brute force, or military might. The Europeans certainly do not deserve military glory or fame, but their contributions in helping a country back on its feet after a war may allow them, in the best cases, to exercise long-term influence in these societies. The EU and its member states are providing varied assistance in the (re)building of social institutions: Germany and others in Central and Eastern Europe; the European Union in Palestine and other conflict-ridden parts of the world; France and the United Kingdom in Africa; and of course the EU, France, Germany, Britain, and others in the Balkans. When a country's constitutional framework, legal order, and economic rules are established by European experts, with inevitably some similarity to the rules that apply in Europe, the investment is not necessarily wasted. This is indeed what the United States did in liberated Europe and Japan after World War II. Nations and societies built on that basis will tend naturally to turn toward Europe, and not just on domestic matters and societal values. It will also presumably have consequences in terms of foreign policy choices. Europeans are therefore also using their comparative advantages, and with a greater effectiveness than many Americans would concede.

The European Union and its member states must extend the European model internationally and accord the model legitimacy on a scale sufficient to prevent anyone from characterizing it as merely a hidden will to power. In fact, this is precisely one of the manifestations of influence to which the United States was accustomed until the middle of the twentieth century. The current propensity in Washington to subsume these influences under the notion of weakness no doubt relates to Americans' newfound preference for displays of classic European power. This characterization is far from being faithful to reality, however. In fact, the international influence that the United States thus concedes to Europeans because of domestic constraints on U.S. policy paradoxically results in a reduction of its own influence. Joseph Nye argues persuasively in his most recent book that the use of military force, or the affirmation of power without concessions, which we would call exercising traditional nationalism, can in reality reduce America's influence in real terms by reducing its ability to attract the best minds among its foreign partners.[11]

The fact that the Europeans have become specialized, perhaps by default, in the area of nonmilitary power can give their foreign policies greater legitimacy than those of the United States and provide them with a greater capacity to create ad hoc coalitions on issues where the United States stands isolated. This would not be the case if they were overly aggressive in asserting their positions. Conversely, would not a certain moderation in U.S. tone and attitude with regard to the International Criminal Court make it easier for the United States to be listened to on other issues?

On the other hand, the creation of a new European entity, bringing together nations of diverse traditions and interests, makes it difficult to translate the resulting mass into power. Because common policies are difficult to reach, often the result of formal rather than real diplomatic compromises, action at the EU level tends to be constrained, thus hardly facilitating the kind of flexibility on which diplomatic success depends. This is why the simple addition of gross capacity is not the same as greater power. Contrary to what most French people currently think and say, bigger does not necessarily mean stronger.

The process of EU enlargement can be used as an illustration since each stage has led to a period of withdrawal by the union in the international context, albeit followed by a more forward-looking phase designed precisely to prevent cracks from appearing in the European house. That is the reason why "Europe puissance" is a slogan or an aspiration rather than a reality. Perhaps it is even a contradiction in terms. Europeans differ on the very concepts of what constitutes a nation, what is a political society, and the ends these entities are meant to pursue.

The historical experience of the past century is interpreted differently in Germany, France, and the United Kingdom. Briefly, one must recall that the Germans disdain both a centralized German state, which brought them great ills, and reproduction of that model at the European level. More than anything else, they detest the use of military force, which brought disastrous consequences for Germany as well as its neighbors. It is not surprising then that a majority of Germans describe Switzerland as the model that they envisage for the European Union once complete. For the French, the state is, by contrast, an expression of the nation, and the European venture is seen as a means of increasing French influence in the international sphere while also reproducing the characteristics of the French state at European level—hence, the hesitancy of the French to expand European competencies, which are perceived as centralized and thus incompatible with the spirit of true federalism and which, if pushed to their logical conclusion, would tend to abolish the prerogatives of member states, an evolution that most French citizens would abhor. As for the British, their concept of the legitimate use of military force places them at opposing ends of the table from the Germans since they can legitimately read contemporary European history as a practical, and indeed moral, justification of the use of armed forces. Their reading of the value of alliances places them at odds with the French.

If one then adds the specific problems of the small member states—which distrust nothing more than an agreement brokered by their larger European partners that would challenge their ability to defend their own interests, as well as the image of "Europe puissance," or a Europe capable of using traditional instruments of international power—it all becomes very problematic. This situation is well illustrated in the largely declaratory style of the European Security and Defense Policy (ESDP) and its previous incarnations. This is indeed a principal reason why the Europeans have specialized in the area of soft power.

One should not force the point, however. First of all, it is extremely loose to talk of "Europe" at all: the British and, to a lesser degree, the French have a more traditional concept of power than many of their partners. They are prepared to use force when other means have been exhausted. This was clear in the Iraqi disarmament debate, on which the French and British positions were closer fundamentally than they appeared; both were concerned with strengthening the role of the UN Security Council, but both were also ready to take up arms if Saddam Hussein refused to meet his international obligations. Spain and Italy affirmed, at least in principle, a similar position. Germany assumed a very different stance, but it stood alone in this. In addition, when other countries have bilateral problems to resolve, such as Spain with its difference with Morocco over the desert island of Perejil, it is not uncommon for the language of force to be heard. The vision of Europe that often prevails in Washington these days is far too influenced by the legalistic quibbling prevalent in Brussels.

CONCLUSIONS

The French believe, like many others in Europe and beyond, that the United States, whatever its reservations about any of its European partners, is not and cannot become a power that knows no limits even if it remains a nation without peers. Indeed, American actions remain curiously pusillanimous at times. During the U.S. campaign in Afghanistan, for example, launched in response to the criminal and unprovoked attack of September 11, 2001, the United States demonstrated a positively "European" restraint—in Kagan's sense—when pursuing Al Qaeda operatives into the caves of Tora Bora and allowing in the process most of the them to escape. A characteristic U.S. reluctance to engage the enemy directly, and hence avoid unnecessary exposure of U.S.

personnel to enemy fire, is understandable, but it is not the expression of a country animated by a strong martial spirit. Conversely, it is hard to picture British or French forces in comparable situations allowing enemy combatants and Al Qaeda leaders to escape without a fight. The Euro-American dichotomy on matters of force is no doubt less pronounced than what is commonly believed in Washington.

The real transatlantic challenge relates primarily to the divergent concepts of international action that are found on either side of the Atlantic and in various European countries. What form of power is relevant in today's world and what capacity for action—military might or persuasion (soft power)—is true in specific events are not self-evident. In an increasing number of cases, military force cannot be used and therefore becomes irrelevant. This is obvious in the context of relations among Western countries, but it also holds true even more generally. The use of force was never an option during the standoff in the South China Sea early in the Bush presidency; a reason why the United States has been relatively unsuccessful in imposing a resolution of the Palestinian-Israeli conflict is its acknowledged inability to bring its military force to bear on the situation, as is well known to both parties; with regard to North Korea, the stated preferences of U.S. allies in that region made a recourse to U.S. force too risky to be contemplated seriously. These examples, among many others, do not suggest an ingenuous, or even contemptuous, analysis with regard to the relevance of military tools: if nothing else, the Balkan experience demonstrated the continued relevance of military force. Yet, the latter must be adapted to meet specific situations (i.e., weapons must not be so dear as to preclude their use, such as is the case with Apaches and B-2s). Even in situations requiring the use of force, however necessary it may be, force is unlikely to prove sufficient.

It is important that France with other European countries, and Europe with the United States, move closer together on these points: before proclaiming their aspiration to make Europe a global power, the states of Europe will have to strengthen their military capabilities and do the humdrum work of addressing the crises that have to be settled. In this perspective, the conclusion to be drawn from the Balkan experience is that an ad hoc intervention by one or several European countries, initiated when Milosevic threatened Dubrovnik, would have been preferable to the various ambitious institutional scenarios that were tried out. As for the Americans, they must not become prisoners of their military power and thus neglect the other capabilities needed for crisis resolution. Always allowing the Europeans to reconstruct after U.S. troops have left the battlefields will help Europe to rise as the moral center of the world at the expense of, but hardly as a substitute for, an increasingly disputed U.S. leadership.

Notes

[1] On the war in Kosovo, see Guillaume Parmentier, "Redressing NATO's Imbalances," *Survival* 42, no. 2 (Summer 2000): 96.

[2] On the U.S.-French bilateral relationship, see Michael Brenner and Guillaume Parmentier, *Reconcilable Differences: U.S.-French Relations in the New Era* (Washington D.C.: Brookings Institution Press, 2002).

[3] See Philippe Roger's excellent book, *L'Ennemi Américain: Essai de Généalogie de l'antiaméricanisme en France* (Paris: Le Seuil, 2002), as well as its review by Tony Judt, "Anti-Americans Abroad," *New York Review of Books*, May 1, 2003, pp. 24–28.

[4] Robert Kagan, "Power and Weakness," *Policy Review* 112 (June/July 2002): 3–28.

[5] On the other hand, foreign policy and public opinion in Canada are strongly "European" in Kagan's sense of the term, as shown by the Canadian official and public positions on the Iraq War. See the results of the *Worldviews 2002* survey commissioned by the German Marshall Fund of the United States and the Chicago Council on Foreign Relations; available at www.worldviews.org/key_findings/transatlantic_report.htm.

[6] One could take missile defense as an illustration of the first category, and the Apache helicopters and B-2 bombers as an illustration of the second. While the current U.S. policy places a high premium on countering the proliferation of WMD, the threat posed by WMD is much more likely to come from a terrorist attack rather than from a rogue state launching a ballistic missile. While the value of the traditional strategy of deterrence against regimes as erratic as Kim Jong-il's Democratic People's Republic of Korea is questionable, the likelihood of a missile-delivered WMD attack by such a rogue state remains extremely low. Furthermore, the benefit of defending against such an unlikely event is far outweighed by the destabilizing effect on the current strategic weapons balance that the development of missile defense systems could cause, as recently demonstrated by statements from China indicating that it may respond to the development of those systems by augmenting its own strategic strike capability.

[7] In summer 2002, 65 percent of Americans opposed action in Iraq without a UN mandate and the support of U.S. allies. (See *Worldviews 2002*, "American Public Opinion and Foreign Policy," p. 27.)

[8] On this, see Anne C. Richard, *Superpower on the Cheap? The Difficulty of Funding U.S. Foreign Relations* (Paris: Centre français sur les Etats-Unis, ifri, 2003).

[9] Pierre Hassner, *United States: The Empire of Force or the Force of Empire*, Chaillot Papers, no. 54 (Paris: European Union Institute of Security Studies, September 2002).

[10] Richard Holbrooke, *To End a War* (New York: Random House, 1998), pp. 64–67.

[11] Joseph Nye, *The Paradox of American Power* (New York: Oxford University Press, 2002).

SEVEN

A GERMAN REVOLUTION WAITING TO HAPPEN

VISIONS OF AMERICA AFTER SEPTEMBER 11

Michael Stuermer

In February 2003 at the Munich Conference on Security Policy, Secretary General Lord Robertson, tirelessly working to save the North Atlantic Treaty Organization (NATO) and its future against post–Cold War blues, U.S. unilateralism, *l' exception française*, and German departures, described his position as "Mid-Atlantic: Cold, wet, and very, very much alone." He was careful not to go into specifics. Yet it is no secret that while the United States and Britain were pulling in one direction, Germany and France were pulling in the other. Faced with muscular U.S. crisis management in the Greater Middle East and the likelihood of war, the transatlantic system was falling apart at an unexpected pace. What happened was not so much head-on collision but a drifting apart, at first almost inadvertently and casually, more motivated by domestic concerns than by any long-term strategy to create—let alone steer—a European foreign policy that would be independent of, and in open conflict with, the United States. Both sides, to paraphrase Benjamin Disraeli's famous phrase about how Britain acquired its own empire, stumbled upon that crisis almost by accident. Yet, as in the British case, strong underlying forces were at work.

On the Franco-German side, tactical maneuvering met with fundamental resentment against U.S. hegemony and the Bush administration. On the French side, economic interests invested in Iraq and its strongman also added to this resentment. On the German side, it was more a combination of weak leadership and demagogic temptation. Whatever the divergent causes, the Franco-German combination resulted in a deep rift that was not so much between Europeans and Americans as right across Europe.

The Iraq blitzkrieg did not settle the scores. Neither was the U.S. administration willing to be magnanimous in victory nor did the French and German governments find a way to sneak back into the tent of the U.S. alliance. Instead of remembering the wisdom of German statecraft—since Konrad Adenauer, Germany has invariably relied on creating a cocoon of trust and treaties around itself; "wrapping" Germany into its alliances, Chancellor Helmut Kohl used to say—the German government and many of its public sympathizers have recently rediscovered the charms of "sovereignty" writ large and made absolute, while ignoring its ominous overtones in a Europe integrated by treaties that aim specifically at reducing classical notions of sovereignty and making them obsolete and impotent.

The official quest for "multipolarity"—trumpeted by French president Jacques Chirac, German chancellor Gerhard Schroeder, and a whole host of intellectuals and supporters across the country—likewise tends to set an imaginary Europe against the United States. Such a stance ignores not only that most Europeans prefer to be allied with the United States rather than among each other, but also that it is only on the military chessboard that the United States is towering above the rest; on the economic chessboard and in the soft-power dimension, to use Joseph Nye's expression, Europe and North America play in the same league.[1] Moreover, on various issues—Iraq's postwar reconstruction being the most prominent one—the U.S. administration is already coming to terms with the limited usefulness of military might and the need to rely on allies and friends to secure long-term success. Churchill's seasoned words of wisdom that "The only thing worse than having allies is having no allies" is as a reminder not only to Germany but to the United States as well.

Meanwhile, the mistrust goes deep, in fact to the very heart of the transatlantic relationship. No one is going to win in the process, and everybody is bound to lose in the long run. Much as this prospect is bleak and frightening, it is indeed the one and only ground for optimism in the present turmoil because, in the end, both sides of the Atlantic equation will have to come to the conclusion that it is better to repair the marriage and stay together—until further notice—rather than stay the current course.[2] Putting Humpty Dumpty together again will require, however, more than routine reactions, soft-pedaling communiqués, vainglorious chest beating, and overcharged rhetoric. It will need magnanimity on the U.S. side and a combination of

Staatskunst [statecraft] and *Fingerspitzengefühl* [fingertip sense] on the German—and possibly the French—side. All of this has been in short supply before, during, and after the defining events leading to the war in Iraq.

When it comes to transatlantic architecture, the U.S.-German relationship remains—Cold War or not—the most important link between Europe and the world's sole remaining superpower. If it is severed beyond repair, the whole of Europe will suffer and alienate its security lender of last resort, while the United States risks losing the continental European wing of its global security edifice. In 2003, and for the foreseeable future, German-American relations are in disarray —politically, strategically, and morally. Yet it is not only the Berlin-Washington relationship that has soured; in natural consequence, the entire European security architecture is shaking while America is facing serious overstretch, at home and abroad, financially and strategically.[3]

WELCOME BACK TO THE GERMAN QUESTION

Center stage, Europe and the United States are having an unexpected encounter with a ghost from the past called the German Question. The post-1990 Euro-Atlantic "interlocking institutions," instead of working like a clockwork of international security, are falling apart.[4] The reasons are to be found not only in the differences of opinion about the practicability and legitimacy of going to war against Iraq, but even more so over the say that the United States should have in European affairs.

Britain is, as always, firmly anchored in mid-Atlantic. France is pulling in its own direction, living out Gaullist instincts and follies of *grandeur*, while Germany, forever unsure of its history and destiny and with its economy ailing, its welfare system imploding, and its leadership disoriented, rebels against the tradition of a half century of pro-Atlantic policies—from Konrad Adenauer through Willy Brandt and Helmut Schmidt to Helmut Kohl. While the economic elites are still clinging to the illusion that nothing much has changed and are seeing the current imbroglio as just an isolated episode to be ridden out, a tsunami of pacifism, anti-Americanism, and isolationism unleashed by Schroeder is shaking the country to its foundations. NATO will survive—and so will the European Union (EU)—but with deep fissures and ruptures all too visible. Still, the paths may well divide in a moment of truth ushered in by the next global crisis over weapons of mass destruction, global terrorism, and early military intervention. In transatlantic affairs, there is no return to square one.

With France and Germany both acting as the proverbial loose cannon on deck, there is little chance that the symbiotic world of NATO and the EU will ever again have the energy and thrust that was evident during the past decade and even in late 2002 at the NATO and EU summits in Prague and Copenhagen, respectively. A point of no return has been reached, and the best days of postwar Europe and the Atlantic Alliance may well be over. There are times in history when pessimism is amply warranted. One such moment is now—and at center stage in the new drama are both the United States and Germany.

Ever since the formation of the early modern state system in Europe the German Question had two parts, both closely linked: To whom should the Germans owe their loyalty, and to whom should Germany belong?[5] Most of the time this question, owing to history and geography, was not up to the Germans alone to answer (and when the Germans tried to do so unilaterally, the attempt ended in catastrophe). After World War II, the Cold War kept the German Question suspended, Germany becoming the chief prize of the secular contest. Defeated and divided, Germany was down and almost out. Yet the piece of European territory that is Germany held the key to dominance in Europe, in fact in the world. That is why in the three great contests between the United States and the Soviet Union—the Berlin blockade of 1948–1949, the second Berlin crisis of 1958–1961, and the 1975–1987 crisis over Intermediate-Range Nuclear Force (INF)—Germany, inevitably, claimed center stage not because of its strength but because of its division.

The German Question dictated that whoever would clinch the answer to it would be the master of Europe. In the Cold War, each side was strong enough to deny the opponent the defining power over the whole of Europe but not strong enough to impose its own solution, until the Soviet Union eventually cracked. For more than 40 years, until 1990, the Eastern part of the answer held the key to the Soviet Empire; the Western part held the key to the Pax Americana in Europe. In the fine print, and even in the full text of the Two-Plus-Four Treaty, the rulers of united Germany, Chancellor Kohl and his foreign minister, Hans-Dietrich Genscher, promised to continue the country's role as a model student in both the Atlantic class and the European class. The enlargement of NATO and the EU, the Kosovo war, and even the war on terror saw Germany not only as a team player but as a leader as well.

NO CERTAIN IDEA OF EUROPE

Once the Cold War no longer provided the organizing principle of the Atlantic Alliance and NATO's military setup, the national egos, vanities, and idiosyncrasies were bound to work their way back to center stage.[6] In the United States, Clinton's reluctance to take up the burden of world order—"it's the economy, stupid"—was topped by the George W. Bush administration when the latter turned its back on, among other things, the Anti-Ballistic Missile (ABM) treaty of 1973 and the Kyoto Protocol on climate change, both dear to the heart of most Europeans. The United States invested in the Revolution in Military Affairs (RMA), widening the technological gap between U.S. forces and the rest of the world, including most, if not all, European partners. Moreover, while the U.S. administration, especially after 9/11, saw its Hobbesian worldview vindicated and the threat of an alleged axis of evil confirmed, most Europeans insisted that the world could be kept on a course of détente and cooperation. Robert Kagan, when confabulating about power and impotence in the pages of *Policy Review*, gained much fame—and notoriety. His muscular vision of the United States, coupled with open contempt for European impotence—"Paradise and Power"—seemed to sum up the new worldview in Washington, while many Europeans had misgivings about U.S. overstretch, hubris, and unilateralism.[7] The Old World, living among the ruins of empires past and visions broken, as Henry Kissinger once said, found it difficult to share the growing U.S. belief in military solutions to political problems.

The transatlantic drift affected most parts of Europe, with the possible exception of the NATO and EU aspirant countries in Central and Eastern Europe. Theirs was a desire, once in a millennium, to be on the side of the stronger battalions, to overcome their Russian trauma, and to shed their old and well-justified hang-ups, not only over Germany but also over Britain and France. The difficult experience that British and French decisionmakers and generals had gone through with U.S. intervention in the former Yugoslavia since 1991 and, even more so, their anger over the style and substance of the 1995 Dayton negotiations prompted the St. Malô initiative. Launched by President Chirac and Prime Minister Tony Blair in December 1998, this initiative called for the creation of a European rapid reaction corps, which the British envisaged evolving inside and the French outside of NATO.

Germany, for the time being, tried to bridge the gap and to continue its traditional role as a go-between with France. Owing to the precautions taken by Chancellor Kohl in the course of Germany's unification, the great sea change of 1990—especially the Two-Plus-Four Treaty between the Four Powers and Germany—did not immediately threaten the architecture of the West anchored around NATO and the EU. On the contrary, German unification was turned into a powerful force for more integration at both levels, European and transatlantic. Consistent with the policies of Adenauer and all of his successors, every gain in power was quickly translated into more integration, thus creating a cocoon of commitments working in all directions. "Sovereignty" was not a term any German government would dwell on. The greatest fear of German diplomacy was that of one day waking up alone in the world, without allies and friends. Within a half century, German uncertainty about the country's past, present, and future had been transformed into a healthy instinct of eat well, sleep quietly, and try never to be alone. The Maastricht treaty—as well as NATO's transformation and, a few years on, enlargement—were meant to confirm older commitments and extend them across the old continental divide. "Europe whole and free" was the vision up until NATO's Prague summit and the EU's Copenhagen summit in November and December 2002, respectively. NATO was to overcome its old out-of-area shyness, become a force for global stability projection, and even encourage the development of special capabilities among its members. Three months later, however, most of these new departures looked illusory.[8]

IRAQ: NOT A CAUSE BUT A CATALYST FOR STRIFE

The major turning point occurred in the run-up to the German national elections, when, faced with electoral defeat, Chancellor Schroeder and his party apparatchiks saw their last hope in drumming up antiwar and anti-American feelings. Suddenly, German politicians in government were beating their chests while shouting "sovereignty" in the direction of Washington. France, in a rehash of old-style Gaullism, joined the rebellion. Iraq was merely a pretext, and so was peace, but ever since, the Euro-Atlantic system has been out of joint.

Europe's security is a function of NATO. NATO's security is a function of the Pax Americana. If German angst and French arrogance combine against the Bush administration, the Pax Americana comes apart. How to put Humpty Dumpty together again has become a vital question for Europe as a whole, let alone for Germany and France. The Franco-German challenge to U.S. leadership sends ripples throughout Europe—old or new, no matter. Nothing can be taken for granted any longer. It is not only the settlements of 1990 that are at stake; even the post–World War II foundations are being shaken. Such is the hidden architecture of Europe that, if the United States is no longer able and willing to act as Europe's security lender of last resort, NATO will fall; and if the Atlantic Alliance falls, the EU has no chance but to follow. Neither NATO nor EU is chained to the heavens.

Since time immemorial, gratitude is nothing but a footnote in the annals of history. Without GI Joe, Hitler's successors would probably still hold sway over Germany and Europe. Without U.S. resolve, Berlin would have fallen twice, in 1948 and 1961. Without U.S. guidance, German reunification would have foundered on the rocks of European resentment organized by French president François Mitterrand and British prime minister Margaret Thatcher. For Germany, the U.S. alliance is a matter of national interest. As Chancellor Kohl famously put it in 1983, when the INF crisis was at its climax, "*Bündnisfähigkeit* [alliance capability] is at the heart of German *Staatsraison* [reason of state]." For some time now, however, the tectonic plates of Europe have been shifting. It is probably too late for a return to the state of affairs that existed before the recent transatlantic crisis. It is not too late, however, to devise ways and means to forge a new European consensus and translate that into a new transatlantic relationship.[9] Too much is at stake for all players in this game to let NATO and, by implication, the EU go the way of all flesh.

AMERICA WATCHES THE WORLD, GERMANY WATCHES ITSELF

For most Europeans, including Germany, the defining moment of the world is November 9, 1989, when the Soviet Union—as George F. Kennan had predicted in his seminal *Foreign Affairs* article of 1947, "The Sources of Soviet Conduct"—imploded, when the Berlin Wall came down without a single shot being fired, and when the nations of Eastern and Central Europe were, step by step, coming in from the cold.

Meanwhile, for most Americans, the moment of truth was September 11, when, on a clear sunny morning, at 8:45 a.m., Eastern Standard Time, the intelligence community's nightmare became reality. On that infamous day, the United States experienced a newfound existential vulnerability, global interdependence demonstrated its destructive power, and the war on terror was declared. In its Brussels headquarters, NATO immediately invoked Article 5 of its treaty. Yet, beyond a symbolic expression of solidarity, the Europeans failed to convey what exactly they were trying to say. Nor did the Bush administration, congenitally bent on unilateralism and on disdain for the NATO allies' military effectiveness, understand that there are times when political cohesion is even more important than technical efficiency.[10] Since then, the transatlantic system has been adrift, and so is the European subsystem optimistically called the European "union."

Still, the war on terror—from U.S. airspace guarded by NATO's high-flying AWACS aircraft; to the Arabian Sea where NATO maritime patrols were on the lookout; to the mountains of the Hindu Kush where U.S. Rangers, German special forces, and British commandos had been fighting side by side—did not tear the West apart. It was only when Iraq became the focus of U.S. wrath that the Western alliance began to tear apart at the seams.

The gulf between the European end-of-history dreamworld, inspired by November 9, 1989, and the U.S. doomsday nightmare, augured by September 11, 2001, widened into a transatlantic schism when translated into strategy.[11] The apocalyptic horsemen of the twenty-first century now seemed to rely on the destructive use of weapons of mass destruction, global terror, religious wars, and breakdown of civilization—in addition to more traditional horrors. In the U.S. view, by and large shared by the British government, this required a whole new set of international rules, including global intervention and preemptive war.

The Bush administration is driven by an assessment of the future that sees weapons of mass destruction in the hands of terror networks, supplied by rogue states, as the ultimate threat not only to faraway countries in the Greater Middle East but close to the U.S. homeland. Some Europeans are siding with the United States, not so much because they share that fundamental analysis about the evolving international security environment, but because they want to side with the stronger battalions. Meanwhile, both Germany and France relive the 1960s, this time without the grim discipline once imposed by the specter of the Soviet Union and the Cold War.

The German Left, in and out of government, is returning to its nationalistic roots and reliving its frustration over the Vietnam War and the INF crisis. The miserable economic and financial situation of the country puts a premium on value-oriented policies. When the 2002 *Bundestag* elections were going badly for Schroeder, he gave a boost to his flagging campaign by turning against the United States and appealing to the isolationist and anti-American instincts of the old and new peace camp in Germany—red, green, churches, and intelligentsia—irrespective of the outcome of negotiations at the United Nations.

Meanwhile the Chirac government, forever cultivating its anti-American resentment, by contrast insisted on a controlling stake in the upcoming showdown at the UN Security Council. At the same time, the French president saw the crisis over Iraq as a momentous chance to construct a Paris-oriented European system, with Germany politically isolated and weak but supplying much of the economic weight. Initially, the leaders in Berlin and Paris, both gifted demagogues, played adventurous tactical games. Soon, however, their overtures assumed a life of their own, and the silhouette of a united European continent, led by France and Germany possibly with some encouragement from Vladimir Putin's Kremlin, against the United States and Britain got some attraction.

It may well turn out to be the work of the sorcerer's apprentice, but this time around the old master may not care to save the day and restore everything to normal. Instead, once the trust is broken and the alliance has been torn apart over questions of life and death, the implications may well be of a strategic magnitude, destroying any notion of the West that may have survived the Cold War. Meanwhile, the smaller nations of Europe, especially those on the other side of the former East-West divide, are alarmed, assuring Washington of their undiluted loyalty. Iraq, not the war on terror, has divided the Europeans much deeper among themselves than from the United States. In all this, Germany has had a key role to play, not only because of its economic weight but also because of its central location in the heart of Europe. The question is not whether NATO can return to its former role and status; NATO has been in transition ever since November 9, 1989. Rather, the questions are whether out of this turmoil and strife a new transatlantic system can emerge, and, in natural consequence, whether the European Union will ever be more than an alliance of economic convenience, a halfway house between a customs union and a global player.

The 1990 high-flying vision of "interlocking institutions" has not stood the test of time. It was the retired admiral, Sir James Eberle, then director of Chatham House, who at the time of the alliance's invention called it "a bugger's muddle." NATO is torn apart; the EU's European Security and Defense Policy (ESDP) is nothing but paper; and the European Union, en route to constitution making, has awakened new doubts. In this context, the Berlin government has contributed to the divisions, driven not by a grand strategy of realignment but by hopes for electoral gain. Concomitantly, more than a few old demons have risen from their shallow graves.

1949: REINVENTING GERMANY AND EUROPE

The Federal Republic, when it emerged in 1949, was not a country in search of a foreign policy but the product of U.S. foreign policy in search of a state. It was President Truman who described the rationale in terms of a U.S. containment strategy. Without the territory between the Elbe and the Rhine, he said, the defense of Western Europe would be nothing but a rearguard action on the shores of the Atlantic Ocean.

On the eve of signing the North Atlantic Treaty, Truman invited the foreign ministers of the future NATO countries to a working dinner in the White House—no German representative was present as the Federal Republic was still in the making. In the U.S. administration's deliberations, however, Germany was center stage. Truman and the newly appointed secretary of state, Dean Acheson (*Present at the Creation* being the title he gave subsequently to his memoirs), impressed on the European and Canadian visitors that the Soviet Union was out to conquer the world—not necessarily by brute force, but by sowing misery and discontent so that Communism would flourish. Germany and Japan were crucial for the future shape of the world balance. Both countries—down but not out—held the balance between East and West. Therefore, everything had to be done to tie them firmly to the West.

So the promise of nuclear and conventional defense against Stalin's Soviet Union was coupled with the condition that the Europeans should never again repeat the post–World War I mistakes, including putting their economies together and co-opting Germany, or what was left of it. The United States would not only keep the Red Army at bay but also see to it that Germany would not, once again, endanger the repose of Europe. This was the bargain that called the entire European postwar system into being—greatly helped, of course, by the grim shadow of Marshall Stalin behind the Iron Curtain and his brutal handling of the nations under his thumb.

At that time, the U.S. offer—backed by nuclear power, around 50 percent of the world's GNP, and infinite amounts of soft power—was impossible to refuse. Residual European doubts—the British foreign secretary wanted Germany rebuilt into a socialist model state, his French colleague wanted Germany even further dismembered and divided—were firmly put to rest by the Truman administration. The U.S. president told his European interlocutors, firmly and decisively, that this was not on the agenda, and that was the end of the story.

PAX AMERICANA: THANK YOU AND GOODBYE?

It was Konrad Adenauer who, among the bewildered and disoriented Germans, understood the U.S. grand design even before it was ever pronounced, and saw the chance it offered West Germany to rise, once again, from the status of "enemy nation"—the term used in the UN Charter—and from the ashes of moral and material defeat to become a major player on the European scene. In early 1946, he wrote to an American friend a letter that set forth his concept of European reconstruction, which envisioned Germany as an integral part of the future transatlantic alliance:

> Asia stands at the Elbe. The danger is great. Nothing but an economically and psychologically sound Western Europe, led by Britain and France, a Western Europe which would of necessity include the non-Russian occupied part of Germany, can put a halt to the further intellectual and political advance of Asia. . . . Europe cannot be saved without help from the USA, and to save Europe is also essential for the United States.[12]

As the product of post–World War II U.S. foreign policy, Germany's role and status during the Cold War were dependent on the United States' benign intervention in Europe. From the Berlin blockade to the creation of the Federal Republic in 1948–1949, from NATO to the European Economic Community in 1954–1958, from the fall of the Berlin Wall to the Two-Plus-Four settlement in 1989–1990, the United States remained throughout the senior partner in the Atlantic Company—leading in May 1989 to President George H. W. Bush offering "partnership in leadership" to Chancellor Kohl and his country. More than France, before and after Charles de Gaulle, and even more than the United Kingdom—never mind Echelon, nuclear cooperation, and the rest of the "special relationship"—Germany became the hub, politically and strategically, of the U.S. role in and for Europe.

This relationship was built on strategic protection and economic cooperation, but also on common values and a shared worldview. German security needs were looked after by the U.S. containment policy, while European fears of Germany were put to rest in an informal system of "dual containment."[13] Germany became the bridgehead of the Pax Americana in Europe in every respect, from defense to the dollar zone to free trade and cheap oil supplies. American missionary zeal, going far beyond the initial postwar drive for reeducation, and the German need for moral rehabilitation and psychological reassurance were made to match. Forgive and forget—*oblivio perpetua et amnestia*. The old art of making peace was practiced between two nations that, at the beginning of the twentieth century, had both challenged the traditional balance of power not only in Europe but in a world still faintly reminiscent of the Vienna Congress and its Realpolitik wisdom. Both powerhouses had combined a forward thrust in technology and economic energy with an unwillingness to take anything for granted. Twice they met in anger, in 1917–1918 and 1941–1945, but before and after these periods the relationship was of a more cordial kind. Prior to 1914 it was, more or less, mutual admiration. The 1920s saw Washington and Wall Street stabilize the ill-fated Weimar Republic. After 1945 the Germans—at least those lucky enough to be on the Western side of the national dividing line—were co-opted by the superpower and, on Washington's insistence, by the West Europeans alike. It was, driven by grim necessity, the beginning of a wonderful friendship.

Ever since, the United States has guaranteed the Europeans' strategic protection while making it clear that the nuclear umbrella had limits. The 1956 British-French-Israeli invasion of the Suez Canal drove home the realization that the United States would not protect the control of empires lost. It was a defining moment. Britain fused its nuclear forces with those of the United States whereas France opted for independence, distancing itself from NATO's military structures while remaining part of the North Atlantic Treaty. Meanwhile, having renounced production and possession of atomic, biological, and chemical (ABC) weapons in 1954 as a precondition of sovereignty and of membership in the Western European Union (WEU) and NATO, Germany was left in the lurch. The brief flirtation with France to "study nuclear devices" in the Algerian desert came to naught. Soon after, the Multilateral Force, promising nuclear participation to non-nuclear NATO partners, including Germany, was sunk by the White House before it ever set sail.

Germany found itself, once again, among the nuclear have-nots. The U.S. answer was an invitation to join NATO's Nuclear Planning Group, a forum important for targeting policy and arms control, while the German answer was to acquire nuclear platforms as a means of becoming a quasi member of the club.

Had it not been for the United States, Germany—by now the biggest economic player in Europe—would have been marginalized in matters of strategic and symbolic importance. Meanwhile, Britain once again cultivated the special relationship, while France under de Gaulle embarked on a policy of maintaining its special status. In the direction of Britain, the French general put in a veto against British entry into the Common Market; in the direction of Germany, he pronounced a clear rejection of any nuclear sharing with Germany. Instead of a nuclear capacity, German reassurance lay in the presence of 300,000 U.S. troops and their dependents in the West German heartland stretching from the Fulda Gap to Ramstein.

From the deutsche mark that was tied to the greenback to the fiercely independent status of the Bundesbank, from the *Fräuleinwunder* made in Hollywood to the reconstruction of the German media, from consumer values to international investment—in so many ways, postwar Germany was recast in America's image. Movies not made in the U.S. dream factories had little impact; abstract painting and sculpture received their most important impulses from the New York art scene; all the major works of contemporary literature were dutifully translated and read. Academic careers would not take off without a spell at U.S. elite institutions; military officers attended U.S. staff colleges; and aspiring managers flocked to Stanford and Harvard to obtain an MBA. The only major section among the German elite rarely exposed to real life in the United States, beyond the world of cliché, were the politicians. Few of them wasted any time outside their own little career patterns in the corridors of politics—local, provincial, and federal.

France, to this day, finds it difficult to forgive GI Joe for having rescued the country twice from German occupation. Surprisingly, mixed feelings were less pronounced in Germany despite the bombing of German cities and the country's subsequent occupation, which was accompanied by few friendly scenes and evoked deep suspicions, curfews, and a strict no-fraternization policy from the U.S. side at the beginning. Yet whatever Germans may have believed or known about America, their prayers went to the U.S. occupiers rather than to some

Russian liberators. The hair-raising stories about the Red Army soon converted West Germans to the reality that, whatever their dislikes about defeat and U.S. occupation, they had ended up with the better lot.

Some residual anti-American feeling among conservatives of both major denominations remained, but it was soon dissipated by the reassuring feeling to be allied with the stronger side. German prewar nationalism had been more a thing of the Right than of the Left. After the Nazi regime it became the other way round. For almost a decade, the Social Democrats (SPD), by and large, did what they could to stop Adenauer's policies of Western integration—be it in the context of the early European Coal and Steel Community (ECSC) of 1952 or its successor institutions, the European Economic Community (EEC) and the European Atomic Energy Community (Euratom) of 1957–1958. With even more vigor, the Social Democrats opposed the development of the *Bundeswehr* and its integration, without a national command structure, in NATO. The prevailing argument was that, absent a German peace treaty, this would make eventual reunification impossible. For the Socialists, it was always national unity first, Western integration second. Adenauer, who never forgot that he was, as he once put it, "the chancellor of the vanquished," knew only too well that West Germany's paramount national interest lay in building trust in the West while keeping the question of eventual reunification in legal and political suspense. Not so the SPD. When in 1959 the dashing young mayor of Berlin, Willy Brandt, with his impeccable record first in the German resistance and then as a cold warrior in beleaguered Berlin, presented to U.S. secretary of state John Foster Dulles the SPD's plan for German unification under the banner of neutrality, the U.S. response dispersed any hopes there might have been at the time: the United States and Russia might be at loggerheads over many things, but they agreed on one thing—never allowing a united Germany to tip the scales of world power to one side or the other.

On the intellectual level, it is important to note that after the U.S.-sponsored *Neue Zeitung* left the field in 1949, the great German newspapers and the vastly influential *Neue Zürcher Zeitung* largely supported Adenauer's policy of Western integration and Economics Minister Ludwig Erhard's policies of open markets. Yet, some increasingly influential weeklies like *Stern*, edited by a prominent former Nazi, and *Der Spiegel*, edited by Rudolf Augstein, cultivated a condescending image of America while they encouraged a picture of Germany and the Germans based on self-pity and often caricature. Adenauer was accused of being a late originator of another "federation of the Rhine," this time under U.S. aegis. Kurt Schumacher, the SPD leader, called Adenauer in parliament the "chancellor of the allies"—without ever caring to apologize. Even Axel Springer, the most successful German newspaper tycoon, took some time and Soviet experience to be converted to the pro-American cause. It was not before the summer of 1960 that Herbert Wehner, the one-time Communist and by now grim taskmaster of the SPD, publicly embraced Adenauer's *Westpolitik*. This conversion came not out of any admiration for the old man or out of any particular love for America, but because of the clear realization that the SPD had no chance of ever being in government without first making its peace with the Pax Americana—late but not too late.

This state of affairs did not last very long, however. When the East Germans, with Moscow's support, built the wall through Berlin's four-power status, Willy Brandt complained bitterly: "The curtain went up, and the stage was empty." Not that he had advocated World War III; he just gave expression to the feeling that the United States had reached the limits of its power and it was time to think beyond the Pax Americana. On the streets of Berlin, Heidelberg, and other places of higher learning, the ugly American was discovered by a younger generation of Germans. It was the Vietnam War that did much to destroy the German image of America the beautiful. Driven by a late-Freudian Oedipus complex, hundreds of thousands of young protesters were taking to the streets. The slogan "Ho, Ho, Ho Chi Minh" merged with the rebellion against the traditional universities and against the alleged boredom of the Adenauer years that were, in a bizarre misunderstanding of the vast changes taking place in their daily lives, labeled as Restoration. The East German Stasi added fuel to the fire, recruiting no small number of future journalists and academics, some paid and some unpaid, for its particular kind of "peace work" throughout academia and the media.[14] The "sixty-eighters," as the protesters called themselves in Germany as well as in France and elsewhere, were not only up against what they called in Europe the Establishment—meaning anything from political parties to dancing lessons to monogamy—but also against the American way of war and peace. Anti-Americanism was their lowest common denominator. By denouncing America as the devil's own country, they also condemned the country that had been recast in America's image.

While the Christian Democratic Union (CDU) was largely unaffected in its structures and programs, the SPD was shaken to its foundations. The old oligarchy tried to divert the Marxist doctrinaires and the intellectuals away from politics and into the education system—only to see them return in force. The long march vowed by the sixty-eighters increasingly affected the SPD's organization and composition. While on the commanding heights, the messianic Willy Brandt—a medium of public sentiment, if ever there was one—was replaced by the pragmatic Helmut Schmidt. Frustrated under the new austerity imposed by the post-1973 oil price hike, the party was becoming increasingly restive, as Helmut Schmidt himself noticed. Schmidt's policy was to influence U.S. politics from within—an occasional shouting match not excluded. The endgame came when the second oil crisis drove German welfare budgets out of control and when the party rank and file deserted the chancellor over NATO's dual-track decision. The SPD's electoral motto of March 1983—"*Im deutschen Interesse*" (in the German interest)—aimed its pacifist-nationalistic tune against the Kohl/Genscher government, NATO, and the United States. No U.S. missiles were to be deployed on German soil. The SPD lost the elections, but out of the same pacifist/anti-American/nationalist instinct the Green Party was born. Four years later Ronald Reagan and Mikhail Gorbachev concluded the "double zero" agreement, foreshadowing still more important changes to come.

NOVEMBER 9: PAX AMERICANA TRIUMPHANT

The fall of the Berlin Wall was good news for most Germans—except for the East German SED and the West German radical Left—and it was bad news for some among Germany's neighbors. British prime minister Thatcher frantically tried to build barriers, hoping for a very long period of negotiations. French president Mitterrand, when faced with Kohl's modest plan for a long-term German federation, threatened to recreate a blocking entente with Moscow and London.

None of this materialized owing to U.S. leadership, Soviet weakness, and French willingness to trade a French veto for the end of the deutsche mark and the Bundesbank. In the future, and as a quid pro quo, monetary policy would have to be in the hands of a European Central Bank. Kohl asked for political union to secure the common currency through common policies. Unable to be more precise, however, he had to settle for the two Maastricht dossiers: one, very precise, on Economic and Monetary Union (EMU); the other one, very imprecise, on political union. The Common Foreign and Security Policy (CFSP) of the EU—whose German abbreviation is, aptly, "Gasp"—has since then produced no small amount of paperwork on every world event and still failed to unite the Europeans in time of crisis. In fact, were that policy to be subjected, today or in the future, to majority voting in the European Council, any serious crisis would blow it to smithereens.

Without U.S. leadership, notably from the White House and the State Department, the last great East-West crisis might have ended in tears and confrontation. While continuing German membership in the European Community was a given, this was not so concerning NATO. Russia's Politburo and Germany's Socialists and Greens were united in wanting to see the reunited country leave NATO. The Kohl government and the first Bush administration wanted nothing of the kind—and they prevailed. In the end, George H. W. Bush and James Baker convinced the Europeans that while Germany continued residing in its cocoon of integration and contractual agreements, the perennial German Question had been put to rest. Washington and Bonn agreed on continued stationing of U.S. troops in sizable numbers in Germany, not only to watch the Soviets retreat but also to reassure the Europeans. On top of this, Kohl repeated the traditional renunciation of ABC weaponry and saw to it that German divisions were organized in multinational corps. Once again, the United States gave reassurance to the whole of Europe, including Germany, that the post–Cold War world would be even more comfortable than the bipolar system that was about to disappear. "Germany unified and Europe transformed" was the title of a book that summed up the official U.S. view—riding into the sunset and on to the end of history.[15]

Instead of a sunset, however, Europeans and Americans were exposed to a cruel test during the first Gulf War. German politicians of all descriptions first warned the Americans against war—never an acceptable means to any end—and then sent their regrets, together with DM 17.6 billion to help with the expenses. Meanwhile, while retreating Iraqis were setting Kuwaiti oil wells on fire, the early flames of burning villages in Yugoslavia sent the first signals of future turmoil. All of this not only reduced Europe's CFSP to a heap of paper, but it also reminded Europeans that without the U.S. cavalry the Balkans and the Middle East could be dangerous neighborhoods. The Europeans were slow to come to grips with the hot reality that had succeeded the Cold War. When, in December 1998, President Chirac and Prime Minister Blair met at St. Malô, they decided that Europeans had better pool their military resources to reduce somewhat their dependence on U.S. intervention. A year later, at the Helsinki European Council, the Finns insisted on giving some muscle to the pious wishes: the Headline Goals were born. Meanwhile, the British started pulling in the direction of NATO; the French, in the opposite direction.

When the Muslims of Kosovo became the victims of Serb ethnic cleansing, Germans realized, to their panic, that hundreds of thousands of refugees were heading toward Munich and Frankfurt. In this situation, the new red-green government took heart—"Never again Auschwitz" was the somewhat overblown slogan—and joined the NATO allies in their fight against Serbian forces and sent in ECR (electronic combat reconnaissance) Tornadoes. The fact that the UN mandate was less than clear, owing to Russian foot-dragging, did not cause too much headache. The most important lesson, however, was lost on the Berlin government: that without U.S. support the Europeans would always have to live "*sous l'oeil des Russes*" (under the eyes of the Russians), as the saying was in the nineteenth century.

After Chancellor Kohl was forced to leave office following 16 years at the helm of German politics, he remarked to an old friend that whoever would follow him could never leave the deep furrows that every chancellor since Adenauer had ploughed. Little did he know that, after only four years, the Iraq crisis would give Germany the occasion to join a Franco-Russian rebellion against U.S. leadership on the world scene.

The red-green government, against all odds, had sent German ECR Tornadoes to lead the battle for Kosovo. After 9/11, the chancellor pledged "unconditional solidarity"— notwithstanding the subsequent caveat that the U.S. administration stay away from "adventures"—and allowed the NATO Council to invoke Article 5 of the North Atlantic Treaty. Special forces were later deployed in the foothills of Afghanistan's Hindu Kush to go after Al Qaeda operatives, and ABC armored personnel carriers (APCs) were sent to Kuwait—just in case. What case, however, these APCs might be called to serve was never specified.

When, early in 2002, the U.S. administration began to identify Saddam Hussein as the next object of its wrath, reactions in Berlin, from the government as well as from the general public, were muted. It was only when zero growth, rising unemployment, and general disenchantment combined to render the electoral prospects of Schroeder and his red-green majority government unpromising that—reportedly in a meeting between the chancellor, his chief of staff, and the SPD's secretary general in the chancellor's office—Schroeder's "German way" was laid out: antiwar, anti-American, and anti-NATO. It was as if the past years and decades had been obliterated. In an about-face, the government that fewer than four years ago had joined its NATO allies in waging war in the Balkans had gone back to its antimilitaristic, peace-movement roots of twenty or forty years ago.

These tactics succeeded in mobilizing support across an already fading left-wing political spectrum and even in shaving off some percentage points from the former Communists. Against all odds, Schroeder won the election on September 22, 2002. Shortly afterward, however, the red-green coalition was caught in a web of its own arguments—drifting into a massive confrontation with the United States, tearing apart whatever existed of the fabric of Europe's not-so-common foreign and security policy, making the EU's constitutional convention look ridiculous, and losing the trust of most NATO allies. German diplomats, when carrying the bad news into NATO meetings, began apologetically, "Don't shoot the messenger for his message." An ill wind was blowing to no one's good.

THE INDISPENSABLE NATION

What has happened, and continues to happen, is the unraveling of that postwar cocoon, transatlantic and European, that granted Germany's third chance in the twentieth century. The transatlantic rift, with its reverberations throughout Europe, is not an episode but a defining moment. It may have started as a minor local difficulty, with nobody of any importance seriously predicting it would end up tearing the transatlantic fabric apart. By now, however, not only has NATO been severely damaged but also, as a natural consequence, Europe's political union is in limbo—ironically, at a moment when the great and the good are working hard to frame a constitution for Europe, when the line for entry into the EU tends to grow almost daily, and when a European rapid reaction force should already be ready to march.

Europeans tend to see November 9, 1989, as the point of departure of a long period of peace, while Americans instinctively recognize September 11, 2001, as the birth date of global turmoil that will turn against the West unless stopped in time. Europeans have lost the stomach for a global role and engage in prevention with great reluctance, while

Americans feel they have no option but to defend against anarchy, if necessary through preemption. It was not inevitable that after the Cold War national sensitivities should be free to destroy the institutions that had been created for European reconstruction and reinforced to accommodate not only a reunited Germany but also the Central and Eastern European nations coming in from the cold. The United States seemed willing to continue to act as the security lender of last resort. Yet there was the implicit assumption that leadership, by definition, would fall to the Americans, and that the United States would remain anchored in Europe, a "European power" indeed.[16] Iraq and the next likely global challenges, from Iran to North Korea to the containment of China, will tear this assumption apart.

The chimera of a Paris-Berlin-Moscow axis does not deserve lengthy discussion; when it comes to the crunch, each and every partner tends to recognize that being in the camp of the empire is more rewarding than posturing against it. Yet what the recent crisis over Iraq has reminded most Europeans—with the possible exception of France, Germany, Belgium, and Luxemburg—is that without the Atlantic Alliance serving as a reinsurance system against both the old demons and the new global threats, the European project will never go much beyond the present state of a customs union de luxe, the single market, and the 100,000 tedious pages of *acquis communautaire*—and even that could be threatened should a long global recession coincide with more global challenges of the likes of Iraq. For most Europeans, the EU is a union of convenience. In contrast, the alliance with the United States is a question of existence—to be or not to be. It would be unwise for Paris or Berlin to continue to force an EU-only choice upon other European countries. Such posturing is likely to result not in a stronger Europe but in the self-destruction of Europe.

From Adenauer to Kohl, German statecraft has been about managing the European and the Atlantic power equation, with Germany as the crucial link between the two. Inexperienced in international affairs, with Vietnam in the 1960s and the antimissile deployment protests in the 1970s as their formative experiences, Germany's present leaders, under the applause of their foot soldiers, are unleashing forces beyond their understanding and control.

It has happened once before: the elites of Wilhelmine Germany were deeply ambiguous over the German-British informal alliance, most of all the Kaiser who at the same time admired and loathed the British empire. So, during the Boer War he orchestrated a hate campaign. Earlier on, it had been Benjamin Disraeli, leader of Her Majesty's opposition in the House of Commons, who had recognized the potential for disaster once Germany refused to play by the rules and decided to upset the repose of Europe. He termed it the "German revolution" and went on to say, in an analysis that preceded Bismarck's careful maneuvering:

> Not a single principle in the management of our foreign affairs, accepted by all statesmen for guidance up to six months ago, any longer exists. There is not a diplomatic tradition which has not been swept away. You have a new world, new influences at work, new and unknown objects and dangers with which to cope, at present involved in that obscurity incident to novelty in such affairs.[17]

Notes

[1] Joseph S. Nye Jr., "This Is No Time for Unilateralism," *Boston Globe*, April 14, 2002, and "Redefining the National Interest," *Foreign Affairs* 78, no. 4 (July/August 1999): 22–35.

[2] Pierre Hassner, *The United States: The Empire of Force or the Force of Empire*, Chaillot Papers, no. 54 (Paris: European Union Institute for Security Studies, September 2002).

[3] For a critical assessment of the limits of U.S. supremacy, see Immanuel Wallerstein, "The Eagle Has Crash Landed," *Foreign Policy* 131 (July/August 2002): 60–68.

[4] The concept of "interlocking institutions" dates back to the Rome Declaration on Peace and Cooperation issued at the NATO Summit Meeting in November 1991. According to the declaration, "The challenges we will face in this new Europe cannot be comprehensively addressed by one institution alone, but only in a framework of interlocking institutions tying together the countries of Europe and North America. Consequently, we are working toward a new European security architecture in which NATO, the CSCE [later OSCE], the European Community [later the European Union], the WEU [later integrated into the EU] and the Council of Europe complement each other."

[5] Michael Stuermer, *Die Kunst des Gleichgewichts: Europa in einer Welt ohne Mitte* (Berlin; Munich: Propyläen, 2001) and "Balance from Beyond the Sea," *The Washington Quarterly* 24, no. 3 (Summer 2001): 145–153.

[6] Christopher Coker, *Globalisation and Insecurity in the 21st Century: NATO and the Management of Risk*, Adelphi Papers, no. 345 (London: International Institute for Strategic Studies, 2002); David Calleo, *Rethinking Europe's Future* (Princeton: Princeton University Press, 2001).

[7] Robert Kagan, "Power and Weakness," *Policy Review* 113 (June/July 2002): 3–28.

[8] Strobe Talbott, "From Prague to Baghdad," *Foreign Affairs* 81, no. 6 (November/December 2002): 46–57.

[9] See, e.g., Ronald D. Asmus and Kenneth M. Pollack, "The New Transatlantic Project: A Response to Robert Kagan," *Policy Review* 115 (October/November 2002): 3–18.

[10] Steven E. Miller, "The End of Unilateralism or Unilateralism Rex," *The Washington Quarterly* 25, no. 1 (Winter 2002): 15–29.

[11] Daniel S. Hamilton, *Die Zukunft ist nicht mehr, was sie war: Europa, Amerika und die neue weltpolitische Lage* (Stuttgart: Robert Bosch Stiftung, December 2001).

[12] Letter to William F. Sollmann, March 16, 1946.

[13] Wolfram F. Hanrieder, *Germany, America, Europe: Forty Years of German Foreign Policy* (New Haven: Yale University Press, 1989).

[14] Hubertus Knabe, *Der diskrete Charme der DDR: Stasi und Westmedien* (Berlin; Munich: Propyläen, 2001).

[15] Condoleezza Rice and Philip Zelikow, *Germany Unified and Europe Transformed: A Study in Statecraft* (Cambridge: Harvard University Press, 1995).

[16] Richard Holbrooke, "America, A European Power," *Foreign Affairs* 74, no. 2 (March/April 1995): 38–51.

[17] Speech in House of Commons, February 9, 1871.

EIGHT

ITALY AND THE UNITED STATES

FROM OLD TO NEW ATLANTICISM—AND BACK

Marta Dassù and Roberto Menotti

The image of the United States in Italy is somewhat paradoxical: for more than five decades, the country's foreign policy has been consistently pro-American and has assumed a special relationship with the United States. Yet, deeply rooted and persistent elements of anti-Americanism (or, more precisely, critical attitudes toward America) are evident in all the core components of the Italian political system and society.

A related paradox is that the post-1945 link to the United States not only has been a foreign policy issue but has also emerged as an essential element of the country's political balance after the Fascist experience, the defeat in World War II, and the presence in Italy of the largest communist party in the West. In many ways, the Cold War fault lines were reproduced inside Italy, making pro-Americanism and anti-Americanism a source of legitimacy (and delegitimization); inevitably, this internal condition gave the American Question an intrinsically ideological trait.

As a consequence, until the end of the Cold War, relations with the United States were treated as taboo—an expected ritual but rarely a topic of open debate—and, to some extent, they have remained so over the past decade. The latest crisis over Iraq is, in essence, the first time a section of the traditionally pro-American establishment has taken a critical stance—a rather substantial shift that might mark the onset of a looser and less ideological transatlantic relationship at the bilateral level.

THE STILL PRESENT PAST

In the early postwar years, Italy was occasionally labeled "the Bulgaria of NATO"—clearly a derogative term meant to describe a markedly passive attitude vis-à-vis the United States combined with a free-rider posture. At the same time, the political culture of the dominant party in Italian politics throughout the Cold War—the Christian Democratic Party—was not instinctively pro-American. The tradition of regarding the United States as Italy's best ally was based on reasons of hard-nosed realism (after all, it was thanks to the United States, certainly not to France or Britain, that Italy had recovered an international status after the defeat of 1945) and of domestic legitimation—even as this same orientation posed a potential threat to some of the party's fundamental values. An example of this tension was the decision by Alcide De Gasperi, Italy's first Christian Democratic leader, to impose the country's accession to NATO on a reluctant political constituency.[1] Yet, even as the Christian Democrats ruled the country for more than four decades, enjoying a significant level of U.S. support, a strong minority (partially influenced by the often anti-Western influence of the Vatican) never fully accepted Washington as Italy's closest natural ally, but rather as a senior partner of convenience.

Against this background, Italy's Atlanticism has always been tempered by a strong dose of Europeanism (the often-quoted "two circles" of Italian foreign policy) and by a degree of freedom of maneuver at Europe's periphery (particularly in terms of openings toward the Arab world). The survival of certain components of the former Christian Democrats as part of the post-1991 center-right coalitions leaves the Italian political scene constantly vulnerable to internal rifts when it comes to relations with Washington. This is why Italy, invariably, finds itself at odds whenever the Atlantic and European circles can simply not be reconciled. In such circumstances, the choice so far has been the United States first, but with increasing difficulties.

As for the Italian Communist Party (PCI), it was only in 1976 that it officially dropped its opposition to Italian membership in NATO. Even that momentous decision was made for paramount domestic reasons—in order to allow participation in the so-called national unity coalition government. Following its transformation into what is now a mainstream European social democratic party (PDS and, more recently, DS), the successor to the PCI has sailed in very troubled waters. On the one hand, the link to the United States continues to be viewed as a decisive source of legitimacy (it was especially so for Massimo D'Alema in becoming the first post-Communist prime minister at the end of 1998); on the other hand, this link has become a constant issue of contention among the diverse forces within the center-left, whose most radical wing is closely aligned with the antiglobal and pacifist movements.

This means that whenever hot issues, including especially issues of war and peace, come to the fore, the Italy-U.S. relationship is a factor of structural fragility for the center-left, which needs an internationalist Democratic administration in the White House to limit the divisive potential of the transatlantic link. Conversely, with a Republican administration in Washington—particularly one as outspoken as the George W. Bush administration—the center-left, now in the opposition, is harshly critical of the U.S. stance. Such criticisms range from the use of military power to the long-standing U.S. support for Israel in the Middle East peace process, or, more recently, from the U.S. shunning of the International Criminal Court to the rejection of multilateral environmental commitments.

Despite the radically different social, economic, and security context of our times, the legacy of the early Cold War years—as the formative years of Italy's contemporary democratic system—still resonates today. Since the founding of the Italian republic—as opposed to pre-Fascist or Fascist Italy—Italians of all political convictions have learned to view the United States as an integral part of the country's domestic politics, for the better or worse. In fact, all political parties have deliberately exploited (and somewhat rationalized) both pro-American and anti-American sentiments to serve political ends and as a way of mobilizing their constituencies and legitimizing important decisions.[2] The complexity of the Italy-U.S. relationship, the transatlantic alliance, and the U.S. society is such that, as an Italian observer once concluded, "each Italian finds the America that he is looking for."[3]

In addition, there is a lingering sense that at critical times in the past, "big brother" in Washington has influenced key foreign policy decisions by Italy's elected officials, including, on occasions, the composition of coalition governments.[4] The more ominous and conspiratorial version of this view holds that the shadowy and unaccountable emissaries of the CIA on various instances exercised decisive pressure on government leaders and opinion makers. According to its milder, more reasonable version, Italian leaders seem to feel a systematic pressure to prove their genuine friendship and loyalty to the United States as a precondition for full (domestic and international) legitimacy.

In terms of bilateral relations, the consequence has been to encourage a rather passive attitude, as well as a lack of transparency, on the Italian side. Witness the fate of bilateral arrangements reached in the 1950s on the utilization of military facilities on Italian soil, which remain secret to this day. While justified on grounds of security, this secrecy is a source of recurring problems—as demonstrated by the public reaction to the 1999 deadly incident that involved a U.S. Prowler conducting an exercise over the Cermis mountain.

Even among the moderate and centrist factions of the political spectrum, analysts such as former senior-level diplomat Sergio Romano are still making the case, based on sophisticated and historically grounded arguments, that the Italian political elite should behave in a more dignified manner and should, on occasion, stand up to U.S. pressures.[5] This is symptomatic of a broader public attitude toward bilateral relations with the United States that are based on the nation's pride and long-term credibility rather than on short-term political convenience alone, to put it in the simplest form.

Others, such as leading historian Ennio Di Nolfo, direct their criticism at Italian leaders for bringing about or facilitating an unnecessary subjugation of Italy to foreign influence with profound domestic repercussions.[6] Such a perception of the political elites as proponents of a rhetoric of the most loyal ally is obviously a breeding ground for, at least, a mild form of anti-Americanism—tempered, to be sure, by some appreciation for the benefits Italy has reaped as a member of the Western alliance but still fundamentally resentful of U.S. predominance. This distinction in public attitudes should be kept in mind when assessing the significance and ramifications of America's images in Italy.

The linkage between America's image as external guarantor and its repercussions for Italy's domestic outlook was the distinctive feature of Italian-U.S. relations. Not only Italy's internal stability but also gains in terms of international status, as well as various economic benefits, were tightly linked to the U.S. security guarantee. This has also nurtured the idea of a special relationship between Italy and the United States, reinforced by the geopolitical advantage of the Italian peninsula in confronting (mostly deterring) threats from south of NATO. On occasion, bases on Italian soil were of special strategic value to the United States in staging operations of various kinds in the Mediterranean basin, North Africa, and the Middle East. On the other hand, overemphasizing the special nature of the bilateral relationship (reinforced by emotional and almost mythical images of a permanent bond created by large waves of Italian emigration to the United States) seems unwarranted on objective grounds and risks leading to excessive expectations.

With the partial exceptions of the Vietnam War and the decision to deploy cruise missiles in five NATO countries between late 1979 and the early 1980s, the pre-1989 period did not fully test the resilience of the bilateral relationship. Even so, in the course of the 1980s, several diplomatic and security issues began to complicate the original picture, requiring a more active foreign policy stance on the part of a middle-sized power such as Italy. Between 1983 and 1987, the coalition government under Socialist Party leader Bettino Craxi most aptly symbolized this gradual shift with the Sigonella episode, when Italian authorities refused to let U.S. troops arrest Palestinian terrorists in transit through the Sicilian military base. In the history of recent Italian foreign policy, Sigonella epitomizes Italy's more mature state of relations with the United States, with instances of close cooperation but, at times, also open differences of opinion.[7] However, a few years later, the fall of the Berlin Wall was to test the nature of the relationship even more directly than ever before.

THE POST–COLD WAR ADAPTATION OF THE 1990s

The end of the Cold War raised wide expectations about a major adjustment of the original transatlantic arrangements. A debate did, in fact, start in Italy on the assumption that the country could no longer enjoy the benefits of a secure condition at relatively little cost (which, traditionally, meant hosting a domestic political fault line within the larger international East-West divide). No longer able to benefit automatically from its geographical location and act as a mere consumer of security, Italy would have to become more willing and capable of accepting active responsibility in foreign policy issues. Such an attempt at policy adjustment, with a renewed emphasis on the European circle of Italy's foreign policy, came in 1996 under the government of Romano Prodi—the first postwar Italian prime minister to pay the inaugural state visit to Bonn instead of Washington.

This effort was only partially successful, however, for two main reasons. First, Italy, overwhelmed by its own crippling domestic problems, was now paying the price of its deep-seated internal political fault line: the implosion of the first republic in the early 1990s had not ushered in a second republic but, rather, had given way to a long and tortuous transition, marked by a series of scandals and the decapitation of a large portion of the old political class. In such a political vacuum, the new arrival of Forza Italia under Silvio Berlusconi (a strong proponent of U.S.-style business models) and the birth of a regionally rooted, anti-Rome, but also Euroskeptical force such as the Northern League should not be surprising. The first coalition government to be formed on this new basis was short-lived, lasting only a few months in 1994, to be soon replaced by Prodi's newly formed center-left coalition, whose successful efforts to meet the criteria for economic and monetary union confirmed Prodi's commitment to the centrality of the European circle of Italy's foreign policy.

The second obstacle to this priority relates to events in the former Yugoslavia, which exposed the structural weakness of the EU in the field of foreign and security policy. In early 1999, especially, NATO's intervention in Kosovo revived the U.S. connection after years of excruciating European divisions in the Balkans and the EU's patent inability to assume concrete responsibilities on its own—to the point that Italy had to run a self-led, ad hoc coalition for Operation Alba in 1997.

The Kosovo war was critical to Italy's first post-Communist premier, Massimo D'Alema. Like its German counterpart, the Italian center-left saw the NATO intervention as a decisive test for its ability to overcome the party's traditional constraints regarding the use of force and its pacifist-neutralist temptations. Italy was ready to assume a greater international burden and more direct responsibilities in the name of the humanitarian duty to intervene even without an explicit UN mandate.

Yet, a particular aspect of this delicate problem manifests itself whenever the use of military force becomes a topic of serious debate. As pacifist movements (both Catholic and leftist) tend to share an anti-American bent (expressed at the time of Kosovo by the formula "no to NATO, yes to the UN"), any possible Italian contribution to a military operation quickly turns into a sort of referendum on the United States, with uncertain results. Therefore, the domestic debate and controversy surrounding the deployment of military forces—a natural and healthy phenomenon in any democracy—invariably risks spilling over onto the overall relationship with the United States. In the Kosovo case, the center-left succeeded in its bold interventionist shift only thanks to a peculiar bipartisanship involving the support of the opposition on the occasion of the parliamentary vote on this issue.[8]

At a different level, the political cohesion around a common Third Way ideology shared with other center-left European governments (in Germany, France, and the UK) and even with President Clinton's Democratic administration, though of little practical consequence, eased the task of combining Europe-first attitudes with a working relationship with the United States. It allowed for a potential relaxation of the security-oriented character of the bilateral relationship in favor of a broader transatlantic dialogue involving issues of international governance and the future of the liberal-democratic Left. The Italian Left supported the joint efforts of President Clinton and Prime Minister Tony Blair to find common ground between the European Left on the one hand—including France's much more skeptical prime minister, Lionel Jospin—and the U.S. Democrats on the other.

Yet, an unexpected factor intervened to complicate the emerging scheme: right after the conference on the Third Way, held in Florence in fall 1999, the antiglobal movement made its first strong appearance at the World Trade Organization summit in Seattle. In a way, the Seattle protests were a reaction against the European Left's search for a common policy on global governance. "Progressive" governance at the transatlantic level, the message from the protests seemed to be, was already generating its own discontents. In any case, as long as Clinton remained in the White House, the pacifist movement in Italy—including its traditionally neutralist or hesitant Catholic wing—remained just that: a movement or, rather, a collection of disparate groups and interests.

As a result, in the 1990s, clear-cut choices between the two circles of Italian foreign policy were simply postponed owing to the wide popularity enjoyed by the U.S. president in Italy as well as his relaxed attitude toward a growing international role for the EU. The rhetoric of democratic enlargement emanating from Washington facilitated a temporary compromise. The Atlantic link could thus be preserved in a rebalanced form, involving a stronger European pillar to be supported by an enlightened and internationalist U.S. administration. This reasoning enjoyed a rather solid bipartisan support in Italy, so that the losses in terms of popularity on the (mostly far) left were offset by the conditional support of large sectors of the center-right.

One issue that still produced some serious controversy was the decision to enlarge NATO to include former Warsaw Pact countries. For the Italian government, the day was won in Parliament by making a highly political—not military—case for enlargement; this was coupled with a sense that the planned EU enlargement would be complementary and that an enlarged NATO and an enlarged EU would be mutually reinforcing. Essentially, it was a new variant of the traditional policy of the two circles. Thus, by the end of the decade, a new post–Cold War synthesis—based on the reconciliation of Europeanism and Atlanticism and reinforced by Italy's direct engagement in stabilization missions in the Balkans—could be envisaged through a merger between the moderate conservative and moderate leftist souls of Italian politics. A type of bipartisanship, Italian-style, appeared as a distinct possibility in foreign and security policy. Since the events of September 11, however, this consensus has come under renewed pressure.

THE ELITES AND THE AMERICAN QUESTION

The preceding analysis would not be complete without mentioning a growing awareness of Italy's harshly competitive economic environment, including the overall performance of the state's institutions and regulatory mechanisms. In short, the dominant view, shared by the country's business community and the political elites, is that the economic future of Italy is structurally tied to Europe—an aspect reinforced further by Italy's membership in the eurozone—and, given Europe's dependence on a dynamic U.S. economy, to the transatlantic space.

Broadly speaking, while usually full of admiration for the American economic model, the business world in Italy is not necessarily committed to a pro-American stance on concrete policies ranging from trade disputes to issues of international governance and the promotion of universal principles. The United States is recognized as the leading power in many key sectors, but U.S. administration policies are assessed on a case-by-case basis. Equally important is a long tradition of Italian business initiatives pursued in open competition with U.S. interests, particularly in the Mediterranean and Middle East: the most conspicuous case was that of the major oil company ENI in the 1950s, which enjoyed strong Italian government backing.

Thus Italy's search for a new balance between Atlanticism and Europeanism in the 1990s reflected domestic priorities more than anything else, given the ongoing efforts—such as its successful crash plan to cut the budget deficit to the EU levels set at Maastricht in December 1991—to avoid being excluded from the European single currency. At the time, the internal debate on the costs and benefits of the euro had already revealed a "British" temptation among minority sectors of the Italian elites. On a European scale, the alignment with London is the functional equivalent of the U.S.-first approach to global security issues: the two attitudes often come together, although one political rationale behind the Britain-first option is the attempt to resist what is perceived as Franco-German domination in Europe.[9]

The launch of the euro undoubtedly changed the economic debate. The liberal, pro-British view of Italian economic interests that is in favor of an Anglo-Saxon socioeconomic model now mostly calls for a different economic policy in Europe (particularly a European Central Bank that should act more like the Federal Reserve, labor market reforms as the domestic priority, and a loosening of the Stability Pact). But the fact remains that a domestic cleavage has apparently crystallized along a particular axis. On one side is the pro-British, pro-U.S. orientation, linked to a model of economic reform that finds strong support among members of Berlusconi's Forza Italia—though not within the center-right majority as a whole. This is at variance with the pro-German orientation that tends to correspond with a social-democratic model. Therefore, the debate on Italy's alignments in Europe and across the Atlantic intersects important domestic trends and cannot be confined to security motivations.

As for professional diplomats, the commitment to the Europe-first approach is probably rising, partly owing to the ever-growing amount of time and effort devoted to EU matters as opposed to transatlantic affairs. Diplomats may also feel more comfortable with the negotiating style of other Europeans than with that of their counterparts in the United States. In addition, although no break with the Atlantic tradition has ever been envisaged, the growing emphasis on the international role of the EU is often described as a way to constrain the United States' freedom of action. This assessment of a sort of benign constraint is privately shared by a vast majority of Italian policymakers, professional diplomats, and opinion leaders.

The attitude of the Italian military, on the other hand, is shaped by Italy's traditional role as the central Mediterranean outpost of NATO's southern flank. In strategic terms, this was the essential comparative advantage that the country was able to exploit over more than five decades. The reality of U.S. leadership—and U.S.-led interoperability—in the NATO context has further strengthened this strong link, which includes an important industrial dimension. The recent decision to opt for a U.S.-made transport plane as an alternative to the long-planned A-400M (seen as a key step toward a more integrated European defense pole) confirms this orientation, generally perceived as a manifestation of Euroskepticism on political as well as budgetary grounds.

What all the components of Italy's elites seem to have in common is a vested interest in an internationalist and multilateral United States. Indeed, too many Italian interests rest on the U.S. willingness to keep its multilateral obligations and remain engaged with its allies and partners internationally. This is truly the underlying logic of Italy's relationship with the United States. Thus, the positive Italian vision of America is that of a responsible player in the multilateral arena: if this condition holds, the Euro-Atlantic link can serve as the linchpin of a stable international order. As will be shown, the events of September 11, 2001, changed the equation that the end of the Cold War seemed to have affected but had not radically altered.

ITALIAN PUBLIC OPINION

A simplified picture of Italian public perceptions of the United States would probably reveal the latter as a very powerful and useful ally although at times exceedingly demanding and arrogant, a great democracy but often blind to some of its worst defects, and a uniquely dynamic society that (for all the ties and mutual contacts) remains alien to most Italians. There is, in particular, a widespread sympathy toward the United States and an admiration for U.S. achievements in the economic field.

A recent, wide-ranging analysis of Italian public opinion shows that a straightforward anti-American versus pro-American divide is hardly applicable and probably misleading.[10] According to the study's results, the Italian public exhibits the following characteristics: very pro-American after 9/11 (more so than the EU average and second only to the British)[11] and very internationalist, favoring Italy's participation in multilateral efforts. At the same time, Italy also appears to be very pro-European (more so than the EU average) and very reluctant to resort to military force.

Positive feelings toward the United States have been and remain consistently widespread among the Italian public: in June 2002, only the EU as a whole, but no individual European country, enjoyed a higher positive rating. Another interesting but still inconclusive finding is that as many as 76 percent of Italians reportedly wish the EU to become a superpower like the United States, the second-highest rate after France and 11 percentage points higher than the European average.[12]

It is worth noting, however, that in Italy as well as elsewhere the level of sympathy toward the United States dropped dramatically as a consequence of the Iraqi crisis—down to 34 percent in March 2003 from a peak of 70 percent in summer 2002 (with most recent postwar levels showing again a rise to 60 percent).[13] Most significantly, opposition to the Iraq War was not confined to the pacifist movement and the leftist Catholic world. A considerable segment of the establishment, including influential media such as *Repubblica* (radical Left) but also the *Corriere della Sera* (traditionally a centrist mainstream newspaper), shared that antiwar sentiment.

Even these general observations are sufficient indication of a certain tension that has become inevitable at the different levels of the complex Italy-EU-U.S. relationship. In practice, as long as the two dimensions of the country's foreign policy stance remain in balance and do not pull in opposite directions, wide public support is almost ensured. However, as soon as the two spheres begin to diverge, any Italian government finds itself walking a domestic tightrope, with the risk of losing at least a portion of its voters. Against this background, the worst possible combination is therefore a situation in which military force comes under serious consideration in a climate of transatlantic divisions and European disunity—in other words, the 2002–2003 Iraqi recipe.

Another central finding of the 2002 public opinion study is that oscillations in attitudes toward the United States have been widening, reflecting greater sensitivity to short-term changes in the perception of U.S. foreign policies. This amounts to the gradual emergence of a more conditional and, possibly, more sophisticated attitude toward U.S. policies. Such an evolution is partly the result of the more uncertain post–Cold War environment, but also of the coming of age of new generations that are less committed to the early transatlantic relationship in its original and rather static form.

As demonstrated by the precipitous drop of sympathy toward the United States during the first three months of 2003, the favorable feelings toward the American people are not matched by a positive evaluation of the foreign policies of the United States (particularly under President Bush), which instead receive very mixed grades. In sum, if between one-fourth and one-third of the Italian population declares to have "no sympathy" for the United States,[14] the ideological anti-American dimension is probably less crucial than a sort of political anti-Americanism, motivated by specific policy decisions by the U.S. administration: the United States is criticized for what it does, not for what it is.

Still, the polls also show that the reaction to the 9/11 shock was one of great solidarity, which translated into a solid majority supporting the U.S. (and international) intervention in Afghanistan that followed the attacks on U.S. soil, including an active Italian contribution to the campaign that did not materialize in the first stage. The level of presumed anti-Americanism reflected in the conclusion that the United States has, at least partly, contributed to the causes of the terrorist attacks was significant (about 50 percent of Italians) but still lower in Italy than in the major European countries. More significantly, however, the genuine flurry of sympathy and solidarity with the American people that came in the immediate aftermath of September 11 from all sectors of the Italian society may have led the government to overestimate its freedom of action.

THE NEW-ATLANTICIST TEMPTATION AND THE IRAQI CRISIS: THE END OF A CONSENSUS?

In 2002, the Berlusconi government saw a practical opportunity to push forward a forceful U.S.-first agenda. The decision reflected various converging trends. First, it underscored the prime minister's penchant for close personal ties with President Bush in order to compensate for Berlusconi's difficulties dealing with key European leaders such as French president Jacques Chirac and German chancellor Gerhard Schroeder.

Second, it relied on preexisting Euroskeptic tendencies in a center-right coalition that includes pro-British elements within Forza Italia, the "sovereigntist" and antifederalist discourse of Alleanza Nazionale, and the Euro-bashing coming from the Northern League. It is no accident that Foreign Minister Renato Ruggiero, known for his strong pro-European credentials and wide international reputation, resigned in early January 2002 after just a few months in office (officially because of a cabinet row triggered by the launch of the euro) and following a series of open differences with some coalition partners, cabinet members, and the prime minister himself. Until the Nice European summit of December 2000, the Italian center-left government had, with the support of the president of the republic, pursued a pro-integration strategy based on preferential relations with Berlin. However, the Berlusconi government—well before the Iraq debate came to a head—had been attempting to build up preferential relations with the UK and Spain. This reassessment paved the way for the emergence of an "Atlantic Europe" perceived as a counterweight to continental Europe.

This turning point in Italy's European priorities further encouraged the pro-U.S. offensive conducted largely by Berlusconi himself, both as head of the executive and as interim foreign minister until the end of 2002. The need to send an unambiguous message across the Atlantic in the hectic aftermath of 9/11 appeared to vindicate the priority assigned to the U.S. connection. In this climate, a small but rather diverse group of openly neo-Atlanticist intellectuals and opinion makers has emerged.[15] This group has been using arguments that are quite dismissive of Europe's international weight, openly favoring a close alignment with Washington that, at times, appears even more "British" than Blair's approach. The underlying notion is that the pro-EU policy of previous Italian governments had failed to promote key national interests.

What we may call Italy's "new Atlanticism" also had the effect of putting the center-left opposition on the defensive, thus shattering the hopes for a bipartisan consensus on foreign and security policy. This rift became evident in early 2003 with the failure to ensure the opposition's support for the renewal of the mission in Afghanistan, which involved the dispatch of a 1,000-strong contingent of Italian mountain troops.

In 2001–2002, the new Atlanticist line evolved around the strong support for the United States in the fight against global terrorism and was supported by practical efforts at intensifying antiterrorist activities, including in the EU area of justice and home affairs. As long as this remained the focus of Italy's action, the government faced little risk domestically while it gained somewhat internationally. In addition, various initiatives mostly centered on the prime minister himself were pursued to raise Italy's profile in foreign policy, giving that policy a marked personal-diplomacy character. The Berlusconi government has sought to project an image of unusual international activism, particularly in cultivating relations with Russia and in advocating a more forthcoming EU policy on the issue of Turkey's accession process. Although one might question or suspend judgment on the long-term impact of some high-visibility declaratory policies and events—such as the proposal first announced in October 2001 of a "Marshall Plan" for Palestine or the hosting of the NATO-Russia ceremony at Pratica di Mare in May 2002—other instances of international cooperation are of real consequence. The presence of Italian troops in Afghanistan, for example, is a tangible sign of Italy's active contribution to a very demanding multinational operation.

Thus, according to the advocates of this new Atlanticist line, a strong partnership with the United States should serve as the anchor of the country's entire strategy. Only a solid link to Washington enables Rome to play a self-confident role in the diplomatic big league, including on the European scene. The problem with this strategy is that the domestic consensus it demands is, at best, untested, beginning with the governing coalition itself. The recent policy shift is thus constantly in danger of collapsing.

Given this political uncertainty and in light of Italy's legacy of caution—the search for a balance among the Atlantic Alliance, the EU, and the UN's legitimizing role—it is all the more remarkable that the prime minister has openly stated his support, even if only in principle, for preemptive interventions, arguably the most contentious of the Bush administration's post-9/11 security policies. Admittedly, argued Berlusconi in response to Bush's West Point speech of June 1, 2002, "the choice of preemption should be made in a cautious and judicious manner." However, the prime minister added, "particularly after September 11, the precautionary principle has assumed two faces on the international scene: one can be incautious due to excessive haste, but also, if one moves on to necessary action late, too late."[16] Given the strong criticism preemption has attracted in Europe and elsewhere, this rather favorable Italian assessment of official U.S. policy is telling.

Initially, the pro-American attitude developed by the Berlusconi government in the wake of 9/11 did not carry any significant consequences, but it assumed a different meaning once the transatlantic and intra-European discussions over the Iraq intervention turned sour. Between September 2002 and March 2003, when Italy was forced to clarify its stance vis-à-vis the new U.S. priorities, the Italian decision—culminating in Italy's inclusion among the signatories of the NATO members' Letter of Eight—was made in favor of Atlantic Europe.[17] Indeed, Italy's decision was an important choice because if Italian support went to the Franco-German position—as argued by the opposition and part of the antiwar camp—the EU's founding members would have been united in opposing the U.S. decision to go to war against Iraq.

By acting otherwise, Berlusconi has unmistakably positioned Italy outside the mainstream European fold—a commitment that is hard to keep given domestic criticisms. Hence the almost desperate need, until the very last minute, for an explicit UN Security Council resolution authorizing an attack against Iraq, also as a basis for reconciling European positions along the way.

The central concept guiding the government's policy can be summed up in the words of Foreign Minister Franco Frattini in a February 2003 speech at the French Parliamentary Assembly—the very heart of Old Europe:

> Each European country has, after all, a distinctive "instinct" in foreign policy: this reality complicates, as we have seen in recent months, the search for common positions; but it can also represent an enriching element for the overall foreign policy of the Union. The underlying instinct of Italy's diplomacy, and its distinctive contribution to the common foreign policy, is to successfully combine European integration and Euro-Atlantic solidarity. . . .[18]

Quite obviously, the government has been walking a fine line in a most charged international and domestic climate. The breaking point was the collapse of UN Security Council diplomatic efforts in mid-March 2003, which marked the end of the constructive overlap of the transatlantic and UN dimensions that had strengthened the government's argument for an alignment with Washington. Indeed, in the final week of diplomatic frenzy in New York, the prime minister had gone so far as to personally characterize a hypothetical U.S.-led intervention without explicit UN Security Council authorization as an "ominous event." When that event did materialize, the government orchestrated an exit strategy that was based on lending diplomatic support to the war without contributing militarily. This was done by giving a restrictive interpretation of Article 11 of Italy's constitution, which prohibits the use of force in any international action lacking the authorization of international organizations.

With the collapse of the UN diplomatic track, a key element of the "British" line also became untenable; after a phase of proud Atlanticism in 2002, Rome seemed to revert to traditional Atlanticism, based on the formula "yes, but. . . ." This was an indication that the British option will likely remain what it has always been: a temptation. Yet alongside the government's ambiguity, the opposition, too, retreated to its earlier political tactics by voting against opening Italy's airspace and bases for U.S.-led operations in Iraq. The Iraq debate has brought the country back to a rather ideological analysis of its foreign policy interests, with mutual charges of excessive pro-Atlanticism and anti-Americanism.

The particular evolution of intra-European alignments in this specific instance also had a significant impact on the decisions made in Rome, perhaps even pushing the Berlusconi government to commit itself beyond its original intentions. To be sure, the modality of the Franco-German initiative in January 2003 (formally to prolong the inspections in Iraq but practically to oppose the United States in the UN Security Council by speaking in the name of "Europe") engendered a negative reaction.

However, given the unambiguous public opposition to the use of force against Iraq—both before and during the war—the government appears to have taken a calculated but certainly high risk in catering to the section of Italian voters in favor of a close alignment with the United States, while dismissing the antiwar opposition as a temporary phenomenon easily reversible by a quick U.S. victory. Yet, a deep-seated interest in cultivating working relations with key Arab regimes could represent additional costs to the government's decision. Italy's tangible engagement in postwar stabilization and reconstruction in Iraq—with the dispatch in June 2003 of an almost 3,000-strong contingent in addition to humanitarian assistance and a field hospital in Baghdad—is partly motivated by the will to emphasize the constructive nature of the pro-American stance taken by the government.

LIFE AFTER IRAQ: REALIGNING EUROPE

There are two possible interpretations of the intra-European spat over Iraq: both are plausible and equally hard to verify. The first is that the 2002–2003 crisis was a trigger for a fundamental realignment that had been delayed for more than a decade but is now under way. In this perspective, the end of the Cold War structure has made the old transatlantic–intra-European bargain untenable, together with the mutual images of the United States and Europe that accompanied it. The disappearance of a straightforward unifying security threat, Germany's evolving role on the international scene, the advances in EU integration, the EU and NATO enlargements, the reorientation of U.S. strategic priorities—all these elements have combined to alter the cost-benefit analysis for each of the allies. The 9/11 earthquake may thus have been the final blow of an already crumbling deal within the West.

If this is the case, the Iraqi crisis has brought to the fore the reality of a fragmented Europe trying to deal with a traumatized, yet reenergized, America in search of a whole new system to increase its level of security. The realignment is inevitable because Europe is divided on the central issue of what should be the overall relationship with the United States. When forced to choose, it appears that Continental Europe places the priority on EU integration and coordination, whereas Atlantic Europe—also referred to as "rimland Europe"—places the priority on hard security and the U.S. connection, thus finding itself more in tune with Washington's approach.

More specifically, the countries of Europe's South—Italy, Spain, and Portugal—share with Britain a concern over current security trends in the Greater Middle East and worry about an excessive shift in the EU's center of gravity to the Northeast. Together with London, they also believe that only a transatlantic strategy can realistically help shape the future of this large and diverse region—even more so in the aftermath of the Iraq War than before. As a consequence, cooperation with the United States, however difficult, is a prerequisite for effectiveness and a primary security interest in itself, much more relevant than any theological discussion on "status" between the United States and France.

Thus according to a first interpretation of the recent intra-European rift, the structural shift currently under way is pitting a neo-Gaullist vision of Europe—whose character is defined by its differences with the United States—against a neo-Atlanticist vision, according to which the security framework for a more active Europe remains the transatlantic alliance. Yet, such an interpretation of the debate over Iraq presumes a high level of strategic coherence in the behavior of all parties involved. If we are to take into account other factors, such as short-term political expedience or the leaders' personalities, the picture looks quite different.

At some risk of oversimplifying, both the French and the British positions on the Iraq debate are fundamentally rooted in a rather predictable and well-understood conception of their respective national interests. By comparison, the Italian and (possibly) the German positions reflect primarily the inclinations of each country's current government majority. In other words, under different domestic circumstances their positions might have been substantially different.

If this analysis is correct—at least with respect to Italy—we can trace a deep-seated motivation for the rather contingent politics of foreign policy witnessed over Iraq: the lack of a solid bipartisan tradition in foreign policy and a shared understanding of the main national interests. Here we return to our initial point that the (image of the) United

States is truly a domestic factor, affecting Italy's internal political configuration and the Italian "politics of identity."

Prime Minister Berlusconi's choice to play an American card in dealing with his fellow European leaders is based on the firm belief that raising Italy's profile in a Europe currently in flux requires a preferential relationship with the United States. The motivations are manifold: cultural admiration for the United States and the "liberal" leanings (in a European sense) of some elements within the coalition government, particularly Defense Minister Antonio Martino; Berlusconi's repeated personal difficulties within the EU in the absence of strong ties with either the German chancellor or the French president; and an overall political penchant for berating Europe's limitations in the context of the very open debate on the EU's institutional arrangements. Although this is far from a uniquely Italian phenomenon under broad conditions of diffuse Euroskepticism, a certain aloofness toward the EU is perhaps the most consequential difference between the current center-right government and its center-left predecessors, as well as the Christian Democratic tradition of Italian foreign policy. The primary allegiance seems to be to the West, not to Europe. This constitutes a major break with long-standing diplomatic practice, especially when it comes alongside a recurring effort to extol the virtues of the Anglo-Saxon model and a conservative platform on various domestic issues.

In fact, the shift in emphasis has been controversial among Italy's professional diplomats who, for decades, have been the custodians of the concentric-circles theory—seeing the solemn-commitments-to-the-EU circle and the transatlantic circle as perfectly compatible and in permanent balance. It is certainly no accident that as long as a more cohesive Europe remains compatible with a strong Atlantic community, squaring the foreign policy circle is possible while addressing most Italian concerns. Italy has committed itself to help heal the rift, presenting its mediation efforts as a great service to the transatlantic cause. The task, however, becomes daunting if the temptation to equate Europe with "un-America" prevails.

This softer, more contingent representation of Rome's stance on Iraq also helps explain the signs of moderation in Prime Minister Berlusconi's declaratory policy that followed the formal end of hostilities in Iraq. The markedly pro-American line, centered on post-9/11 solidarity, was already becoming increasingly difficult to maintain in the context of a war that was waged without a UN mandate and of a public that remained distrustful of U.S. motivations in waging that war. With the Vatican totally opposed to the war, the Catholic forces within the government coalition, as well as the rightist Alleanza Nazionale (which has virtually no Atlanticist credentials), began to press for moderation— taking stock of the gulf that had developed between the official line and the vast majority of public opinion. Italy's rotating presidency of the EU in the latter part of 2003 was thus seen in early summer 2003 as a perfect opportunity to try to fix the relationship between Europe's two opposite camps during the Iraq War.

With Pope John Paul II condemning the war and the president of the republic—in his capacity as custodian of the constitutional order— calling for full respect of the ban on war enshrined in Article 11 of the constitution, the potential weaknesses of a proactive security policy had become evident. The natural tendency was, therefore, to find refuge in the well-tested old Atlanticism: cautious, EU-friendly, and perhaps less able to meet the Bush administration's expectations. After all, this is a challenge shared by most Europeans most of the time.

Beyond Italy's specific views and perspectives, a central lesson of the Iraqi crisis must certainly be that questioning the solidity of the transatlantic link in security affairs tends—at least in the short term—to divide Europeans instead of uniting them in common opposition to the United States. While there is indeed a common concern with, and possibly even a common interest in, constraining Washington, there is, as yet, no Europe-wide consensus when it comes to laying the foundation for a distinctively European international stance.

In honesty, part of the responsibility for the crisis in transatlantic and intra-European relations lies with the Bush administration:[19] the unilateralist overtones of U.S. diplomacy have had the regrettable effect of stimulating a sort of Franco-German unilateralism within Europe because the terms of a unified European response to Washington's pressures had not been negotiated in advance. This offers an image of the Euro-American world at its worst: not a functioning security community but instead a fractured alliance, complicated by a bid for intra-European leadership by the Franco-German couple on essentially Gaullist premises. Admittedly, a more careful U.S. diplomacy might have avoided an unnecessary escalation of the dispute. The fact is, however, that a lid could not be kept forever on the deeper, unresolved problems of the transatlantic deal inherited from the Cold War and only marginally adjusted in the 1990s.

When Italians set their sights beyond the Alps, what they see is a paramount transatlantic space forming the preferred framework of Italian foreign and security policy. Even with the growing importance of the European space—from monetary union to issues of justice and home affairs to the embryonic security and defense policy—the transatlantic link remains crucial to the promotion of Italy's primary interests for two main reasons: the reliability of the unique security community enshrined in NATO, which until very recently was still seen as the best guarantee of Italian security particularly to the South and Southeast; and the unreliability of an exclusively European arrangement based on a *directoire* that, in whatever form, is bound to permanently question Italy's standing as coleader in European affairs. A divided Europe is not in Italy's interests, but as long as the multinational leadership of a more cohesive Europe does not adequately guarantee Italy's full inclusion, a contested U.S. leadership is seen as a preferable option.

To be sure, a U.S. administration that views ad hoc coalitions as the most practical solution also seriously undermines the role and reliability of NATO. The systematic adoption of ad hoc coalitions as the main mechanism of Euro-Atlantic action would force a long series of controversial debates in Italy, with major domestic reverberations including a wider gulf between the center-right and center-left, and also put great strain on the internal cohesion of both political groupings. In other words, the disaggregation of Europe could also mean the disaggregation of Italian foreign policy as we know it.

If Italy wishes to preserve the Atlantic link on broader foundations than the purely bilateral relationship (which remains domestically fragile), the practical elements of the transatlantic deal will have to be rethought and restructured. We suspect that without a new agreement on this overarching issue between the major European countries and the United States, all efforts at fence mending are bound to fail. After looking to Washington with great conviction, Italy may start looking again to Brussels.

Notes

[1] Ennio Di Nolfo, *La Repubblica delle speranze degli inganni. L'Italia dalla caduta del fascismo al crollo della Democrazia Cristiana* (Florence: Ponte alle Grazie, 1996).

[2] Massimo Teodori, *Maledetti americani. Destra, sinistra e cattolici: storia del pregiudizio antiamericano* (Milan: Mondadori, 2002).

[3] Pier Paolo D'Attorre, "Sogno americano e mito sovietico nell'Italia contemporanea," in *Nemici per la pelle. Sogno americano e mito sovietico nell'Italia contemporanea*, ed. Pier Paolo D'Attore (Milan: Angeli, 1991), pp. 15–68.

[4] At least in some instances, the historical record partly confirms the perception of a deliberate exercise of U.S. influence on the Italian domestic debate. See, for example, Leopoldo Nuti, "The Role of the U.S. in Italy's Foreign Policy," *International Spectator* 1 (2003): 91–101.

[5] Sergio Romano, *Lo scambio ineguale. Italia e Stati Uniti da Wilson a Clinton* (Rome; Bari: Laterza, 1995).

[6] Di Nolfo, *La Repubblica delle speranze*.

[7] See, in particular, Alessandro Silj, ed., *L'alleato scomodo. I rapporti fra Roma e Washington nel Mediterraneo: Sigonella e Gheddafi* (Milan: Corbaccio, 1998).

[8] In practice, the parliamentary majority that voted to support Italy's military contribution to Operation Allied Force was different from the governing majority.

[9] In an interview after the Iraq War, Prime Minister Berlusconi stated this logic of intra-European (re)balancing in very explicit terms: "In foreign policy we have clear guidelines. We ally ourselves with the U.S. and belong to a Europe which must no longer be subordinate to decisions that were once made only in *Mitteleuropa*, by the countries of Central Europe." (*La Repubblica*, April 24, 2003, p. 7.)

[10] Pierangelo Isernia, "Meno antiamericani di altri," *Aspenia* 19 (2002): 242–263.

[11] The rate of approval for the United States was around 75 percent on the eve of 9/11 compared with an average rate of 65 percent in the period 1952–2002.

[12] The German Marshall Fund and the Chicago Council on Foreign Relations, "European Public Opinion and Foreign Policy," in *Worldviews 2002*; released on September 4, 2002; available at www.worldviews.org/key_findings/transatlantic_report.htm (June 3, 2003).

[13] *Views of A Changing World 2003* (Washington, D.C.: Pew Research Center for the People and the Press, June 3, 2003), http://people-press.org/reports/display.php3?ReportID=185.

[14] See, for instance, Renato Mannheimer, "Un Italiano su quattro 'giustifica' Bin Laden," *Corriere della Sera*, October 22, 2001.

[15] These include Giuliano Ferrara, the editor of the conservative daily *Il Foglio* and an informal adviser to Berlusconi; journalists such as Carlo Rossella; Gianni De Michelis, a former Socialist foreign minister; and such unique cases as war correspondent and novelist Oriana Fallaci, who has suddenly become a favorite of some neoconservative circles in Washington and New York after her highly passionate pro-U.S. call to arms following 9/11.

[16] *Il Foglio*, September 11, 2002, p.1

[17] "United We Stand," *Wall Street Journal*, January 30, 2003.

[18] "Ciascun paese europeo mantiene, in fondo, un suo specifico "istinto" in politica estera: questa realtà rende complicata, come abbiamo visto in questi mesi, la ricerca di posizioni comuni; ma può costituire anche un elemento di ricchezza per l'insieme della politica estera dell'Unione. L'istinto di fondo della diplomazia italiana, l'apporto specifico dell'Italia alla politica estera comune, è di riuscire a combinare integrazione europea e coesione euro-atlantica (. . .)." (Authors' translation), www.esteri.it/attualita/2003/ita/interventi/index.htm (June 3, 2003).

[19] Most moderates across the Italian political spectrum recognize that various levels are at work: short-term difficulties due to the particular policies of the current U.S. administration, traditional differences in perspective between the two sides of the Atlantic, and ongoing structural changes. A good example is Giuliano Amato (interview), "Gli Stati Uniti che abbiamo. E quelli di cui abbiamo bisogno," *Aspenia* 19 (2002): 10–19.

NINE

THROUGH RUSSIAN EYES AND MINDS
POST–9/11 PERCEPTIONS OF AMERICA AND ITS POLICIES

Dmitri Trenin

Attitudes toward the United States and its policies play a dual role in Russia. On the one hand, they reflect the kind of country Russia (i.e., its leaders, its elites, and its people) wants to be. On the other hand, they reflect the Russians' perception of their own place and role in world affairs. In Soviet times, the United States was the one country the Russians routinely used as a benchmark. America was setting the standard to which the Russians usually aspired. The United States was often laying down the rules of competition. Rivaling the United States on the principal parameters of national power, especially in the military field, was the official policy goal. At the same time, there was obviously no wish to emulate America's democracy, its market system, or its societal organization. The Soviet leaders wanted the USSR to be at least as strong on the Cold War battlefield as the United States, but they were generally uninterested in U.S. domestic institutions. In short, America was "the other"—foreign, alien, and yet the one to be constantly measured against.

The Soviet people generally were far from hostile toward the United States. The two sides had never gone to war against each other, U.S. military intervention—a couple of skirmishes that left virtually no scars—in the Russian North and in Siberia during the 1918–1920 Russian civil war notwithstanding. Indeed, a half century earlier, during America's civil war, Russia had sent warships to New York and San Francisco in a gesture of support for the Union. In both world wars, the United States and (Soviet) Russia fought on the same side. Their combined forces on the Elbe in late April 1945 marked the triumph of the anti-Hitler coalition. During the Cold War that followed soon after, the Soviets learned to know—and appreciate—Americans even better.

In fact, both Communist ideology and Soviet propaganda were making a clear distinction between the American bourgeoisie and the working masses. While the former was considered a class enemy, the latter was a friend and potential ally. Of course, there was never any illusion about a socialist revolution in the United States, but hatred of America and Americans as such was virtually absent in the Soviet Union. Moreover, there was a genuine recognition of the United States' technological prowess, its business acumen, and its consumer-oriented economy. As the Soviet system started to decline, America as a model began to look attractive, even natural. Post-Soviet Russia originally sought to achieve a double feat, remaining a fellow superpower to the United States while borrowing U.S. institutions for their subsequent transplantation onto Russian soil. The early reformers soon failed on both counts. Not only was the "friendly bi-hegemony" a pipe dream, but U.S. political and social importations fared badly in the rough and intemperate Russian climate. Indeed, the reformers, dubbed romantics, had to admit, to quote the title of a popular (and virulently anti-American) book, that "Russia is not America."[1]

The disenchantment of the mid-1990s prompted a new approach, which soon evolved into the mainstream. Proponents of this new attitude argued that the United States had become too strong, as evidenced by its intervention in the Balkans, its continued post–Gulf War harassment of the Baghdad regime, and especially its deep penetration into territories only recently controlled by the Soviet Union—Eastern Europe and former Soviet republics from Ukraine to Uzbekistan. As a result, the United States had displaced Russia as the dominant power in Eurasia. The crunch came in 1999, with the U.S.-led NATO war against Yugoslavia. This sudden and massive imbalance was a clear challenge to Russia, most politicians and pundits agreed. The problem was how to deal with it, given Russia's weakness and internal incoherence.

There was never a question of Russia confronting U.S. power single-handedly. Moreover, Moscow was not alone in fearing the consequences of U.S. global domination and military interference. Thus, it appeared possible to create a "coalition of the resentful," under the general rubric of a multipolar world, with the purpose of limiting and possibly resisting American hegemony. President Boris Yeltsin himself, a self-declared friend of the United States and clearly opposed to any new confrontation, saw merit in efforts to restrain U.S. expansionism. Yeltsin's cultivation of the Chinese leadership from 1996 onward is a testimony of this attitude.

The shock and awe of Russia's early economic transition and its mixed results were blamed on the team of reformers devoted to the precepts of the Chicago school. The 1998 financial collapse was blamed, in part, on the government for following the advice of the International Monetary Fund (IMF) and the so-called Washington consensus. By the end of the 1990s, American institutions were pronounced unfit for direct transplantation, and it became fashionable to call for a better use of both Russia's own experience with modernization and reform in the nineteenth and twentieth centuries and the experience of Western Europe, now deemed closer to Russia than faraway America.

While the domestic recommendations made some sense, the international implications of a multipolar strategy were sending Russia's foreign policy straight into a dead end. However, the pull appeared irresistible. The Russian elites, who only a decade earlier were roundly hailing America as the new model, were now exhibiting various degrees of anti-Americanism.

In the early twenty-first century, attitudes toward the United States remain crucial for Russian domestic transformation and, even more so, Russian foreign policy. Like everyone else, Russia will have to learn to live in a U.S.-dominated world. The outcome of this learning process will shape Russia's place and role in the emerging world order. This chapter will examine the main conditions and parameters driving this process. It will start with the presidency, consistent with the view, deeply held in Russia, that foreign policy in general, and relations with the United States in particular, are the "privilege of the czar" (whatever the czar's current title). The following section will focus on the elites, or various vested interests, whose role is of key and growing importance in the formulation of Russian foreign policy. Public opinion, another important barometer of Russia's state of mind, although limited in its impact on a quasi democracy such as Russia, is also considered.

THE PRESIDENT

President Vladimir Putin is credited with an ability to be in the right place at the right time. On September 11, 2001, he lost no time in appearing on Russian television to show his indignation at what had happened a few hours earlier in New York and Washington and to express solidarity with the United States in the global war on terrorism. That the fight against international terrorism had also been the official Russian justification for the second Chechen campaign, launched by Putin two years earlier when he was prime minister, was not incidental in the president's reaction. For Putin and his security and defense colleagues, international terrorism and Islamic fundamentalism have always been issues that extended beyond Chechnya.[2] For years, Russian leaders had been trying to convince the West that Russia was waging an antiterrorist campaign in the North Caucasus, not a colonial war. Now at last, from the Kremlin's point of view, the United States was joining Russia in the fight against a common enemy, and President George W. Bush was hailed as Putin's comrade-in-arms.

This had important and wide-ranging implications. September 11, 2001, changed the course of Russian foreign policy by giving Russia's second president a powerful and long-sought reason to dispense with the image of the United States as an adversary, which seemed to frustrate his presidency's central project. Ever since coming to office on New Year's Eve 2000, Putin has been pursuing a modernization agenda. In his celebrated "millennium article," published just days before he assumed the Russian presidency, Putin clearly stated that, whatever Russia's problems, they were of domestic origin and not to be explained away by some "foreign conspiracy."[3] The residual confrontation with the United States, implicit in the multipolar concept, had not only lost all rationale for Russia; from the new president's perspective, it was an obstacle to be overcome.

As prime minister during the high-intensity phase of the second Chechen war in the fall of 1999, Putin refused to be provoked into a verbal confrontation with the Clinton administration over the Russian federal forces' strong-arm tactics in the rebellious province. Even as Russia's relations with the West had reached their post–Cold War nadir (as a consequence of both Kosovo and Chechnya), Prime Minister Putin was praising the White House for upholding the principle of Russia's territorial integrity while totally ignoring Washington's criticism of Moscow's methods of upholding that principle. Putin's early policy toward the United States could thus be summarized as "no confrontation with the United States." Soon it went beyond that.

The secretary general of NATO at that time, Lord Robertson, was among the first Western dignitaries to visit Moscow. The visit, less than two months into Putin's acting presidency and which took place against the preferences of the Russian military establishment still reeling after the 1999 Kosovo crisis, essentially normalized relations between Russia and the Atlantic Alliance, traditionally viewed in Moscow as the prime instrument of U.S. policy in Europe. The Putin-Robertson meeting of February 2000 also launched a process that went beyond mere normalization of relations and represented a genuine attempt at positive cooperation between Russia and the U.S.-led alliance.

Robertson's landmark visit to Russia was succeeded, in short order, by that of the UK prime minister, Tony Blair. As Robertson's former boss and Clinton's close friend, Blair assumed the task of bridge building between Russia's new leader and the leadership of the West. In doing so, he followed the hallowed tradition of British leaders like Harold Macmillan, Harold Wilson, and Margaret Thatcher, who during the Cold War had sometimes functioned as facilitators of the political dialogue between Washington and Moscow. Putin appreciated the help offered by London, which he, like most Russian foreign policy experts, regarded as a gateway to the White House.

Putin's personal need in reaching out to Washington should not go unstated. At the start of his presidency, which had come so unexpectedly to him and to everybody else, Putin clearly craved recognition and acceptance as a fellow world leader, a peer among peers of the exclusive G-8. That recognition, he understood, could be granted only by the United States. As a true pragmatist, however, Putin chose not to invest too heavily in the relationship with the outgoing Clinton administration, and he waited for the results of the 2000 U.S. elections. When George W. Bush was eventually pronounced the winner of the 2000 race, the Kremlin started lobbying hard for an early U.S.-Russian summit. After months of indifference on the part of Washington, a brief Bush-Putin encounter was indeed organized in Slovenia in June 2001. The Russian president, eschewing the nuances of negotiations, saw in this his chance to establish a one-to-one relationship with the newly elected president. In the end, the summit proved a greater success than Putin must have hoped for. Bush's comment at the conclusion of the summit that he had "looked into [Putin's] soul" and found the Russian president trustworthy has become one of the better-known quotations of recent diplomatic history.

Meanwhile, on the domestic front, Vladimir Putin launched a major economic reform initiative in 2000, even as he sought to consolidate power and prosecute the war in Chechnya. His first and second annual messages to the Federal Assembly (in 2000 and 2001) placed overwhelming emphasis on Russia's domestic needs and outlined a bold reform agenda. In that context, foreign policy was logically defined as a resource for Russia's internal development, rather than the other way around as had been in the Soviet case.

Putin's early plans for optimizing the military establishment, designed and deployed to confront the United States in a World War III scenario, came in the summer and fall of 2000 as a logical consequence of the economic restructuring agenda drafted by Minister of Economic Development and Trade German Gref. In an unprecedented protracted public dispute between Defense Minister Igor Sergeyev and Chief of the General Staff Anatoly Kvashnin over the future of the Russian military establishment, Putin finally sided with Kvashnin, who had advocated a military force essentially designed for local conflicts along Russia's southern periphery. Putin sacked Sergeyev, who was still clinging to a notion of strategic parity with the United States. In the spring of 2001, the Strategic Rocket Forces, the once-proud symbol of Soviet military might and the most powerful argument for U.S.-Soviet equality, ceased to exist as a separate (and de facto senior) service, and drastic cuts in its strength were announced. In the summer of the same year, Putin decided to close the two remaining Soviet-era military outposts overseas, the Cam Ranh Bay naval facility in Vietnam and the Lourdes intelligence-gathering station in Cuba. The latter was a clear signal to the United States that the Russian security agenda had fundamentally changed.

This brief overview of Putin's foreign policy from January 2000 to September 11, 2001, confirms that the Russian president did not suddenly change heart on September 11. Instead, he saw in the events of that day an opportunity to advance his already formed agenda. Incremental changes during the previous 20 months gave Putin a good basis from which to leapfrog ahead. The overriding goal was integrating Russia into the West. The result was a new quality in the U.S.-Russian relationship. This, however, was not an easy feat to perform. In his effort to proceed from an outdated great-power vision of the country to a more modern worldview, Putin had to endure the elites' general unwillingness to welcome and sustain the new momentum.

THE ELITES

In Russia, the political class—they like to call themselves the elite—is essentially composed of persons who have risen through the Soviet system. This is especially true of those involved with conceptualizing, deciding, and implementing foreign, security, and defense policy. These people have by and large shed Communist ideology (which had been ringing hollow even in Leonid Brezhnev's time), but they have mostly remained faithful to the centuries-old great-power mentality. To them, Russia has always been a thing apart, a Eurasia, essentially unfit for Putin's integrationist ideas. This mentality had important implications for the president's new vision.

Putin proclaimed Russia on the side of the United States within hours of the terrorist attacks on New York and Washington. It took him ten days, however, to enter into a true coalition with the United States, complete with material support for U.S. forces in Afghanistan and accepting their presence in the former Soviet South—Central Asia and the Caucasus. To do that, Putin had to overrule Russia's entire foreign policy and defense establishment, whose chiefs had been publicly speaking against U.S. military presence in the Commonwealth of Independent States (CIS).

The establishment's attitude, expressed by Putin's trusted lieutenants, was rooted in a closely held belief that the entire post-Soviet space had to remain, a decade after the Soviet Union's demise, a sort of an exclusive strategic preserve of Russia. Under the national security concept and the military doctrine, both signed by Putin in 2000 but prepared at the end of the Yeltsin presidency, deployment of third-party military forces in the newly independent states (NIS) as well as alliance relations between those states and a third party (which in both cases really meant the West) were treated as security threats to Russia. Even in a much-weakened country, great-power instincts continued to be strong.

The elites also resented Putin's implicit recognition of U.S. primacy in world affairs. They had been visibly sulking over the loss of Russia's former superpower status under the Soviet Union. While Cold War–style parity between the two former rivals had ceased to be sustainable even in the late Gorbachev years, the notion of being a junior partner to the United States was difficult to accept. Bandwagoning was never an option. Rather than joining the United States in some kind of unequal partnership, the Russian elites preferred to engage in balancing acts, entering into coalitions with other international players to offset U.S. power and influence. Acting against the United States, even in a coalition with regimes of doubtful international reputation, was psychologically more comfortable to the members of the Russian establishment than joining the U.S. camp as a junior ally.

The default position of the elites was most eloquently and consistently advocated by Yevgeni Primakov in his posts as director of Russia's Foreign Intelligence Service, foreign minister, and prime minister. In Primakov's view, Russia was (and is) a great power among other centers of power in the world, including the United States, the European Union, China, Japan, and India. The United States may be a primus inter pares, but its hegemony, or dominance, was regarded as unacceptable and even inimical to the interests of other powers, especially those not aligned with the United States, such as Russia, China, and possibly India. According to that logic, to prevent the emergence of a unipolar, U.S.-centered world, Russia would have to join forces with other willing power centers to restore international equilibrium. This was the essence of the multipolarity doctrine that prevailed during the second Yeltsin presidency and has not been forgotten.

As long as Putin showed resolve to chart a different course, the elites followed reluctantly. Not one among the high-level officials who doubted the wisdom of siding squarely with the United States deemed it wise to publicly oppose the president after he had made his decision. Not one among them has been sacked by Putin, either. Thus, the chief was unchallenged, but his troops remained unconvinced. As a result, the elite followed as long as Putin was willing and able to lead, and he took the political class a long way indeed—from the acceptance of U.S. withdrawal from the Anti-Ballistic Missile (ABM) Treaty in late 2001, to Russia's acquiescence to the presence of U.S. military personnel in Georgia in early 2002, to the lack of response over the 2002 invitation to the Baltic states to join NATO. Meanwhile, frustrations within the elite were rising.

True, during the 15-month honeymoon in U.S.-Russian relations, roughly from September 2001 through January 2003, a large number of senior politicians, opinion leaders, and establishment journalists in Russia routinely criticized the new rapprochement with Washington. Since this was often done by means of government-owned or Kremlin-controlled electronic media, questions were raised about Putin's credibility or, alternatively, the sustainability of his course. In the winter and spring of 2002, the Russian media czars launched a particularly vicious anti-American hysteria in connection with the corruption scandals and the overall dismal performance of Russian athletes in the Salt Lake City Winter Olympics. Eventually, Putin himself had to intervene in order for the hysterics to be turned down.

However, Putin's apparent success in handling elite resentment had an underside. He had failed to explain to his associates and the broader elite groups why he had consistently refused to pick fights with the United States. Instead of laying out a strategy of integration with all its related conditions and obligations but also its vision of a modernized Russia as an integral part of a "new West" or "the North," Putin allowed the internal discussion to be reduced to the issue of quid pro quo. This was a losing proposition.

Naturally, the elite, accustomed as they were to trade-offs and instant swaps, constantly demanded U.S. counterconcessions on a wide range of issues. They made no secret that they operated on the principle of "I give if you give," a principle they viewed as the only fair and durable tenet of any foreign policy. Because of his apparent failure to produce the required quid pro quo, Putin was becoming a feeble figure before his associates, almost a latter-day Gorbachev (an especially vicious accusation in the eyes of the elite and probably of Putin himself). Apparently, Moscow's secret probing during 2002 and early 2003 regarding Washington's willingness to protect Russian interests in Iraq in exchange for Russia's tacit support for a U.S.-led military operation had come to nothing. No assurances on the Iraqi debt repayment and the Russian oil contracts had been offered before the Iraq War began. That could have been the straw to break the Russian camel's back. In the end, Putin himself may have begun doubting the effectiveness of his no-contest course.

It has been important that the mutual empathy of the two presidents, which by and large survived the Iraq War crisis, has not been supported by close interaction at the elite level. Very few senior Russian politicians or top bureaucrats enjoy easy access to U.S. politicians or officials. Even fewer can speak English. Contacts between the State Duma and the U.S. Congress are stilted. The Russian business community is yet to be accepted into the world business elite. There is not, nor is there likely to emerge, anything like a Russian lobby in the United States. All this makes the relationship rather shallow and distant.

The U.S. refusal to make a deal on Iraq with Russia before attacking Saddam Hussein may have been for valid reasons. Yet, it is also true that after September 11 the Bush administration made no serious attempt to reach out to the Russians as part of a long-term agenda. This was not an omission but a reflection of the ad hoc nature of U.S.-led coalitions. Partnership between the United States and Russia was repeatedly proclaimed, but it remained largely at the level of diplomatic communiqués. Having lost its centrality to Washington as a geostrategic problem, Russia did not arouse much U.S. interest afterward as a partner. When Russia's high-level emissaries traveled to the White House armed with lists of complaints and demands ranging from U.S. steel quotas to Russian interests in Afghanistan, those complaints were usually waved away.

Evidently, the United States believed it owed Russia nothing. After all, had Washington not toned down its criticism of the war in Chechnya, played alongside Moscow on the issue of terrorist presence in Georgia's Pankisi Gorge, recognized Russia as a market economy, and, above all, eliminated in one stroke the most serious threat to Russian-CIS military security posed by the Taliban regime in Afghanistan? Was that not more than enough U.S. quid for the Russian quo—all the more so as the Russian so-called concessions were not really that? Besides, could Moscow have really prevented U.S. troop deployments to Central Asia, or the Baltic states' membership in NATO, or the U.S. withdrawal from the ABM Treaty? Russia could have chosen to oppose Washington on each of those issues and would have certainly lost, at a heavy price for Russia itself.

This argumentation may ring true, but it fails to address a larger question: did the United States need Russia as a serious partner for the long haul in the post-9/11 environment? Assuming it did, what would be the realistic terms of that partnership? How would Russia be best integrated into the U.S.-led system? What means and mechanisms were to be used? These questions were never answered, assuming they were asked at all.

Not everyone in Russia, of course, was ready to accept integration even on the best of terms. A much smaller, less advanced, but rather vocal section of the elite was led by geopolitical and ideological rather than pragmatic and material considerations. To them, the United States under the George W. Bush administration had overstepped the limits of what was acceptable even for the world's only remaining superpower. Their view was that leaving the Bush administration unopposed on the Iraq issue, at a time when the vast majority of U.N. member states, the European public, and a significant part of U.S. opinion was either opposed to or highly skeptical of the military operation, would make it far more difficult to deal with the United States later, when the administration might take on the two remaining links of the "axis of evil," Iran and North Korea. Thus, Iraq promised to turn out to be larger than Iraq.

In comparison with Iraq, Russian vested interests in Iran (among them the nuclear industry and the defense industry) are much stronger and enjoy powerful political support. These interests will be most reluctant to leave Iran, even under intense U.S. pressure. Not even U.S. promises of cooperation to offset the losses in Iran would satisfy many Russian players. Russia as a nation may be compensated (after all, the worth of the Bushehr nuclear reactor project is a mere $800 million), but not necessarily the individual players. Notably, the one area where Putin in 2000 distinguished himself from Yeltsin's earlier commitments to the United States was Iran. Since then, official prospects for Russian-Iranian nuclear energy cooperation have broadened. Even as Moscow is expressing growing unease over nuclear weapons proliferation, it is not prepared to sacrifice what it regards as legitimate nuclear-energy contracts. In the near- to medium-term future, Iran is a very serious problem for U.S.-Russian relations.

Among the Russian government institutions, the State Duma—the lower house of parliament, with a strong Communist and nationalist representation—traditionally has taken a hard line on the United States. A skeptic at best with regard to U.S. policy motives, a critic of most U.S. geopolitical moves, the Duma has become the principal institutional source of suspicion vis-à-vis the United States. Its platform and the parliamentary elections offer wide possibilities for populist exploitation of the great-power complexes of both the elite and the public. Having won overall control over Russia's parliament, Putin has been content to let the Duma function as a safety valve for anti-U.S., anti-Western feelings. Among other things, the domestic hard-liners back home made Putin's negotiating position in Washington stronger.

By early 2003, as the United States was positioning itself to enforce regime change in Iraq and Russia was entering its election cycle, the elites' pressure on the Kremlin had grown in intensity. Demands that Putin adopt a harder line with regard to Washington were bolstered by a sudden hardening of the official French position and the emergence of an opposition to the United States within NATO. Surely, if the United States' own allies could afford to be so independent of Washington, the hard liners argued, Russia had no reason to duck and abstain at the United Nations. In addition, Russian government analysts were predicting a long and bloody war in Iraq rather than the quick military walkover anticipated by many in the United States. A long war would have had major repercussions across the Greater Middle East, including

Central Asia, radicalizing local Islamic movements. With some 20 million Muslims inside the Russian Federation—12 percent of the entire Russian population—Moscow was looking for ways to stay a safe distance from the United States on Iraq. In Dagestan, Chechnya's eastern neighboring republic, some 7,000 people volunteered to go to Iraq to fight Americans; a top Muslim cleric on a visit to Bashkortostan, Russia's autonomous republic near the Urals, declared jihad on the United States. Neither event proved consequential, but both are illustrative of Moscow's predicament at the time.

The Russian president could have ignored the elites' pressure, however powerful and intense; after all, he had been through similar trials before. Clearly, he must have realized that had he instructed the Russian UN ambassador to abstain during the Security Council vote, he would have made himself vulnerable to accusations of a sellout of the national interests and of kowtowing to "his friend George." However, the reason for the adjustment of Russia's foreign policy in early February 2003 probably lay elsewhere. Putin himself was starting to doubt the wisdom of his post-9/11 don't-mess-with-the-U.S. approach.

Still, all this may only be the visible part of the iceberg. However big and vocal, Russia's foreign and defense policy communities exercise limited actual powers. Nearing the end of his first presidential term, during which he has largely refrained from changing the leadership group he had inherited from his predecessor (widely rumored to have been part of the succession deal), Putin might have felt compelled to prevent anyone from accusing him of being a wimp or a patsy to the United States. If he contemplated any serious personnel changes that would alter the balance of power within the elite, he had to ensure that his would-be opponents would be in no position to make of foreign policy an instrument that they could use against him. The security community, which had eventually approved the post-9/11 shift as clever tactics, was growing increasingly wary of U.S. policies. Thus, Putin's abrupt change of policy on Iraq in early February 2003 and his move in mid-March to centralize the security community by concentrating nearly all the powers of the old KGB under the Federal Security Service, headed by a presidential loyalist, appear to be linked.

THE PUBLIC

Two years almost to the day before 9/11, Moscow was terrorized by apartment bombings attributed to Chechen terrorists. As a result of five explosions in the capital and elsewhere, some 300 people died. A year after 9/11, a theater in Moscow was seized by a Chechen commando group that held about 800 people hostage, of whom over 130 died as a result of the rescue operation. Since 2000, Palestinian-style suicide bombings have been rocking the north Caucasus, but not sparing Moscow, either. The Russians, who until the early 1990s had experienced no acts of terrorism, were suddenly learning to live with that new reality. While Chechnya remains the principal source of the new threat, the radical Islamic overtones that accompanied the second Chechen war and the presence of Arabs, Saudis, and Afghans among the Chechens have made ordinary Russians realize that, as targets, they were in the same category as the Israelis or, after September 2001, the Americans.

It is often heard in elite circles that, whereas in Soviet times most Russians were actually friendly toward the United States despite the government propaganda, nowadays the majority mostly take a negative attitude despite the official rhetoric of partnership. The argument looks appealing, leading to the conclusion that the United States wasted a historic opportunity to turn its former Communist foe into a trusting friend. NATO enlargement, the Kosovo crisis, and the Western presence on CIS territory are usually cited as reasons for new Russian negativism toward the United States.

This argument, however, reflects more accurately the elites themselves rather than the general public. From the 1960s to the 1980s, despite the propaganda that some of them helped disseminate, the elites held a positive attitude toward most things American. It was also they who had enhanced expectations for "democratic parity" and a "friendly condominium" in the wake of the Cold War's end. It was they, ultimately, who felt disappointed—starting with Gorbachev himself.

During the Soviet era, there were, of course, no public opinion polls that could be used to gauge the effectiveness of Soviet anti-imperialist propaganda. Yet, at least until the early 1980s, ordinary Russians viewed the United States as a political and ideological competitor and its military posture, above all NATO, as a clear and material threat to their country. There was no hatred for America; but the Russian public, while recognizing U.S. achievements, was far from pro-American (unlike, for example, the Poles). Indeed, opposition to NATO enlargement in the mid- to late 1990s drew much of its fervor from old-time Soviet rhetoric. As Russia entered the twenty-first century, its public's relationship with the United States showed increasing disappointment.

As opinion polls by the Public Opinion Foundation (FOM) show, just under 50 percent of Russian respondents are indifferent toward the United States.[4]

Attitude toward the United States (in %)	May 2001	September 2001	February 2002	March 2002	February 2003
Good	32	38	32	20	25
Neutral	45	47	47	46	46
Negative	17	12	17	29	25

It is interesting to compare this with a friendship index of selected foreign countries as perceived by the Russian public:[5]

Country	Mostly positive		Mostly negative		No opinion	
	1995	2002	1995	2002	1995	2002
United States	77.6	38.7	9.0	45.5	13.4	15.8
Canada	72.8	58.9	2.4	12.9	24.8	28.2
United Kingdom	76.6	64.1	4.2	14.5	19.2	21.4
France	78.9	78.0	3.0	7.1	18.1	14.9
Germany	69.0	68.1	11.5	14.9	19.5	17.0
Japan	68.5	55.3	9.2	22.3	22.3	22.4
Israel	40.8	23.7	20.4	45.9	38.8	30.4
China	41.2	42.7	21.1	30.6	37.7	26.7
India	59.4	62.8	4.8	10.2	35.8	27.0
Iraq	21.7	17.6	34.7	49.0	43.6	33.4

The above table suggests a dramatic public disappointment with cooperation with other countries in the late 1990s. Most Russians had hoped that their own lives would greatly improve and Russia's international prestige would soar after the rejection of Communism and the voluntary dismantlement of the Soviet empire and the Soviet Union itself. As it turned out, the living standards of the majority of the population plummeted (they are only now reaching the 1990 level, according to some estimates),[6] and the country's power rating, which for so many Soviets had been compensation for their dismal private situation, stood at the lowest point since the Russian civil war of the early twentieth century.

The vast majority of Russians welcomed Putin's arrival as the beginning of internal stabilization and the relative restoration of law and order. Putin's high popularity ratings since 1999 reflect people's hopes, not so much their judgment on the president's performance. Modest economic growth (almost 8 percent of GDP in 2000, more than 5.5 percent in 2001, 4.5 percent in 2002, and a similar figure expected in 2003) gave Russians slightly more confidence about their future economic prospects. The feel-better factor has positively affected the public's attitudes toward the outside world, starting with the United States.

Almost three-quarters of the Russians polled a few days after the 9/11 terrorist attacks said they felt "no satisfaction" at the sight of America suffering, but 7 percent said they strongly believed "America had deserved this," and another 15 percent said that the United States had "somewhat deserved this." September 11 brought about a surge of friendliness toward Americans. From September 2001 through February 2002, those who believed the United States to be a friendly country (38 percent) were almost equal in number to those who thought otherwise (44 percent). By September 2002, only 30 percent thought the United States was a friend, and 51 percent believed it was not. In general, just less than one-quarter of Russians think positively of the U.S. world role, against one-half who regard that role as negative. Even the U.S. operation in Afghanistan met with a mere 29 percent approval in Russia, as against 45 percent disapproval. Still, more than 40 percent would want an improved U.S.-Russian relationship, as against 13 percent who want Russia to take an anti-U.S. stand.[7] Putin was widely credited by the general public with having improved the relationship with the West in 2000–2002.

All polling figures are largely notional. Sociological surveys in Russia are new and not all are reliable. Some are expressly ordered to produce a desired result. Most Russians are relatively unconcerned about foreign affairs. What they think about the various topical issues often directly depends on the television coverage and the editorial line usually set or approved by the Kremlin. The effect is especially powerful if this resonates with Soviet-era stereotypes. Thus, in 1995–1997, the first wave of NATO enlargement was perceived by the bulk of the Russian public as a major threat. In 2001–2002, however, when NATO moved to the next stage in its enlargement process and invited the three Baltic countries to join, the Kremlin (and television) downplayed the issue, and the public remained largely unconcerned.

This was not an isolated incident. A similar metamorphosis happened with regard to the fate of the ABM Treaty. As late as summer

2001, public opinion was still agitated, in tune with the Kremlin's apparent resolve to keep the Unite States within the treaty's framework. In December 2001, however, when Putin merely "regretted" the termination of a treaty that for three decades previous had been treated as the cornerstone of strategic stability in the world, the public was quite relaxed.

Conversely, as the wars in Kosovo and in Iraq have demonstrated, media hype can result in a jump in anti-American feeling. In March 2003, just before the start of the Iraq War, 71 percent of Russians regarded the United States as a threat to world peace, as opposed to 45 percent who saw Iraq as a threat. (It is clear that some people saw both the United States and Iraq as a threat.)[8] Typical Russians would rather grumble in private than take part in demonstrations and other street actions. Spontaneous massive expression of political attitudes is simply not part of the Russian culture. The rally outside the U.S. embassy on the first day of the Iraq War attracted a mere 300 demonstrators. This gives Russian leaders formal grounds to claim that "there is no anti-Americanism in Russia"—a statement no less self-serving and wrong than the people who make such statements.

Anti-Americanism among the general public, unlike among the elites, is latent and rarely expressed in public. Only when the government decides to make use of it, for example, by means of a television-driven campaign, is the response likely to be resounding. A mix of pent-up frustration with hard life in general, envy of those who are enjoying an easy life, and wounded pride ignited by the effect of slanted television coverage may indeed result in a temporary steep rise in popular anti-American sentiment. Usually these steep rises are followed by falls, when the rage wave subsides, but the potential is there, always ready to tap into.

CONCLUSION

The Iraq crisis was a major test for the new U.S.-Russian relationship. For the first time since September 2001 the Russian leadership opposed the U.S. administration on a central policy issue. There was a real danger of reverting to the less-friendly environment predating 9/11. Yet, in the end, the Kremlin chose to recognize the reality of unilateral exercise of American power, not brace itself against it; and the elites relished being able, at last, to say "no" loudly to the United States. The Ministry of Foreign Affairs heartily engaged in a trilateral combination with

France and Germany, and the Defense Ministry used the demonstration effect of the war as an argument for more exercises and weapons modernization. The public in Russia, antiwar as elsewhere in Europe, took some satisfaction from the fact that Americans, having been so successful in the war, were later faced with familiar postwar problems from looting and oil pipeline sabotage to becoming sitting ducks for local guerillas. Comparisons with Chechnya were a welcome change from the previous shock-and-awe news coverage. From May 2003, nearly everyone on the Russian side was ready to move on beyond the disagreement with the United States on the war. Nonetheless, the Iraq crisis highlighted some very serious problems that cannot be ignored.

The U.S. rise to dominance in world affairs poses a special set of challenges to Russia, as a recent contender to the United States for international supremacy. Most Russian elites and the general public see their country through the prism of a historical continuum. The current Russian Federation is thus perceived as the latest in the line of the various incarnations of Russian statehood. It follows, then, that the Soviet Union was not another state but was a Soviet period in the historical existence of an eternal Russia. In more than style—so evident in the 2003 tercentenary celebration of St. Petersburg's founding—Putin's Russia looks more czarist than anything else.

In other words, the Russian elites and the public are still recovering from the "loss" of the Cold War. A decade after the end of the USSR, much of the emphasis is still on the losses (in terms of territory, power, and prestige) rather than on the gains (unprecedented degrees of freedom, the beginnings of a market economy, consumer society, and the prospect of the formation of a middle class and political democracy).

The United States, by contrast, is seen as primarily the winner in the competition, and a somewhat unworthy one at that, helped by a combination of ineptitude and treason on the Soviet side. The United States' post-9/11 assertiveness and the U.S. propensity to take unilateral action have not sat well with most Russians despite Putin's opening to Bush. Russians today see the United States taking over the former Soviet legacy as its Cold War booty (Eastern Europe, the NIS) and attacking or pressuring former Soviet clients (such as Iraq, North Korea, and Cuba). For most ordinary Russians, pride in their country's might worked as a compensation for their lack of freedom and their squalid living conditions. U.S. dominance takes away that pride, providing no substitute compensation for the continuing material difficulties. It is a caricature to say that this feeling is uniform or stable, however; in times of crisis such as U.S. military interventions overseas, the usually detached and mildly critical attitude of the Russian public toward the United States gives way to intense resentment.

The immensely wealthier elites, however, are, if anything, even more anti-American than Russia's poor. Despite the high material standards they have achieved, most have not abandoned their latent great-power ambitions. The elites have only grudgingly supported Putin's rapprochement with Washington; they have done little to deepen and further it and are instead waiting for an opportunity to check Russia's "subjugation" to the United States. The unreformed sections of the foreign, defense, and security elites will continue to present the most serious constraint on Russia's adjustment to its much-diminished role in a U.S.-dominated world. Absent a major transformation within these elites, no ideological adjustment will take place on the Russian domestic scene.

The president's role will remain key. Unless the presidency (as an institution) demonstrates sustained leadership and convinces key associates of the need to emerge from the post-Soviet hubris, the Russian president will remain a follower and a de facto captive of the more retrograde elements within the elite. To lead, the president of Russia needs a grand strategy, not just a general (and somewhat fuzzy) vision of integration.

Russia's travails in its search for a post-imperial role highlight one of challenges facing the United States. In the twenty-first century environment, the United States will need both allies and partners to structure a new world order. The Bush administration's intense but narrow focus on the war effort, whether in Afghanistan or Iraq, has been to the detriment of issues of a much higher order in the long term. In spring 2003, it was feared that the Bush administration's frustration with the UN Security Council might reinforce Washington's predilection for ad hoc responses to such issues. With the beginning of the postwar reconstruction in Iraq and the impetus given by Washington to the Israeli-Palestinian peace process, this danger looked diminished. Yet, the United States, in its unprecedented position at the apex of the world system, faces a fundamental dilemma.

To put it starkly, this is the choice between becoming a systemic world leader or turning into a seemingly free global hegemon. The latter is simpler and appears easier, but it forgoes the advantages of burden sharing and thus places on the United States much higher costs, which are likely to be unsustainable domestically over the long term. By contrast, the former option requires going beyond the operational doctrine of coalitions of the willing to redesign and strengthen the United States' key relationships around the world, starting with the traditional European allies and also including new friends such as Russia.

In sum, constructing a durable U.S.-Russian relationship will be neither quick nor easy. Improved communication channels between the White House and the Kremlin will be most welcome. Engaging Russia's elites, however, will be even more crucial. The emergence of constituencies with a clear interest in a strong relationship with the other country is key. The Russians would be well advised to be more active in Washington, engaging the U.S. political and business communities at various levels, learning to know their counterparts better, and identifying potential areas of effective cooperation. For their part, Americans would be wise to welcome these Russian advances and to think of Russia's potential assistance as a resource toward promoting long-term U.S. interests abroad and constructing a stable world order. After all, the central message of 9/11 internationally has been to unite against major systemic threats.

Notes

[1] Andrei Parshev, *Pochemu Rossiya ne Amerika* (Why Russia is not America) (Moscow: Krymskii-Most-9D, 1999).

[2] Cf., *From the First Person*, interviews with Vladimir Putin (Moscow: Vagrius, 2000).

[3] Vladimir Putin, "Rossiya na poroge tretyego tysyacheletiya" (Russia on the threshold of the third millennium), *Nezavisimaya Gazeta*, December 30, 1999.

[4] Public Opinion Foundation (Fond Obschestvennoe Mnenie, FOM), *All-Russian Poll of Urban and Rural Population*, Moscow, May 26, 2001; September 22, 2001; February 9, 2002; March 2, 2002; February 1, 2003; The group included 1,500 respondents. The drastic worsening of the attitude toward the United States in March 2002 is attributed to the perceived maltreatment of Russian participants in the Salt Lake City Olympics.

[5] Based on a report produced by the Russian Academy of Sciences' Institute of Integrated Social Studies and Germany's Friedrich-Ebert Stiftung; cited in *Izvestia*, October 8, 2002, p. 7.

[6] *Rossiya i mir – 2003* (Russia and the world – 2003) (Moscow: Foundation for Advanced Research, 2003).

[7] FOM, *Attitudes toward America: A Year After*, Moscow, September 5, 2002.

[8] VTsIOM (All-Russian Center for the Study of Public Opinion) poll, 1,600 respondents, early March 2003; in *Moscow Times*, March 20, 2003, p. 2.

PART FOUR

CONCLUSIONS

TEN

CONTRASTING IMAGES, COMPLEMENTARY VISIONS

Christina V. Balis

Fifty years ago, a previously little-known phrase by an ancient Greek poet—"The fox knows many things, but the hedgehog knows one big thing"—inspired Isaiah Berlin to write a masterful essay on Tolstoy's vision of history. Berlin's theme has since found recurring use among commentators and political analysts. In the 1990s, some used it to describe the U.S. post–Cold War predicament as that of a hedgehog facing many foxes. To those concerned about the United States' increasing global commitments and rising responsibilities as the world's only reluctant sheriff, the past decade seemed to augur an era of intractable ethnic conflicts, proliferating rogue states, and diffuse multilateralism.[1]

Since the events of September 11 and the transatlantic debate that followed President Bush's January 2002 State of the Union address, have the Europeans become the modern-day foxes ganging up on the American hedgehog? Can the most recent transatlantic divide be an example of what Berlin called

> a great chasm between those, on the one side, who relate everything to a single central vision, one system, less or more coherent or articulate, in terms of which they understand, think and feel . . . and, on the other side, those who pursue many ends, often unrelated and even contradictory, connected, if at all, only in some de facto way, for some psychological or physiological cause, related by no moral or aesthetic principle?[2]

The reader of the preceding essays in this collection is unlikely to conclude positively either way. More disturbingly, even as everyone agrees that realities ought not to be equated with perceptions, the latter have now come to shape, if not transplant, reality. Despite hopes that transatlantic visions prove flexible with regard to a common future, perceptions have become captive of both past and more recent idées fixes. In Simon Serfaty's words, "I lead you, hear you, and like you—and neither do I" is what defines this incoherent flow of mutual accusations across the Atlantic. Suddenly gone are the transatlantic prophets of a new multilateralism. Similarly gone, it seems, are memories of past transatlantic achievements and missed opportunities and whatever lessons they may portend for the future. By fall 2003, what seemed to be left of the 2002–2003 collision across the Atlantic is a bitter aftertaste whose causes point to no single event, and for which the antidote appears even more elusive than its diagnosis.

EUROPE AND ITS DISCONTENTS

From division to unification, from waging war to preaching peace, from imperial policing to community building, Europe's evolution in the past century is as breathtaking as it is counterintuitive. The states of Europe have moved a long way from a pure thinking of raison d'état even as they have yet to define their new raison d'être within an ill-defined union. That sovereignty, according to Michael Stuermer, can still resonate strongly in such pacified and Europeanized a country as Germany should come as no surprise in times when true political convictions are lacking and electoral gimmicks dominate the political stage. Deeper forces are under way in Europe, however. These may not always be evident in the eyes of bystanders, or even among Europeans themselves, but they are there, pushing Europe through a transformation still undefined in duration and scope. Like all transitions, this one is no different in the range of feelings of uncertainty and wariness it evokes—across the Continent no less than across the Atlantic.

At first sight, Britain's embedded Europeanism would seem to have historically and culturally little in common with the European circle of Italian foreign policy, and yet in both cases the centripetal forces emanating from Brussels are unmistaken. Christopher Hill argues that even without the catalytic event of the Iraq crisis, Anglo-American relations would sooner or later have reached a point of reevaluation, not because of some fundamental disagreement within the special relationship—an "entente cordiale of remarkable durability"—but as a result of Britain's gradual Europeanization across most areas of political and economic life. Trends, Hill reminds us, fall outside the control of political elites, and, consequently, the ongoing institutional movements within Europe are bound at some point to reassert themselves upon Britain's long-established patterns of bilateral relations.

Yet it is not only that Britain's politics and everyday culture are increasingly tied to Europe's evolution. The United States, too, will soon experience, if it has not already done so, that it cannot always rely on its junior partner to approve of and follow Washington's policies—especially where these are conducted under the doctrinal banner of preemption. "Why," Hill pointedly asks, "should the United States forgo an eclectic diplomacy for an ally with limited assets and nowhere else to go?" In short, a gradual reassessment of priorities and stakes on both sides has slowly been transforming the Anglo-American partnership into a more pragmatic relationship without the traditional emotional baggage that was once deemed as important as issues of purely strategic interest.

Italy's relationship with the United States may also be termed special but for distinct and rather paradoxical reasons, according to Marta Dassù and Roberto Menotti. If in British politics the traditional defining boundary has been between pro-European and anti-European loyalties, in the Italian case pro-Americanism and anti-Americanism have variably served as the main source of legitimacy for successive governments and their political opponents. As in the British case, such sentiments were not simply a matter of foreign policy; they resonated deeply in domestic debates and had significant repercussions for the country's overall political discourse.

What changed with the end of the Cold War, and even more patently since the September 11 attacks, is not the reality of these polar attitudes toward the United States but rather their mode and scope of expression across Italy's political spectrum. Anti-American expressions of dissent were not uncommon throughout most of the 1990s. What is significant about the current political climate in Italy, however, is that for "the first time a section of the traditionally pro-American establishment has taken a critical stance." Italy's traditional Atlanticism may have suffered its most serious blow in early 2003, strengthening in turn pro-European predilections that, in the past, might have been more directly challenged by pro-American loyalties.

Lacking the traditional Atlanticist penchant of its two neighbors, France appears free of the contradictions that characterize Britain and Italy. Yet, French opposition to U.S. policy in Iraq was more nuanced than the majority of media commentary seemed to suggest at the time.

According to Guillaume Parmentier, the shift of the French mood from one of complete solidarity after 9/11 to one of overt criticism of the United States by late 2002 had as much to do with France's traditional mistrust of U.S. motives and its desire to maintain freedom of action in foreign policy matters as it had to do with an earnest underestimation of the impact of September 11 on the U.S. psyche. Misperceptions in this case resulted from a different reading of the terrorist threat born out of each side's distinct experience with combating organized terror.

Likewise, the reasons behind France's insistence on working through the UN Security Council appear more structural than ideological in nature. France's pro-UN stance during the entire Iraq debate reflected neither a formal attachment to the values of multilateralism, as some commentators and even French policymakers would have us believe, nor some alleged "European" pacifist attitude among the French public and the political elite. Parmentier, partly echoing Robert Kagan's much-cited essay on contemporary U.S. and European views of world order, states that the divergent conceptions of France and the United States on the management of the international system stem from a reversal in the power relationship between the two countries. Rather than being the new creed of French foreign policy, multilateralism is only a means of restraining U.S. power, not an end itself. Opposition to U.S. policies ensues in the name of long-standing U.S. internationalist principles of which Europeans have come to be the most ardent advocates, if not always the most faithful followers.

In Germany, as in France to some extent, the debate over Iraq reflected the country's preference for multilateral institutions in dealing with international security threats. Compared with the French, however, Germans were far more united in opposing the use of force as a matter of principle. In the summer of 2002, even the conservative opposition could at times sound even more adamant in its rejection of the use of preemptive force, although its leaders never committed the glaring mistakes characteristic of Chancellor Schroeder's electoral tactics.

The persistence of the German Question in U.S.-European relations, which Stuermer emphasizes, need not entail that the entire European project is dependent on the continuation of the Pax Americana in Europe. That the European Union (EU) is seriously strained is without a doubt, but the argument that "for most Europeans, the EU is a union of convenience" while "the alliance with the United States is a question of . . . to be or not to be" may be overstated. Understandably, Stuermer has no sympathy for a Germany that "rebels against the tradition of a half century of pro-Atlantic policies" and his "point of no return" with regard to the damage done to the transatlantic alliance evokes as much pessimism as nostalgia for an era when enlightened *Staatskunst* guided the actions of postwar German political leaders. Still, Konrad Adenauer's magnanimity as the "chancellor of the vanquished" could last only as long as true U.S. leadership was on display. If "the unraveling of that postwar cocoon, transatlantic and European, that granted Germany's third chance in the twentieth century" has any culprits to call for, these are to be sought in Europe no less than across the Atlantic.

If Germany's post–Cold War self-perception appears unsettled, Russia's ongoing transformation reveals an even more unstable state of affairs. However pragmatic Vladimir Putin's early policy decision of "no confrontation with the United States" might have been, the ambiguities and contentions within the Russian political scene could never have been easily overcome. By early 2002, facing the elites' increasingly open anti-American rhetoric, the Russian president's stance had become unsustainable. Dmitri Trenin argues in his essay that Putin's 15-month honeymoon with President Bush was rooted less in some newfound personal affection for the outspoken Texan president than in Putin's overriding interest in promoting Russia's economic integration into the West. The feeling that after 9/11 the U.S. administration no longer appeared eager to meet the terms of repeated proclamations of partnership, despite an early sense of common purpose in the fight against international terrorism, encouraged Putin's shift away from Washington and toward Europe's main capitals.

Iraq may have been the first real sore point in U.S.-Russian relations under Putin's government, but the potential for even greater tensions in the future remains, especially with regard to Iran (where Russian stakes are much greater than in either Iraq or elsewhere in the Middle East) or even Chechnya (should Washington reverse its present policy of benign neglect). To a certain extent, Europe holds the key to the future of the U.S.-Russian relationship. Just as most European countries' loyalties remain split between an ever-integrating Europe and a strong transatlantic alliance, the Russian pendulum will continue to swing between Europe and the United States in search of openings to the West.

Trenin makes an early observation that, by and large, resonates in Russia as much as in the rest of Europe—and the world, for that matter. The United States, Trenin comments, not only sets the standards to which other countries aspire but also serves as the measuring stick for each country's self-assessment of its status and role around the world. America is thus the nation to be interchangeably imitated and rivaled, a paragon of both admiration and assault. To be sure, Russia's selective emulation of and traditional sense of rivalry with the United States are not found in the same form elsewhere in Europe. Yet such fixation with the only remaining superpower finds its parallel in most of Europe today.

It is worth reflecting for a moment on how different, indeed paradoxical, an impact the Kosovo war had on Europe's public debate. On the one hand, it prompted strong negative reactions among European publics as a result of the use of military force; on the other hand, it exposed Europe's failure in the area of a common foreign and security policy. The lessons that Europeans drew from this experience proved no less conflicting. If European leaders showed themselves suddenly determined to reverse serious shortcomings in the area of political coordination and military capabilities, the task of selling the implications of this policy reversal to their publics—including the need for higher levels of defense spending—was lost amid the jazzy initiatives and dazzling rhetoric. Ultimately, the consecutive crises in the Balkans throughout the 1990s could not be turned into the defining issue of the transatlantic relationship—not even with regard to Russia and in spite of the latter's historical sensitivities in the region. Notwithstanding some isolated dissenting voices, most Europeans conceded to Americans both the military superiority *and* the higher moral standing for deciding to intervene militarily in Europe's backyard.

Iraq was an altogether different matter. Not only did the crisis extend far beyond Europe's borders, it also raised serious questions about U.S. motives and the risks of creating an international precedent for preemptive interventions. To be sure, the political discourse in Europe has been at times as muddled and inconsistent as in the United States. The range of questions raised by the debate over Iraq, however, underline the seriousness of the latest transatlantic rift, more so than any crisis in the recent and even more distant past.

Early support for the U.S. campaign against Al Qaeda in Afghanistan came spontaneously to all Europeans. Most European nations extended tangible assistance and moral support to U.S. antiterrorist efforts—and, indeed, they continued to do so even after slogans such as "Old Europe" and "axis of weasel" began to emerge. The early response on the part of the EU was as impressive as that of the NATO allies, although the subsequent failure of EU leaders to coordinate a plan of action on Iraq long before the crisis came to a head had become all too palpable by late fall 2002.

It is not that transatlantic solidarity ceased to exist by early 2003. Rather, it is the emergence of a new internal fragility, first revealed by the intra-European fallout in late 2002, that may have provided the greatest blow to the U.S.-European partnership. While the reaction of Eastern European governments was understandable in light of their countries' experiences, the way in which they extended support to Washington—without any prior notification, let alone consultations, with the EU and its members (most of whom would have readily endorsed the wording of the declaration)—was troubling. France's impulsive reaction to the Letter of Eight, essentially shutting the relevant EU aspirant countries down, only aggravated a situation that soon no one, with the exception of Tony Blair who had the greatest interest in keeping transatlantic talks going, wished to reverse through single-handed diplomatic concessions.[3]

In short, developments in the first half of 2003 point to a European evolution whose beginnings can be traced to the collapse of the old bipolar world. In nearly all cases, one can observe a less emotional or ideological interpretation of bilateral relations with the United States. At the political level, pragmatism has replaced previous doctrinal and sentimental attachments. Unlike in the past, European leaders no longer assume an obligation to support U.S. policies unreservedly. While such an adjustment in European attitudes was arguably predictable, post-9/11 U.S. policies—whether declaratory or actual—have contributed to an acceleration of these trends, often in ways that precluded a positive transformation of the transatlantic relationship.

At the level of public opinion, the situation appears more fluid. Neither pragmatism nor crude sentimentalism alone is responsible for shaping long-term attitudinal changes. To be sure, even such sudden changes in public perceptions as could be observed in Britain before and after the launch of U.S.-led military operations in Iraq need not imply a sudden break with the past. A new British political consensus vis-à-vis Europe will not come about easily, and, in that regard, Britain's case may seem hardly instructive of general European trends. Yet, the evolution of the British domestic debate illustrates the emergence of a common, if still spasmodic, awareness among European publics when it comes to issues of security and global governance.

Domestic conditions matter, too, to the extent that they define national leaders' margins of maneuver. The political majorities enjoyed by Britain's Tony Blair and, as of June 2002, France's Jacques Chirac as well certainly eased some decisions at crucial times in 2002–2003. When compared with the electoral worries and internal troubles of Chancellor Schroeder, the contrast becomes clear. To an extent, both Russian president Vladimir Putin and Italian prime minister Silvio Berlusconi could impose their preferences on the internal political scene, but that had more to do with those countries' structural peculiarities than with genuine public support.

In short, both temptations—national and European—are there to stay throughout Europe, and for a considerable time still. Post-national but pre-federal is how the states of Europe appear today—bereft of their former destructive nationalist passions (though not their occasional national caprices) but still lacking a true common European identity (albeit not without some periodic bursts of European pride). This ambiguity between national and European priorities ultimately contributed to Europe's cacophonic response to U.S. initiatives post–September 11. The lack of any effective coordination among "Europe's indispensable three" on Iraq was the clearest manifestation that Europe is far from being a political reality. In the pithy words of three European analysts, "the British should be more European, the French should be more modest and the Germans should be bolder"—or else all aspirations of Europe becoming a serious political force will remain, at best, wishful thinking.[4]

AMERICA'S STRATEGIC (MIS)FORTUNES

Even before September 11, the common U.S. view of Europe, whether on the part of devoted Eurobashers or committed Atlanticists, was one of a continent in disarray, incoherent, and largely self-absorbed.[5] Europe could be distant in its continental preoccupations but also harshly critical when it came to specific U.S. decisions, such as regarding the Kyoto Protocol, the Anti-Ballistic Missile treaty, and the International Criminal Court. September 11 did not alter the reality of Europe's state of confusion, but it gave new ammunition to those who seem more intent on attacking Europe than on providing constructive criticism.

In the view of many U.S. observers, European societies are experiencing a broader malaise, not merely demographic or economic in nature, but mainly intellectual, which disqualifies their elites from thinking seriously and progressively about current international challenges. Neo-conservative writer Michael Ledeen declares that "Europeans have gone brain dead." European leaders are said to use the United States as "a scapegoat for their own malfeasance," while "European intellectuals have turned selfish, utterly materialistic, and lacking in independent thought."[6] Mark Lilla, professor at the University of Chicago, recently credited the European "intellectual crisis of sovereignty" with all that appears currently objectionable in and about Europe. By pointing to "the omnipresence of political ideologies and passions, and the relative absence of serious political thought" in Western Europe, Lilla is clearly distraught at the loss of the Raymond Arons, Isaiah Berlins, and Norberto Bobbios who had come to define an earlier generation of European intellectuals—and whom U.S. intellectuals and politicians alike had learned to respect and relate to. Yet, a question that would otherwise merit serious consideration—and that finds its parallel in Europe's own nostalgia for an earlier "great generation" of Americans—is subsequently lost amidst the writer's feeble claim that the crisis of the European idea of the nation-state ought to somehow explain European intellectual attitudes toward Israel.[7]

Lilla's analysis of European realities is not unique. It stands for a growing U.S. alienation from Europe's ongoing unification project and a general contempt of most things European that smack of opposition to U.S. postures.[8] But for the Europe with that recognizable "life of intellectual leisure in a delightfully scenic setting of old castles and romantic cafés," all other incarnations seem now distant, if not outright hostile to U.S. eyes.[9]

Such cultural interpretations of Europe often combine with a certain degree of "elite europhobia"—a revived Rooseveltian thinking whose adherents, John Harper explains, have concluded that a Europe "retired from the game of power politics and basically irrelevant to the United States" should no longer matter to U.S. policymakers. Since September 11, 2001, this temptation to view the United States as the main force of the future without any need or interest to cultivate close relations with traditional allies—don't call me, I'll call you—has found its strongest expression among so-called neoconservatives. If the 1990s were a reaffirmation of the Europe-first, Achesonian approach, the early 2000s find their Rooseveltian opposites vindicated and confirmed in their anti-European spite. Yet, with the historian's characteristic skepticism, Harper leaves the door open for yet another reversal in U.S.

foreign policy thinking. Should events at home and abroad turn against the wishes and designs of those currently in power, "the 'Rooseveltian' conviction of Europe's weakness and irrelevancy to America's strategic fortunes would then look as hubristic and wishful as it did 60 years ago."

Not necessarily so, retorts Christopher Layne, whose unmistaken credentials as an international relations theorist make for a reading different from the historian's insight. Layne would probably agree with Harper that the United States has traditionally expressed both the embrace and rejection of Europe, but for Layne that ambiguity does not extend to U.S. relations with post–World War II Europe. According to Layne, "[t]he core assumption of U.S. postwar European grand strategy was that either a reversion to multipolarity within Europe . . . or Western Europe's reemergence as an independent pole of power in international politics . . . would be inimical to U.S. interests." Consequently, "a sophisticated grand strategy of subordination, or denationalization" had to be devised, with the goal of establishing U.S. hegemony over Western Europe.[10]

In effect, Harper's analysis leaves off where Layne's thesis picks up. Harper makes a compelling case for the complementary as well as conflicting nature of the visions that have shaped U.S. policymakers' thinking toward Europe since the end of World War II. With history as his flashlight to peer into the future, Harper's conclusion is inevitably open-ended, allowing for more than one possible scenario with regard to the future of the transatlantic relationship. Layne's analysis follows the inverse and rather more prescriptive path. Taking the early 1990s as his starting point, he uses Washington's post–Cold War behavior as his guide for U.S. motivations during the latter half of the twentieth century. His argument that even in the absence of the Cold War the United States would have sought to establish a hegemony over Western Europe is intriguing but merely as an exercise in counterfactual history, not as an actual predictor of events—whose impact on the actual course of states' policies remains most uncertain. By imputing specific post–Cold War motivations to the policies of preceding generations of U.S. leaders, Layne adheres to a logic that some will find hard to reconcile historically.

What deserves attention, however, is the corollary of Layne's argument—that is, why successive U.S. administrations in the 1990s seemed rather unwilling or unable to reconsider remnants of Cold War policies such as military commitments to Europe. In other words, Layne's thesis becomes especially interesting when it assesses possible revisions in the rationale of U.S. strategy toward Europe *following* the end of the Cold War. In this light, September 11 may be seen as merely the culmination of a transformation in U.S. strategic thinking that began with the collapse of Communism but did not come to the surface until the collapse of the World Trade Center 13 years later.

VISIONS OF EMPIRE

"One's view of one's partner is, in large part, derived from one's view of oneself," writes Daniel Hamilton. Accordingly, while the fall of the Iron Curtain on November 9, 1989 (11/9), marked one bookend in Europeans' minds, the fall of the Twin Towers on September 11, 2001 (9/11), marked another dramatic bookend, this time deep in the American psyche. These two experiences have now come to dominate not only each side's consciousness but each other's source of grievances and mutual strategic divergences as well. September 11 changed more than perceptions of transatlantic realities. Inevitably, it also brought about diverging visions of the future role of the world's remaining superpower. If the European vision post-11/9 relied on the benign image of a Pax Americana, since 9/11 it has gradually turned into a visceral condemnation of the Imperium Americanum.

While the inevitability of U.S. global preponderance is undisputed, most Europeans express strong views against the potential follies and excesses of the American empire-in-making. Professor Niall Ferguson's generous interpretation of empires is unlikely to find much resonance among a majority of Europeans. On the other hand, EU commissioner Chris Patten's alternative vision of "a world empire without an emperor, where international rules set the parameters for the legitimate pursuit of interests but where the law applies to all," is likely to be ridiculed by those on the other side of the Atlantic who deem such rules as undue restrictions on the exercise of U.S. power.[11] Meanwhile, European leaders are no less guilty of their own contradictions when it comes to defining their common aspirations to maintaining global order, often allowing anti-American sentiments to hype public frenzy and hijack serious political debates. As Jean-François Revel recently put it, "What is lacking in the European thinking [about the reality of the American superpower] is the search for the reasons of its existence." For only "once we have successfully identified and correctly interpreted these reasons, and only then, can we hope to find the means to counterbalance the American preponderance."[12]

The predicament of correctly defining the United States' role in the world is not merely a European one, however. An empire that is variously defined by representatives of the New World as arrogant, adolescent, compulsive, or even benevolent points to serious ambiguities about the justification and self-perception of that empire.[13] (Notably, no one is any longer questioning the subject-noun, empire.) In one of his most memorable phrases, Dean Acheson once remarked that Great Britain had lost an empire and had yet to find a role. Forty odd years on, America may be said to have found an empire and consequently to have lost its role in the world.

While the two, empire and role (or identity), need not be in disagreement, whatever the United States' choice proves to be—and this time no claim about a reluctant or accidental empire can suffice—will have implications for other countries' receptiveness to U.S. power. "With such [military and economic] power undergirded by a belief in America's moral exceptionalism, the most dangerous threat to American omnipotence may very well come about as a result of the alienation of Europe and Japan, and the wariness of China and Russia." Coming from the pen of Acheson's biographer, these words should not be taken lightly. "It is in fact the height of realism," James Chace continues elsewhere, "not only to advance the nation's interests but also to seek allies among other governments and peoples who share those interests."[14] The anecdotal observation by Assistant to the President for National Security Affairs Condoleezza Rice in the wake of the Iraq War that U.S. policy toward the three dissenting European countries would be to "punish the French, ignore the Germans, and forgive the Russians" may paraphrase Lord Ismay's more serious statement about NATO's Cold War rationale, but in light of the circumstances it suggests a rather short-term vision for the many challenges in postwar Iraq that still lie ahead.

Why, we might ask, should Americans take warnings of imperial overstretch and hubris more seriously today than preceding generations of Americans did during comparable debates in the history of U.S. foreign policy? After all, Daniel Webster's reproach to the imperialists of his own times—"You have a Sparta; embellish it!"—can well apply to current conditions, and the inescapable fact of the United States' unrivalled world status would still hold. Indeed, what makes the present debate, and its timing, so much more critical than at any other point in the nation's history has less to do with that debate's internal dynamics than with its external reverberations.

One of the most readily available indicators of the bearing that U.S. foreign policies have on the rest of the world is world public opinion. Domestic support—"the acid test of a policy," Henry Kissinger remarked nearly 50 years ago—ceases to be merely domestic when the impact of such a policy extends beyond the welfare of one country's citizens and when foreign leaders no longer feel free to conduct their states' external affairs according to commonly understood bureaucratic practices.[15] No political leader whose survival is tied to the expectations of a domestic audience can ignore the reality of public opposition to decisions that link the country's fate to the actions of another country, let alone when the latter is the world's new imperial power.

Despite their external flavor, however, many of the sources of European public discontent vis-à-vis the United States are distinctly pragmatic, not merely ideological in nature. With respect to Italian public attitudes toward the United States, Dassù and Menotti argue that "the United States is criticized for what it does, not for what it is." The image of the Ugly American abroad is ultimately not a measure of SUVs, eating habits, or religious predilections, but rather an assessment of the U.S. government's conduct around the world.

In short, the gap between the United States and Europe, though substantive, is more structural than cultural in origin—the product of a tumultuous twentieth century and not the inevitable outcome of two culturally diverging societies. In their desire for prosperity, innovation, and entrepreneurship, Europeans continue to look to Americans as their natural allies. F. A. McKenzie's *The American Invaders* of more than a century ago were armed not with rifles and bayonets but with manufactured products and seductive ideas of the land of plenty.[16] Today, "improvised Americans" are no less in vogue than "improvised Europeans" were during the early part of the past century. True, Europeans have mostly "tendered small-circulation currency for mass culture: paying for Levi's with Levi-Strauss, for Bart Simpson with Roland Barthes, for Disney with Derrida, for Burger King with Baudrillard, and Michael Jackson for Michel Foucault." Yet, culturally no less than economically, there is more that unites the two societies across the Atlantic than there are divisive issues.[17]

By contrast, structural differences between the two sides—differences related to diverse experiences and, hence, different readings of history—

are more crucial than are purely cultural interpretations.[18] To some extent, this distinction goes beyond Dan Hamilton's 11/9 versus 9/11 thesis. If England was "the unwitting protector of American isolationism" for the better part of the nineteenth century, a century later America had become the unwitting protector of Europe's return to regionalism.[19] In both cases, history proved generous to both sides. Yet neither historical analogy can be sustained any longer. Today neither (American) isolationism nor (European) regionalism is a real option for a West defined not as a homogeneous entity to be protected from the readily available image of an Other, but as a common ground for taking necessary action beyond narrowly defined spheres of interest.

STRATEGIC (DI)VISIONS, MULTILATERAL DILEMMAS

Containment, deterrence, prevention, preemption—all have been variedly employed and/or propagated, and yet a transatlantic consensus on a new concept of geostrategic stability is not in sight. The greatest challenge, it seems, is not so much agreeing on the root sources of international threat as laying out a common strategic vision for countering them—agreeing on the cure after establishing the symptoms of a common disease.

The response of critics—American as well as European—to the latest U.S. doctrine of preemption is reminiscent of George F. Kennan's reaction in 1947 to the alarmist tone of the Truman Doctrine and its neat division of the world into a "free world" and an "enslaved world." Fifty-five years later, Kennan can still inspire those who see fault in President Bush's black-and-white approach to global challenges. "I deplore doctrines," a 98-year-old Kennan remarked in the wake of the first anniversary of the September 11 attacks, referring not only to the Bush administration's proposed preemptive intervention in Iraq but also to the early theory of containment—a word he arguably never meant as the foundation for a doctrine. "[Doctrines] purport to define one's behavior in a future situation where it may or may not be suitable."[20]

By contrast, most thinking in favor of a preemptive strategy discards the effectiveness of both containment and deterrence and favors instead direct intervention to bring about the external transformation of pariah states. It is naive and dangerous, the advocates of preemption argue, to defer the use of military force lest we might find out that it can no longer be used to avert an irreversible act of aggression. Nor is it sufficient that the West promotes trade and open markets to seduce others to its values of free trade, democracy, and human rights. Preventive intervention is hence sometimes warranted to forestall future disasters and to bring about faster change among citizens of countries still living under sclerotic socioeconomic and political conditions.

While an optimistic versus pessimistic interpretation of the current international system may arguably explain the difference between these two approaches, this is not strictly the case. Indeed, preemptive strategies are often regarded by their opponents as more optimistic, even naive, in assuming that easy or sudden change can occur in distant places merely by virtue of some benign Western intervention—the United States' postwar woes in Iraq offering the most concrete example of such naïveté. For proponents of preemptive action, pessimism may be what defines their worldview, but optimism is what shapes their perceived ability to change the world. By contrast, their critics are more optimistic about the promises of a globalizing world but less trustful of policies that aim at sudden geopolitical transformations.

The vast majority of Europeans clearly espouses the latter view. In contrast, the inconclusive debate in the United States over the wisdom of preemption as the nation's new strategy in dealing with the rogues of this world leaves many questions unanswered. Indeed, if there is one area where European reservations about U.S. actions are largely justified, this is it. Opaque and elusive as Brussels's signals tend to be and indecisive and slow as Europeans collectively appear, Washington has frequently failed, at crucial times, to convince its European partners that it has a clear conception of its international engagement with the rest of the world.

We know we live in uncertain times whenever the need to define things in concrete ways becomes irresistible. In the process, attempts to define a world as either unipolar or multipolar are confused with policies that have either a unilateral or multilateral streak. Were ours a truly unipolar world, with the United States as its focal point, then multilateralism would be an option only for the United States and a necessity for all others. If, on the other hand, despite all the United States' resources in the areas of hard security and soft security, today's world is accepted as too complex a place for any single nation to manage, let alone lead, then the distinction between unilateral and multilateral policies becomes blurred for all players—leaders as well as followers.

The kind of uni-multipolarity implied in this conception of international politics is, by necessity, a function of the issue and countries involved in each case. This is not to dismiss the continued value of multilateral organizations and other means of multilateral diplomacy—quite the opposite. The role of such institutions in most areas of international cooperation will remain indispensable and is likely to increase in significance. Just as a world can be multipolar economically but unipolar militarily, multilateral institutions are no less a tool of power politics than are unilateral policies.

The main difference is that, in most cases, the payoff is higher and the long-term cost is less for power politics played through institutions than played unilaterally. This is as true for the strongest as it is for the less powerful states of the international system. The United States' predicament is such that it cannot simply opt for unilateralism over multilateralism; rather the choice is between a "unilateralist and disengaged" approach (at the expense of maintaining worldwide influence and leadership) and a "multilateralist and fully engaged" foreign policy (by wielding global leadership and tying international cooperation in with the country's own interests).[21] Conversely, so-called multipolar strategies or "coalition[s] of the resentful," to use Trenin's phrase, that seek to restrain U.S. unilateralism tend to be self-defeating when aimed at the mere establishment of a separate center of power. Tony Blair remarked pointedly in the wake of a victorious U.S.-led military campaign in Iraq, "Those people who fear 'unilateralism'—so-called and in inverted commas—in America should realise that the quickest way to get that is to set up a rival polar power to America."[22]

To be sure, occasional U.S. and European idiosyncratic reactions to specific issues will often do little to disperse European perceptions of an across-the-board U.S. unilateralism on the one hand and U.S. perceptions of dodgy European multilateralism on the other. Nonetheless, the distinction between a system that remains inherently multipolar and policies that are bound to swing between unilateral and multilateral alternatives ought to put to rest pointless generalizations about power and weakness and respective accusations of U.S. unilateralism and European institutional ganging up.

THE LIMITS OF DISAGREEMENT

"There are many angles of vision from which human minds peer at the universe," Arnold Toynbee once wrote, and hence anyone's "view of history is itself a tiny piece of history."[23] Such humility ought to guide all visions and political actions, even as these seek to be bold and inventive. Visions require both foresight and insight. How much foresight and insight the next, if not the present, generation of leaders on either side of the Atlantic is likely to exhibit is unknown but not insignificant. Even as the day-to-day pressures at home and abroad take an immense toll on politicians' ability to think broadly and act preventively, the imperative of conducting policy beyond short-term political expedients cannot be overstated.

The fear now is that some unbridgeable differences in strategic vision or stubborn perceptions of lessened commonalities between Europe and the United States might compel both sides to renounce the socio-economic and political space in which they have come to reside. That both sides of the Atlantic possess distinct capabilities and even certain comparative advantages should be an incentive for strengthened cooperation, not cause for a permanent break. For, as Parmentier points out, translating mass into power is as difficult for Europeans as translating power into influence is for the Americans. Or, as Layne might argue, while Europeans are still incapable of hard balancing, Americans are increasingly ineffective at soft balancing. Both sides' sources of relative power involve distinct assets that are complementary rather than mutually exclusive. It is such complementarity that forms the bedrock of Dan Hamilton's "enabling or empowering relationship" and that ought to guide the thinking of all partners across the Atlantic.

Likewise, aspirations on either side should reflect practical realities. Just as Europeans ought to learn to limit their ambitions to the capabilities at hand—and, conversely, seek to expand available capabilities to meet stated ambitions—so should Americans accept the futility of their own sense of omnipotence when the latter is, in fact, only a function of outside followership or, sometimes, even equal partnership. The largely accepted if often resented formula that "The U.S. will fight, the UN will feed, and the EU will fund" clearly has its limits when it comes to denote a mere division (or distribution) of labor rather than true complementarity. Power means little without influence, and, for influence to be long lasting, power must be legitimated through collective engagement, especially when the stakes in a specific action are not limited to the dominant player.

Nearly all propositions for a so-called new transatlantic bargain or new Atlanticism have a strikingly familiar appeal. Such bargains have been promoted many times in the past, with more or less success. What mattered in each case was the idea that stood behind them, more than the people who initially supported them. Jean Monnet, that visionary par excellence, argued that "There are no premature ideas: there are only opportunities for which one must learn to wait."[24] Assuming that today is such an opportunity to renew the transatlantic relationship, old ideas should not be discarded. Visions are not "things"—*pace* President Bush senior—to be employed and disposed of at will. They do not merely pop up. They gestate for a long time, waiting for the right moment to come to light, sometimes even to resurface after a time of hibernation and neglect through succeeding generations. True, a good deal of groundwork needs to precede the realization of any vision, which is why visions cease to be fully appreciated once they have materialized. Yet, if recent events are any indication of the overall state of the transatlantic relationship, such groundwork has been largely missing on both sides of the Atlantic.

This is not much of a conclusion for the many uncertainties that bedevil the U.S.-European relationship. It has become quixotic to suggest that structural differences between the two sides could be surmounted through greater tolerance for each other's sensitivities. Nonetheless, whatever the inadequacy of prescribed solutions, we have not yet reached the point of no return. Unlike Isaiah Berlin's Tolstoy—whom the philosopher in the end judged to be neither a true hedgehog nor an accomplished fox but rather "a desperate old man, beyond human aid, wandering self-blinded at Colonus"[25]—Europeans and Americans would be best served by discarding simple labels that set them against each other and do justice to neither side. If there is one broad vision that comes out of all the contributions to this volume, it is that of a common transatlantic space defined by new rules of governance and complementarity and reinforced by the shared conviction in long-held values of promoting peace and prosperity across the Atlantic as well as beyond. To concede otherwise is to dismiss the many achievements of the transatlantic relationship to date and to recoil from the responsibility that befalls both sides with regard to the challenges ahead—and thus succumb to a tragic fate similar to that of old, banished, and blind Oedipus.

Notes

[1] Isaiah Berlin, *The Hedgehog and the Fox: An Essay on Tolstoy's View of History* (London: Weidenfeld & Nicolson, 1953). More recently, David Ignatius lamented how among today's world leaders there were too many hedgehogs and not enough foxes—too many "absolutists" as opposed to "more pragmatic people who can maneuver, manipulate, cut the deal, get it done." Ignatius judged President Bush, Israeli prime minister Ariel Sharon, and Palestinian leader Yasser Arafat as hedgehogs who know only "one big thing" ("Day of the Hedgehog," *Washington Post*, April 19, 2002, p. A25).

[2] Berlin, *The Hedgehog and the Fox*, 3.

[3] For a dispassionate analysis of the events leading to the war in Iraq, see the four-part series in the *Financial Times*, "The Divided West," May 27–30, 2003.

[4] Timothy Garton Ash, Michael Mertes, and Dominique Moisi, "Only a Club of Three Can Bring European Unity," *Financial Times*, July 11, 2003.

[5] See, e.g., Michael Kelly, "The Divided States of Europe," and Fareed Zakaria, "They're the Isolationists," both of which appeared in the *Washington Post*, June 13, 2001.

[6] Michael Ledeen, "Europe Loses Its Mind," *American Enterprise* 13, no. 8 (December 2002): 40–41.

[7] Mark Lilla, "The End of Politics: Europe, the Nation-State, and the Jews," *New Republic*, June 23, 2003, p. 32. The argument that "Once upon a time, the Jews were mocked for not having a nation-state. Now they are criticized for having one" makes for a fairly simplistic interpretation of current European views on the Israeli-Palestinian conflict.

[8] For a rather disturbing exemplar of this thinking, see Andrew Sullivan, "The Threat of European Integration: The Euro Menace," *New Republic*, June 16, 2003, pp. 22–25.

[9] For an eloquent analysis of such U.S. attitudes that often mix misleading nostalgia for an Old World with increasing contempt for the New Europe, see Simon Serfaty's essay in this collection.

[10] Layne's thesis about a certain continuity in U.S. strategy toward Europe since the Cold War finds distant echoes in Andrew Bacevich's *American Empire*. According to the latter, "Since the end of the Cold War the United States has in fact adhered to a well-defined grand strategy. . . . Those who chart America's course do so with a clearly defined purpose in mind. That purpose is to preserve and, where both feasible and conducive to U.S. interests, to expand an American imperium." (Andrew Bacevich, *American Empire: The Realities and Consequences of U.S. Diplomacy* [Cambridge: Harvard University Press, 2002], pp. 2–3.)

[11] Niall Ferguson, *Empire: The Rise and Demise of the British World Order and the Lessons for Global Power* (New York: Basic Books, 2003) and "True Lies: Lessons from the British Empire," *New Republic*, June 2, 2003, pp. 16–19; Chris Patten, "America Should Not Relinquish Respect," *Financial Times*, October 3, 2002. However, Ferguson's apologia for enlightened empires apparently does not extend to "empire[s] run on a shoestring"; see Niall Ferguson and Laurence Kotlikoff, "The Fiscal Overstretch That Will Undermine an Empire," *Financial Times*, July 15, 2003.

[12] Jean François Revel, "Contradictions of the Anti-American Obsession," *New Perspectives Quarterly* 20, no. 2 (Spring 2003); available at www.npq.org/archive/2003_spring/revel.html (June 12, 2003).

[13] Fareed Zakaria, "The Arrogant Empire," *Newsweek*, March 17, 2003; James Kurth, "The Adolescent Empire," *National Interest* 48 (Summer 1997): 3–15; Robert Jervis, "The Compulsive Empire," *Foreign Policy* 137 (July/August 2003): 83–87; and Robert Kagan, "The Benevolent Empire," *Foreign Policy* 112 (Summer 1998): 24–35.

[14] James Chace, "Imperial America and the Common Interest," *World Policy Journal* 19, no. 1 (Spring 2002): 8; and "Present at the Destruction: The Death of American Internationalism," *World Policy Journal* 20, no. 1 (Spring 2003): 4.

[15] Henry A. Kissinger, *A World Restored: Metternich, Castlereigh and the Problems of Peace, 1812–22* (Boston: Houghton Mifflin Company, 1957), p. 326.

[16] Fred A. McKenzie, *The American Invaders* (reprint, New York: Amo Press, 1976).

[17] Alex Zwerdling, *Improvised Europeans: American Literary Expatriates and the Siege of London* (New York: Basic Books, 1998), p. 16; and Susan L. Carruthers, "Not Like the US? Europeans and the Spread of American Culture" (review article), *International Affairs* 74, no. 4 (1998): 890–891.

[18] See, for example, "America hatte kein Verdun" (interview with German foreign minister Joschka Fischer), *Der Spiegel*, March 24, 2003.

[19] C. V. Woodward, "The Age of Reinterpretation," *American Historical Review* 66 (1960–1961): 3.

[20] Jane Mayer, "The Big Idea: A Doctrine Passes," *New Yorker*, October 14 and October 21, 2002, p. 70.

[21] Stephen M. Walt, "American Primacy: Its Prospects and Pitfalls," *Naval War College Review* 15, no. 2 (Spring 2002): 26.

[22] Philip Stevens and Cathy Newman, "Confident Blair on the World, the Nation and his Birthday" (interview with the prime minister), *Financial Times*, April 28, 2003.

[23] Arnold J. Toynbee, *Civilization on Trial* (New York: Oxford University Press, 1948), p. 3.

[24] W. W. Rostow, "Jean Monnet: The Innovator as Diplomat," in *The Diplomats, 1939–1979*, ed. Gordon A. Craig and Francis L. Loewenheim (Princeton: Princeton University Press, 1994), p. 265.

[25] Berlin, *The Hedgehog and the Fox*, p. 82.

INDEX

Page numbers followed by the letters n *and* t *refer to notes and tables, respectively.*

ABOUT THE AUTHORS

Christina V. Balis is a Ph.D. candidate in strategic studies at the Paul H. Nitze School of Advanced International Studies (SAIS), Johns Hopkins University, in Washington, D.C. Her current research focuses on European army professionalism. For four years, until June 2003, she was affiliated with the Europe Program at CSIS, most recently as fellow. During that period, Balis made contributions to a number of publications produced by the Europe Program. A native of Greece, with a Greek-German heritage, she has studied and worked in Europe, Japan, and the United States.

Marta Dassù is editor of *Aspenia* and director of policy programs at the Aspen Institute Italia in Rome. She also lectures at the Rome university, La Sapienza, focusing on new conflicts and the role of media. A specialist in international relations and Italian foreign policy, she served as foreign policy adviser to Italy's prime minister from 1998 to 2001. Previously, she was director of the Rome-based Centre for International Political Studies (CeSPI). She has published extensively in Italian and European journals and is the editor of various books, including most recently *Conflicts in the 21st Century* (Aspen Institute, 2002).

Daniel S. Hamilton is the Richard von Weizsäcker Professor and director of the Center for Transatlantic Relations at the Johns Hopkins University's Paul H. Nitze School of Advanced International Studies (SAIS). He also serves as executive director of the American Consortium for EU Studies (ACES). From 1993 to 2001, Hamilton held a variety of senior positions in the U.S. Department of State, including deputy assistant secretary for European affairs, U.S. special coordinator for Southeast European stabilization, and associate director of the Policy Planning Staff. He has authored many works on transatlantic relations, including most recently *Die Zukunft ist nicht mehr, was sie war: Europa, Amerika und die neue weltpolitische Lage* (Robert Bosch Stiftung, 2002).

John L. Harper is resident professor of American foreign policy and European studies at the Bologna Center of the Johns Hopkins School of Advanced International Studies (SAIS), Italy. He has contributed articles and reviews to various publications and is the author of *America and the Reconstruction of Italy, 1945–1948* (Cambridge University Press, 1986), winner of the 1987 Marraro prize from the Society for Italian Historical Studies; *American Visions of Europe: Franklin D. Roosevelt, George F. Kennan, and Dean G. Acheson* (Cambridge University Press, 1994), winner of the 1995 Robert Ferrell Prize from the Society for Historians of American Foreign Relations; and *American Machiavelli: Alexander Hamilton and the Origins of U.S. Foreign Policy* (Cambridge University Press, 2004).

Christopher Hill is Montague Burton Professor of International Relations at the London School of Economics and Political Science. He is the author of numerous scholarly articles and book chapters as well as the author, joint author, or editor of nine books, including *Cabinet Decisions on Foreign Policy* (Cambridge University Press, 1991); *Two Worlds of International Relations: Academics, Practitioners and the Trade in Ideas*, edited with Pamela Beshoff (Routledge, 1994); and *European Foreign Policy: Key Documents*, edited with Karen E. Smith (Routledge, 2000). His most recent book is *The Changing Politics of Foreign Policy* (Palgrave MacMillan, 2002).

Christopher Layne is a visiting fellow in foreign policy studies at the Cato Institute and a consultant to the RAND Corporation. He has held teaching positions at the University of Miami and the Naval Postgraduate School as well as fellowships at the University of California, Los Angeles; University of Southern California; and Harvard University. A prolific writer, Layne has published three widely cited articles in *International Security*: "The Unipolar Illusion: Why New Great

Powers Will Rise" (Spring 1993), "Kant or Cant: The Myth of the Democratic Peace" (Fall 1994), and "From Preponderance to Offshore Balancing: America's Future Grand Strategy" (Summer 1997). He currently is working on a book about American grand strategy, to be published by the Cornell University Press in its Studies in Security Affairs series.

Roberto Menotti is research fellow in the policy program at Aspen Institute Italia, Rome, where he focuses on transatlantic relations. Previously, he was coordinator of transatlantic studies at the Rome-based Centre for International Political Studies (CeSPI). He has been a lecturer at the LUISS University and the John Cabot University in Rome. He has published extensively on international relations and security issues, including *Mediatori in armi: L'allargamento della NATO e la politica USA in Europa* (Guerini e Associati, 1999), "Italy: Uneasy Ally" in *Enlarging NATO: The National Debates*, ed. Gale A. Mattox and Arthur R. Rachwald (Lynne Rienner, 2001), and *XXI secolo: fine della sicurezza?* (Laterza, 2003).

Guillaume Parmentier is founder and director of the French Center on the United States (CFE) at the Paris-based Institut Français des Relations Internationales (IFRI) and a professor of the University of Paris-II. Previously, he was director of studies and research at the French Foundation for Defense Studies (1997–1999) and served in the French defense minister's cabinet with responsibility for international affairs (1995–1997). He has been an associate professor at Sciences-Pô and has taught at Ecole Nationale d'Administration (ENA), as well as at several universities in the United States and in Europe. He has published extensively on European and transatlantic security issues. He is the author most recently of *Reconcilable Differences: U.S.-French Relations in the New Era*, with Michael Brenner (Brookings Institution Press, April 2002).

Simon Serfaty is the director of the CSIS Europe Program and the first recipient of the CSIS Zbigniew Brzezinski Chair in Global Security and Geostrategy, established in 2002. He is also Eminent Scholar and professor of U.S. foreign policy at Old Dominion University in Norfolk, Virginia. From 1972 to 1993, he was associated with the Johns Hopkins School of Advanced International Studies (SAIS), serving consecutively as director of the Bologna Center, Italy; director of the Washington Center of Foreign Policy Research; and executive director of the Johns Hopkins Foreign Policy Institute. His most recent books include *La France vue par les États Unis: réflexions sur la francophobie à Washington* (IFRI, 2002) and *Memories of Europe's Future: Farewell to Yesteryear* (CSIS, 1999).

Michael Stuermer has been chief correspondent for *Die Welt* and *Welt am Sonntag* since 1998 and full professor of medieval and modern history at the Friedrich-Alexander-Universität Erlangen-Nürnberg since 1973. Previously, he was a columnist for the *Neue Zürcher Zeitung* and *Financial Times* (1994–1998) as well as for the *Frankfurter Allgemeine Zeitung* (1984–1994). Between 1988 and 1998, he was director of the Stiftung Wissenschaft und Politik in Ebenhausen, and he has been an adviser for common foreign and security policy at the EU Commission, DGIA. He has authored several books, including most recently *Das Deutsche Reich 1870–1919* (Berliner Taschenbuch, 2002), *Das Jahrhundert der Deutschen*, with others (Bertelsmann, 2001), and *Kunst des Gleichgewichts: Europa in einer Welt ohne Mitte* (Propyläen, 2001).

Dmitri Trenin is senior associate at the Carnegie Endowment for International Peace (CEIP) and director of studies at the Carnegie Moscow Center. Before joining Carnegie in 1994, he served in the Soviet and Russian army. Colonel Trenin's postings included Iraq (with the military assistance group, 1975–1976), Germany (liaison with the Western powers in Berlin, 1978–1983), and Switzerland (INF and START talks, 1985–1991). For several years, Trenin taught area studies at the Defense University in Moscow. He is the author or coauthor of several books, including most recently *The End of Eurasia: Russia on the Border between Geopolitics and Globalization* (CEIP, 2002), *A Strategy for Stable Peace: Toward a Euroatlantic Security Community* (U.S. Institute of Peace, 2002), and *Russia's China Problem* (CEIP, 1999).